THE COMPLETE
GARDENING
HANDBOOK

THE COMPLETE
GARDENING
HANDBOOK

Abbeydale Press

ISBN: 978-1-86147-272-4

1 3 5 7 9 10 8 6 4 2

Published by Abbeydale Press,
an imprint of Bookmart Limited,
Registered Number 2372865
Trading as Bookmart Limited,
Blaby Road, Wigston,
Leicester, LE18 4SE,
England

Material from this book is taken from
The Practical Gardening Encyclopedia,
published by Bookmart Limited
in 1993 and *The Small Garden Handbook*,
published by Bookmart Limited in 1999

Printed in Thailand

CONTENTS

GARDENING BASICS

FLOWERS & FOLIAGE 93

FRUIT & VEGETABLES 171

BIG IDEAS FOR SMALL GARDENS 249

GARDENING BASICS

A garden does not look after itself, and if you want to get the best from your plants you have to think about the basics like watering, feeding, weeding, and pest and disease control. Fortunately, as the following pages show, these need not become onerous chores...and they are well offset by the delights to be discovered in the more 'creative' aspects of gardening such as propagation. Even pruning can be creative, as you learn to shape the shrubs as well as improve their flowering.

Opposite
Propagation is one of the most satisfying aspects of gardening, and if you have a greenhouse the scope is widened enormously.

CHOOSING TOOLS 1: DIGGING AND CULTIVATING TOOLS

Good quality, well-designed tools will often make a job much easier and remove some of the hard work.

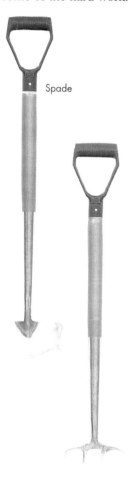

Spade

Fork

SPADES

Choose a spade with a long handle if you are tall, and stainless steel blade if you can afford it.
• A D-shaped hilt provides good grip, but make sure your hand fits with a gardening glove on.
• Choose a full-sized blade if there's a lot of digging to do, or a border spade if planting trees and shrubs.
• A tread on top of the blade makes feet less tired, but the spade heavier.
• Wooden shafts are strong and comfortable, metal shafts should be plastic coated.

FORKS

A garden fork is invaluable for digging and lifting manure and compost.
• A D-shaped hilt is stronger than a Y-shaped one and more widely available than T-shaped hilts.
• Choose a full-sized head with square prongs, for general cultivation.

HOES AND RAKES

A hoe is one of the basic gardening tools ideal for keeping down weeds.
• The Dutch hoe is excellent for weeding between rows and around plants. Its angled head is designed to slice

Left: special trowel designed to fit into separate handle. Centre: traditional hand trowel and fork. Right: narrow trowel, used for rock gardens

Left: weeding trowel.
Centre: patio/paving weeder.
Right: daisy grubber

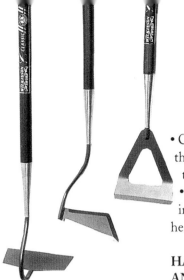

Left: draw hoe. Centre: proprietary three-bladed hoe. Right: Dutch hoe

Hand cultivator head that can be fitted to a long or short proprietary handle

through the weeds with minimum damage to plant roots.
• Choose a long handle so that you have less bending to do.
• An angled hoe has an angled head for taking out flat-bottomed drills for seeds and for drawing up earth around crops such as potatoes.
• Patent hoe designs sometimes have a smaller blade that cuts on more than one side for working close among plants.

A rake is useful in a kitchen garden and for making a new garden.

• Choose a long handle so that you have less bending to do.
• Buy a head that is made in one piece. Riveted heads are not so strong.

HAND CULTIVATORS AND WEEDERS
Hand cultivators are useful for breaking up the ground after digging, and for weeding between rows of seedlings or small plants.
• A cultivator that has removable prongs is more versatile than a fixed-prong type.
• Choosing one with a long handle that can be used with other heads and accessories can be useful.

Special tools are available for grubbing out daisies and other lawn weeds. These are useful, but worth buying only if you have regular use for them.

HAND FORKS AND TROWELS
Trowels are inexpensive and indispensable—you will need them for planting, but they are good for weeding and filling pots and containers.
   You can manage without a hand fork, but it is useful for weeding and loosening soil.
• A wide-bladed trowel is best for planting and general use around the garden.
• A narrow blade is good for confined areas, such as rock gardens.
• When buying a hand fork, make sure that the prongs are strong and the head is firmly fixed to the handle part.

Hand weeder, also called a hand grubber

Left: conventional rake. Above: a proprietary rake design

GARDENING BASICS

CHOOSING TOOLS 2: MOWERS

Almost every gardener owns a mower, but it is important to choose the most appropriate type for your garden.

WHICH MOWER?

Manual mowers are worth considering for a very small garden.

Side-wheel mowers with no roller attachment are the lightest and easiest to use.

Rear-roller mowers are the best choice for a small lawn and a striped finish.

Wheeled rotary electric mowers are the choice for a medium sized lawn if you do not need a striped finish. For a large lawn, where a trailing cable could be a hazard, a petrol cylinder mower is a better choice.

Hover rotary mowers are useful for cutting awkward places, beneath branches and shallow slopes. They are lightweight and easy to manoeuvre.

Although not all rotary mowers have rear rollers or grass boxes, some have both these features. Shop around to see what is available.

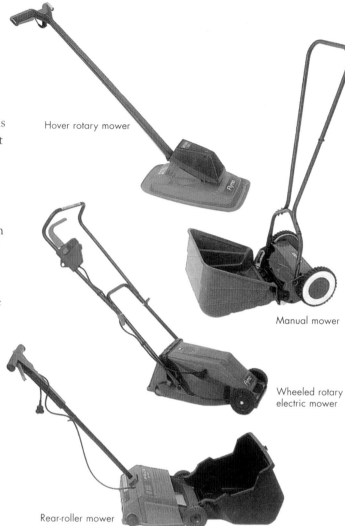

Hover rotary mower

Manual mower

Wheeled rotary electric mower

Rear-roller mower

SHARPENING

You can sharpen mower blades yourself, but it is best to have them done professionally. Rotary mower blades are not expensive to replace. Some can be fitted with plastic safety blades, and you might want to consider using these.

ELECTRICAL SAFETY

Check cables and plugs on electric mowers for damage or loose connections. Do this at the beginning of each season. If you do not have an earth leakage circuit in your house wiring, buy a special power point which has one fitted.

GETTING THE BEST FROM YOUR MOWER

Clean the blades after mowing. Remove any grass on other parts of the mower. Always disconnect the power supply to an electric mower before cleaning.

Adjust the cutting height throughout the year. Cut high in spring, then reduce the height gradually. The adjustments on your mower may vary from the

mower illustrated—consult your manual. Rotary mowers can also be adjusted for height of cut. See the manual for the correct method.

Adjust the blades of a cylinder mower so that it cuts evenly. Use a sheet of paper to check it cuts cleanly along the length of the blade. Rotate the cylinder slowly as you move the paper.

Make any necessary adjustments to the blade setting. Your mower may differ, so consult the handbook for your particular machine.

At the start of the season, and every month or so, put a drop of oil on bearings and chains. This will make the mower much easier to push.

WINTER WORK

Drain the petrol and oil from a petrol mower before you put it away for the winter.

Clean and replace the spark plug. Check your handbook for the correct gap setting.

Before replacing the spark plug, pour a tablespoon of oil into the cylinder and turn the engine over about half a dozen times.

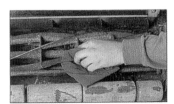

Wipe the mower with an oily rag, or spray with an anti-rust before storing.

Before storing a rotary petrol or electric mower, clean the metal blades with an emery cloth.

Wipe the blade over with an oily rag to prevent rust. If the blade is worn, replace it.

Choosing Tools 3: Trimming and Pruning Tools

Hedge-trimming is one of the most labour-intensive jobs in the garden. Electric hedge-trimmers make light work of the task, but hand shears may be better for a short hedge or trimming shrubs.

HEDGE-TRIMMERS

The longer the cutting length, the quicker you will cut the hedge. The longest blades are found on heavy machines. A 40cm (16in) blade is suitable for a small or medium-sized garden, but if you have a lot of hedges in a large garden, a 60cm (24in) blade will save a lot of time.

• A double-sided cutting edge is useful to cut in both directions.

• If both blades move vibration is likely to be much less. This is called reciprocal action.

• The more teeth there are for a given blade, the finer the finish will be.

• Blade extensions or guards, reduce the risk of injury.

• A hand shield should be included with the hedge trimmer.

• A lock off switch makes accidental starting less likely.

HAND SHEARS

Hand shears must be kept sharp and the pivots or bearings oiled, to reduce the physical effort required.

• Make sure that the blades are easy to adjust.

• Most shears have straight blades.

• A thick-shoot notch in the blade is useful if you have to cut through a thick shoot.

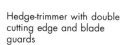

Hedge-trimmer with double cutting edge and blade guards

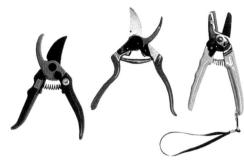

Long-handled pruners, sometimes called loppers

Handles are less important than the blades. Their shape has little bearing on the ease with which the shears are used.

SECATEURS

- Anvil secateurs cut when a sharp blade is held against a flat anvil. The anvil may have a groove to allow sap to run away. They will tear or crush stems if not kept well sharpened.
- By-pass secateurs have a scissor-like action, and produce a sharp, clean cut.
- Brightly coloured handles make the tool easier to see.
- The safety catch should be easy to use.
- Make sure the spring does not hold the blades too wide apart.

LONG-HANDLED PRUNERS

These are sold under a variety of names, such as loppers and branch cutters, but all do the same job: cutting through shoots and branches too thick or high up, for ordinary secateurs.

- By-pass blades may be easier to use in small spaces.
- Long handles have more leverage, so less effort is needed for thick branches.

Secateurs: the two on the left have a by-pass action, the one on the right an anvil action

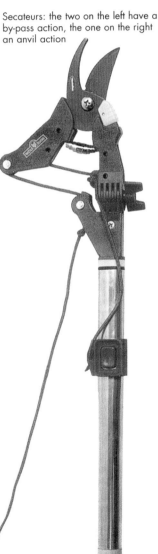

Tree pruner

CHOOSING TOOLS 4: OTHER USEFUL TOOLS

There are newer tools for specific jobs, such as shredding waste or raking moss from lawns. Some of the most useful are described here.

NYLON-LINE TRIMMERS

These are the equivalent of the scythe, but are more versatile. Use them to trim long grass around trees or up to the edges of fences or walls. Brushwood cutters are more powerful machines, suitable for tough undergrowth, having metal discs.
• Cutting guides keep the line off the ground and prevent ground scalping.
• Two handles control the trimmer better and an adjustable shaft handle makes manoeuvring easier.
• An automatic line feed is useful.
• A swivel head allows the trimmer to edge a lawn.

SHREDDERS

Shredders are useful if you like to recycle as much garden refuse as possible, but their cost is usually justified only if you have a lot of waste to shred.

Shredders chop or mash woody and soft material so that it rots down more easily on the compost heap.

• The outlet spout should be high enough off the ground to slide containers below it.

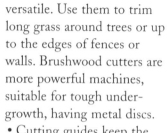

Lawn rake

Traditional spring-tined lawn rake

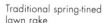

• The inlet funnel should be large to use easily— but you should not be able to touch any moving parts.

• Wheels are very useful as shredders are heavy, and electric models cannot be left outside unprotected.

Half-moon edgers, sometimes called edging irons

LAWN RAKES

These are good for raking out moss and 'thatch' (dead grass and debris) from a lawn. They are also useful for scattering worm casts and raking up autumn leaves.

• There are many kinds of manual lawn rakes, but the traditional fan-shaped spring-tined rake is the most useful.

• Powered lawn rakes save a lot of time on a large lawn, collecting leaves and debris.

• The wider the machine, the more expensive it is likely to be, but on a large lawn this saving in time will make it worthwhile.

EDGING TOOLS

If you have a large lawn with a lot of edges, a half-moon edger (also called an edging iron) could be useful. It is used against a straight-edged piece of wood to straighten an uneven edge.

Although useful, over-use will gradually make your lawn smaller and beds and borders bigger!

Use long-handled edging shears or a nylon-line trimmer with a swivel head to trim grass overhanging the edge. If the edge keeps breaking down, use metal or plastic edging strips to reduce the problem.

Nylon line trimmer

PREPARING THE GROUND 1

Digging helps to aerate the soil and expose pests to predators, and gives you the chance to incorporate humus-forming manures or garden compost. For heavy clay soils it can also help to improve the structure. The autumn and early winter is the best time for digging, but you can finish it off in the spring.

SINGLE DIGGING

1 If you have a large area to dig such as a vegetable plot, or a new garden to cultivate, divide it into two equal areas. Then you can dig to one end and work back down the other side to finish where you began.

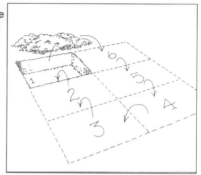

2 **Above** Remove a trench the width and depth of a spade.

3 **Above right** Push the spade into the soil at right angles, no more than a spade's width away from the previous bite of soil.

4 **Right** Push the spade in parallel to the trench, taking a bite about 15–20cm (6–8in) deep. Do not take larger bites as they will be too heavy to lift.

5 Pull back on the handle, using it as a lever to loosen the bite of soil, which will pull free on to the blade.

6 Lift the soil and flick the spade over to bury the weeds. At the end of a row, work back again in the opposite direction.

DIGGING A SMALL AREA

For a small area of ground in the garden, don't bother to divide the area. Just throw the soil forward as you work, then rake it level when preparing the ground for sowing or planting.

PERENNIAL WEEDS

If the soil is inverted properly, most annual weeds will be killed and will decompose to add humus to the soil. Remove the roots of troublesome perennial weeds by hand to prevent their spread.

7 When you reach the end of the plot, fill in the last trench with soil from the first row of the return half.

8 When you have dug the last row, fill in the trench left with the soil excavated from the first trench.

USING A GARDEN FORK

Use a spade for normal digging, but choose a fork to loosen ground that has already been dug recently. A fork is less likely to slice through the roots to leave pieces behind, and by shaking the prongs it is easier to remove difficult weeds.

Loosen the roots with a fork.

Pull up the roots by hand.

PREPARING THE GROUND 2

When planting or sowing seeds, you need to break down the soil to a fine tilth, after digging it and removing weeds. Fine, crumbly soil is essential if you are sowing seeds. For a lawn or an area where appearance is important, you may need to level the surface too.

PRODUCING A FINE TILTH (STRUCTURE)

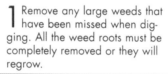

1 Remove any large weeds that have been missed when digging. All the weed roots must be completely removed or they will regrow.

2 If the initial digging was done in the autumn, then go over the ground again, if plan - ting in spring. A fork will open up the soil revealing any weeds.

LEVELLING WITH PEGS

1 Paint or mark 15cm (6in) long pegs 12–25mm (0.5–1in) from the top. Make sure that all the pegs are marked in exactly the same position.

2 Level the ground roughly. Insert a row of pegs about 1m(1yd) apart and check that the painted mark is at soil level.

3 Insert another row of pegs 1m (1yd) away from the first row. Use a spirit level in more than one direction to check all pegs are at the same height.

4 Repeat the process until the whole area has been pegged. Rake the soil, making sure that it is at the same level on each peg.

3 A hand cultivator is good for breaking down large clods of earth and doing some of the initial levelling.

4 Use an ordinary garden rake for the main levelling and smoothing, raking first in one direction and then another.

5 A combination of rake and hoe, produces a fine soil structure for a seed bed. A star-wheeled cultivator like this makes the job easier.

Seeds need a light, fine soil if they are to flourish.

TESTING YOUR SOIL

You can't determine how acid or alkaline your soil is, or how rich or deficient in nutrients, just by looking at it. Simple and inexpensive soil-testing kits will give you quick results, but they are not as accurate as a laboratory test.

TESTING FOR MAJOR NUTRIENTS

1 Gather your soil sample, using a trowel, from 5–8cm (2–3in) below the surface. Take samples from around the garden and test each one separately.

2 Mix 1 part soil to 5 parts water and shake in a clean jar, then allow to settle — this may take from half an hour to a day to become almost clear.

3 Slowly draw off some clear liquid from the top of the mixture for the test, using a pipette.

4 Using the pipette, transfer the solution to the test and reference chambers of the plastic container.

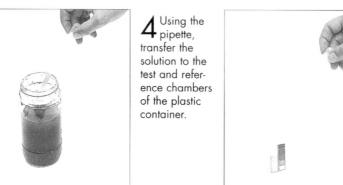

5 Add the powder from the capsule provided into the test chamber. Replace the cap and shake vigorously until the powder has dispersed.

6 Wait for the colour to develop, then compare the result against the chart which accompanies the kit. It will then tell you how to correct any problems.

Left margin: GARDENING BASICS

APPLYING LIME

1 Try not to handle lime unnecessarily. Use gloves and goggles when applying it. Divide the area into 1m (1yd) squares and weigh out the correct amount. Apply with a spade, sprinkling evenly.

2 Use a rake to cover the lime and work it into the ground.

A HANDY TEST

If you are unsure what type of soil you have try the following test:
• Pick up a handful of damp soil and rub it in your hand. If it feels gritty and is difficult to roll into a ball, it is sandy.
• If it is gritty but can be rolled into a ball, it is a sandy loam.
• If it is gritty or sticky and can be rolled into a cylinder, it is sandy clay loam or a clay loam.
• If you can bend the cylinder into a ring, it is clay.

PROBE METER

Meters are even quicker to use than indicator kits, but they need to be used carefully as instructed. Keep the probe clean, some recommend using fine emery paper to do this.

Push the probe into the soil and after a few moments read the pH on the dial. Repeat in different areas to get a consistent reading.

TESTING THE pH

The pH test is different as you don't have to wait for the soil/water mix to settle and only the test chamber is filled with this solution. Fill the reference chamber with clean tap water.

HOW MUCH LIME?

Use the following table as a guide to the amount of lime needed to raise the pH of your soil by 1pH. It is better to make several smaller applications over time than one big dose. Test the soil again after a month, and apply more lime if needed.

Do not apply lime at the same time as manure. There could be a reaction and nitrogen released can harm nearby plants.

TYPE OF SOIL	HYDRATED LIME	GROUND LIMESTONE
CLAY	640g/m² (18oz/yd²)	850g/m² (24oz/yd²)
AVERAGE LOAM	410g/m² (12oz/yd²)	550g/m² (16oz/yd²)
SAND	200g/m² (6oz/yd²)	275g/m² (8oz/yd²)

Chemicals which make the soil more acid do not produce a satisfactory result. It is better to grow plants suited to the soil you have. For the vegetable plot, adding garden compost or manure will raise the acidity by about 1pH.

IMPROVING YOUR SOIL

Healthy vegetables are a good indicator of the condition of your soil.

All soils benefit from adding plenty of garden compost or well-rotted manure. Clay soils improve with drainage.

CREATING A SUMP

It is possible to drain the land into a natural drain or ditch, if allowed. If not make a sump in a low part of the garden and place drains so that water flows into it. The soakaway must be at least 60cm (2ft) deep and filled with rubble, topped with inverted turves and a layer of soil.

LAYING LAND DRAINS

1 Dig the trench at least 30cm (1ft) deep and at a slight fall. Put a layer of coarse grit or fine gravel along the bottom.

2 Both clay or plastic drains can be used satisfactorily. Lay the drains on the bed of gravel or grit.

SOIL CONDITIONERS

1 Dig in plenty of compost, manure or any organic matter that will quickly rot down in the soil. Peat and sharp sand will not rot down but improve the soil structure, aid drainage and moisture retention.

2 If the area has already been planted, use plenty of mulch material. This will eventually be worked into the soil.

3 Clay soil can be improved by applying lime and digging in coarse sand or grit. Concentrate on one area at a time. Also add plenty of compost or well-rotted manure.

3 Use a T shaped connector for side drains.

4 Pack coarse sand or fine gravel around the drains to improve drainage further and reduce the chance of the pipes becoming clogged.

MAKING GARDEN COMPOST

Garden compost is always valuable so make as much as you can. It is best to buy a bin or compost maker, or make one from scrap wood.

CONSTRUCTING A WOODEN BIN

1 The simplest way is to buy a kit. The wood is precut, ready to assemble by slotting the pieces together, or by nailing the slats to the corner pieces provided.

2 The kit above is quick and easy to make. The pieces are hammered into the slots forming a sturdy bin. Once full, simply lift the entire bin away and start a new compost heap.

READY-MADE COMPOST BINS

A proprietary compost bin with lid.

This bin is suitable for compost or leaves.

MAKING COMPOST

1 To improve airflow, place twiggy material at the bottom, then add kitchen and garden refuse.

2 Adding a layer of manure after every 15cm (6in) will speed up the rotting process.

TIPS FOR QUICK COMPOST

• Use a large container to produce more heat, increasing the rate that the material will rot down at.
• Keep material moist.
• Cover the top in wet weather.
•Let in plenty of air at the base and sides.
•In winter, cover the whole heap to keep it warm and prevent waterlogging.
• To speed up the rotting process, fork out the compost after a few weeks, then fork it back into the bin, putting the old material from the outside towards the middle.

3 A thin layer of soil can be substituted instead of manure which will add bacteria into the heap.

4 Compost activators will help speed up the rotting process by encouraging bacteria to grow. This will not be needed if manure has been added to the compost.

Fertilizers and Manures 1

Most gardeners use a combination of organic and inorganic fertilizers, some prefer the organic-only approach. Feeding does make a difference, especially to vegetables, seedlings and plants grown in containers. The benefits to trees and shrubs is less obvious, so feed only in response to a known deficiency.

1 Apply fertilizers evenly. Divide unplanted ground into strips 90cm (3ft) wide, work along these in 90cm (3ft) 'bites', scattering the fertilizer. A wheeled fertilizer spreader will do the job well.

2 Raking in the fertilizer, distributes it evenly as well as working it into the soil.

3 Scatter fertilizer either side of the vegetable rows, keeping it off the leaves. Hoe in later.

4 Scatter fertilizer in a circle around shrubs and large plants. This concentrates it where the active feeding roots are. Keep away from the stem, and do not apply beyond the spread of the plant.

5 Hoe in the fertilizer so that it penetrates more rapidly. Water in thoroughly, unless rain is forecast, so that the plants benefit more quickly.

INORGANIC FERTILIZERS

Ammonium Sulphate supplies nitrogen, but makes the soil more acid.

Nitro-chalk supplies nitrogen without making the soil more acid.

Potassium sulphate supplies potassium.

Superphosphate of lime supplies phosphorus. Triple superphosphate is similar but almost three times stronger. Make sure that you apply the correct lime at an appropriate rate.

Balanced fertilizers (such as Growmore in the UK— a formulation, not a trade name) contains all the main nutrients: nitrogen, phosphorus and potassium.

Compound fertilizers are usually the same as balanced fertilizers, but do not contain all three major nutrients.

Controlled- and slow-release fertilizers contain the major nutrients in a form that is released slowly over a period of months. Controlled-release fertilizers are regulated by the temperature of the soil.

Ammonium sulphate

Nitro-chalk

Potassium sulphate

Superphosphate of lime

Compound fertilizer

Slow-release fertilizer

Growmore

FERTILIZERS AND MANURES 2

Organic gardeners prefer to use fertilizers that occur as natural products.

ORGANIC FERTILIZERS

Blood, fish and bonemeal contains all the major nutrients. The nitrogen content is released quickly.
Bonemeal is a slow-acting fertilizer containing mainly phosphorus and nitrogen. Unsterilized bonemeal carries a very small risk of disease.
Dried animal manures contain a full range of trace elements but only a small amount of the major nutrients.
Dried blood is a fast-acting nitrogen fertilizer, when plants need a quick boost in summer.

Fish meal contains nitrogen and phosphorus.
Hoof and horn contains nitrogen in a form that is released slowly. It is a more suitable source of nitrogen than dried blood.
Liquid animal manures contain a small amount of all the major nutrients, plus a full range of trace elements.
Liquid seaweed contains a useful amount of nitrogen and potassium, but only a trace of phosphorus. Good for supplying trace elements and growth hormones.
Seaweed meal contains all the major nutrients, plus many minor ones and trace elements. It is a very good all-round fertilizer, but is best applied when the soil is warm so that the bacteria can break it down.

Wood ash— the exact chemical analysis depends on the material burned, but there will be a useful amount of potassium and a small amount of phosphorus.

BULKY MANURES AND COMPOST

Garden compost, well rotted animal manures and bulky organic materials are invaluable. They improve the soil structure, its water holding capacity and the ability of the soil to retain nutrients from other sources.

Dried chicken manure

Blood, fish and bonemeal

Bonemeal

Dried blood

GREEN MANURING

1 Green manuring is a way of adding humus to the soil without making a compost heap. Fork over the cleared ground first of all.

2 Scatter mustard seed, covering the ground quite thickly.

3 Rake over to bury the mustard seed completely.

4 When the mustard is 30cm (12in) high, and before it flowers and sets seed, dig it into the ground. It will eventually rot, releasing humus and nutrients for a later crop.

Liquid seaweed

Fish meal

Seaweed meal

Hoof and horn

WATERING

Watering by hand is hard work but an automatic watering system will eliminate that and be better for the plants.

DRIP FEEDS

1 A system like this will run both spray and drip nozzles off the same system. Connect the master unit to a hose from the mains. The master unit reduces water pressure and contains a cleanable filter.

2 Run the main supply tube so it is not too visible.

4 Use drip-feed heads to water containers and individual plants in borders. Pegs hold the tubes in position.

3 Connect the smaller-diameter branch tubes wherever you need to take water.

5 Use a spray head for more general watering in flower beds or vegetable plots. Various sizes of nozzles are available.

CHOOSING AN APPROPRIATE SPRINKLER

Oscillating sprinklers are useful for rectangular lawns and seed beds as they are adjustable.

Static sprinklers are intended mainly for lawns, generally watering in a circular pattern, so moving them around is necessary to achieve an even coverage.

Rotating sprinklers water in a circular pattern. The rotating arms throw out droplets by water pressure and cover a wider area than static sprinklers.

To water a flower bed or vegetable plot, you will need to buy a version with a head on a long spike.

Pulse-jet sprinklers have a single jet on a central pivot that rotates in a series of pulses, ejecting a spurt of water. They water in a circular pattern but can cover a very wide area. Lawn versions have a low base.

Static sprinkler

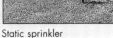

Rotating sprinkler

Pulse-jet

Oscillating sprinkler

TAPS AND TIMERS

An outdoor tap is essential if you have a drip-feed watering system. Kits are readily available with fitting instructions. In the UK a non-return valve must be fitted by law.

If you have installed an automatic watering system, consider installing a tap computer to turn the water supply on and off automatically.

SEEP HOSES

Seep hoses are designed for long-term watering. The tiny perforations deliver the water slowly so that it seeps down into the soil. Use in flower beds, borders or rows of fruit or vegetables.

SEEPAGE HOSE

Some seepage hoses are made of porous rubber and can be laid on top of the soil or buried in a shallow slit trench 10–15cm (4–6in) deep.

WEEDING BEDS AND BORDERS

Weeds look unsightly and can affect the growth of your plants by competing for water and nutrients. Once you have a plan of action, weeding should be no more than an occasional chore.

HAND-WEEDING

1 Some hand weeding is always necessary, but forking out deep-rooted perennials need only be done when you are clearing the ground. Use a fork to loosen the roots so that the whole root system is removed.

2 Hand forking will control perennial weeds while they are still young.

3 Hoeing, in dry weather, keeps most weeds under control. A Dutch hoe, like this, is good for slicing off the tops of weeds. Other designs are available.

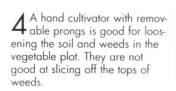

4 A hand cultivator with removable prongs is good for loosening the soil and weeds in the vegetable plot. They are not good at slicing off the tops of weeds.

CHEMICAL WEEDING

1 The quickest way to clear the ground of weeds, is to use a chemical weedkiller. Choose the correct weedkiller for the job and area of the garden.

Spray on a calm day so no spray drifts onto plants or grass. Keep one watering can especially for weedkillers and label it clearly.

2 Most weedkillers act quickly within days. Some products are inactivated by contact with the soil, allowing planting as soon as dead growth is cleared. Translocated weedkiller acts to kill difficult perennial weeds, and once top growth is dead the weed can be removed.

3 Where spraying is impossible, paint a translocated weedkiller (such as a glyphosphate) on to individual weeds.

MULCH CONTROL

2 In areas where appearance matters, cover any bare ground with a 5cm (2in) layer of chipped bark or other decorative mulch.

1 Black polythene sheets controls weeds effectively in areas of no importance. It can be secured with soil or pegs or weighed down with bricks.

PREPARING THE GROUND 1

A weed-free lawn or path is no longer a dream with the selective weedkillers available today. They attack the weeds but not the grass so you can achieve a superb lawn and clear paths with just one or two applications.

LAWN WEEDKILLERS

1 Most selective lawn weedkillers are diluted and applied as a liquid. To ensure even coverage, use two lengths of string to mark out the width of the dribble bar used with your watering can.

2 At the end of a row, move one of the strings across for the next strip. Always carefully follow the instructions for the rate of coverage.

3 If the lawn also needs feeding, use a weed-and-feed for lawns. This combines fertilizer and weedkiller and can be applied with a fertilizer spreader to save time.

4 If there are isolated weeds in small patches, do not apply weedkiller to the whole lawn. Use instead a wipe-on stick containing a selective weedkiller, applied directly onto the weeds.

HAND-WEEDING A LAWN

1 Weeding trowels are useful for prising up weeds such as dandelions and daisies.

2 Firm the soil afterwards to prevent seedlings germinating in the area. If a large bare area is exposed, it is worth sprinkling grass seeds over the patch.

DEALING WITH COARSE GRASS

Small clumps of coarse grass growing in your lawn can either be dug up and the area reseeded, or keep slashing through it with a knife. This will weaken it allowing fine grasses to grow over the area.

PATH WEEDKILLERS

1 Path weedkillers kill all plants that they touch, remaining active in the soil for months. Great care should be taken to avoid spray blowing onto plants or grass.

2 Shield plants with a sheet of board, wood, or plastic if applying weedkiller near a border.

PEST CONTROL 1:
APHIDS AND OTHER SAP-SUCKERS

G A R D E N I N G   B A S I C S

Sap-sucking insects weaken the plants they feed on by transmitting virus diseases by injecting infected sap from one plant into another.

IDENTIFICATION

Aphids are well known pests, greenfly and blackfly are the commonest ones. Some species attack the roots rather than the leaves. Sticky foliage is caused by the honeydew excreted by the aphids—with a black mould.

CHEMICAL CONTROL

Leaf-sucking insects hide on the undersides of leaves, so spray both sides of the leaves.

Chemical control with contact insecticide for aphids. Systemic insecticide will be more effective on ornamental plants.
Green controls include insecticidal soaps and pirimicarb.

Leaf hoppers are usually green or yellow insects which leap when disturbed.
Chemical control with most contact and systemic insecticides.

Red spider mites are tiny creatures. Their silky webs and pale mottling on the upper surface of leaves are an indication of the pests presence.
Chemical control with a contact insecticide.
Green control is achieved with the predatory mite *Phytoseiulus persimilis* and high humidity.

Scale insects are immobile and scale-like in appearance, usually yellow, brown, dark grey or white.
Chemical control with a contact insecticide for scale.

Thrips are narrow brownish-black insects. Affected leaves have a silvery-white discolouration on the upper surface.
Chemical control with a systemic insecticide.
Green control is best with relatively harmless insecticides such as those based on pyrethrum, sprayed frequently.

Whitefly look like tiny white moths which rise up in a cloud when disturbed.
Chemical control with any contact insecticide for whitefly but spray frequently.
Green control is with a parasitic wasp, *Encarsia formosa*, but only in a greenhouse.

BIOLOGICAL CONTROL

Encarsia formosa is a parasitic wasp that helps to control whitefly. Hang the pack on the plants you want to protect, emerging parasites will feed and start to breed.

Blackfly   Whitefly   Red spider mite   Leaf hopper   Scale

PEST CONTROL 2:
LEAF- EATERS

Leaf-eating pests destroy plants, identifying the culprit is not always simple unless they are caterpillars.

IDENTIFICATION

Caterpillars come in various sizes and shapes.
Chemical control with derris dust or other suitable contact insecticide.

CHEMICAL CONTROL

Slug pellets are effective at controlling slugs and snails. Most are coloured blue to discourage birds. To protect pets eating the bait, place bait in a piece of narrow pipe.

Green controls include picking off by hand and spraying with *Bacillus thuringiensis.*

Earwigs are yellowish-brown insects with curved pincers at the rear.
Chemical control with insecticidal powders dusted at the base of plants at dusk.
Green control by making a trap of a pot filled with straw, on top of a cane where the insects gather during the day. Empty regularly.

Slugs and snails are so well-known that they need no description. They either make holes or eat all the leaves. Their slime trails show their route.
Chemical control with slug pellets.
Green control involves making or buying beer traps so that the pests drown in a state of intoxication. Coarse grit sprinkled around crowns and new shoots in spring, will help protect them.

Weevils eat irregularly shaped holes around the edges of leaves. The mature insects are usually grey or black with a short snout and elbowed antennae.
Chemical control by spraying with an insecticide for the pest, preferably at dusk.
Green control by biological control is under development.

BIOLOGICAL CONTROL

Many kinds of caterpillars can be controlled by a bacterium that causes disease in the insects. If you spray the food plants of the pest species (such as cabbages) you should not upset the health of decorative butterflies that feed on weeds.

Mix up the spray according to instructions supplied and spray before the problem has become a major one.

Caterpillar damage

Snail damage

Earwig damage

Slug damage

Weevils

PEST CONTROL 3: ROOT-EATERS

Root pests often go unnoticed until the plants collapse, but control is possible if you are vigilant.

IDENTIFICATION

Cutworms and leatherjackets Cutworms are caterpillars of moths, and have a caterpillar shape. They are usually brown and live in the soil. The base of the stem is usually gnawed, the plant slowly dies.

Leatherjackets are the larvae of daddy-long-legs, or crane flies, and have tubular bodies.
Chemical control by treating the affected plants with a soil insecticide as soon as damage is seen.
Green control consists of winter digging to expose the grubs to birds, and picking the pests off by hand.

Root flies are numerous, affecting carrots and onions but also bulbs. There are many different species and it is the larvae eating the roots which cause the damage.
Chemical control is difficult and impossible once the grubs are in the roots. Use a soil insecticide when planting vulnerable bulbs and seeds.
Green control consists of firming the soil around roots when planting or thinning. Carrot fly can be deterred by placing a polythene barrier around the plants 45cm (18in) high — this works as the pests fly close to the ground.

BIOLOGICAL CONTROL

Carrot flies keep close to the ground so a low physical barrier such as mesh or plastic sheeting may prevent them laying their eggs around the plants.

Weevils It is the grubs which damage the plant roots. If you find small curved white grubs with brown heads and no legs on the remains of the roots, these are likely to be weevil grubs.
Chemical control is difficult, and soil insecticides have little effect.
Green control is possible with a nematode, which affects the grubs, this is not widely available yet.

CHEMICAL CONTROL

Use recommended soil pest products, either in powder or spray formula for affected areas.

Root fly larvae

Root fly damage

Grubs of weevils

DISEASE CONTROL 1: LEAF DISEASES

Fungus diseases affect the leaves of many plants so grow disease resistant varieties. Spray or remove affected leaves immediately.

Downy mildew

IDENTIFICATION

Downy mildew looks like fluffy white growth on the surface of the leaf. Brown or yellow blotches may be seen on the top surface.
Chemical control by removing affected leaves, spraying plant with a fungicide for downy mildew. Powdery mildew treatments will not be effective for this disease.
Green control consists of removing affected leaves, improving ventilation and plant space

Leaf spots affect many plants, rose black spot is just one kind. The spots are usually black, brown or yellow.
Chemical control is best achieved by a systemic fungicide — not on edible crops.
Green control by destroying affected leaves promptly.

Powdery mildew looks like a white powdery deposit most commonly found on the upper surface of leaves.
Chemical and green control are as for downy mildew with a wider choice of chemicals.

Leaf spot

Powdery mildew

Rust

BIOLOGICAL CONTROL

Removing diseased leaves as soon as they are visible, prevents the spread of the problem. Never use these leaves for compost, destroy them.

Rusts vary in appearance, but most cause yellowish patches on the upper surface of leaves and small brown or orange patches on the reverse sides.
Chemical control with a fungicide for rust. Remove affected leaves to control spread of disease.
Green control is best achieved by removing all affected leaves, improving spacing of plants and increasing ventilation.

CHEMICAL CONTROL

Roses prone to fungus diseases are best sprayed on a regular basis with a systemic fungicide.

DISEASE CONTROL 2: ROOT DISEASES

Most root diseases are of a minor nature, but club root is a serious problem that restricts the types of plants you can grow.

IDENTIFICATION

Blackleg affects cuttings. The base turns black, shrinks, softens and eventually dies.
Chemical control is impossible once blacklegs takes hold but use of a hormone rooting powder at planting may prevent an attack.
Green control is impossible.

Club-root affects members of the Cruciferae family, especially brassicas and wallflowers. The roots swell and growth is very stunted.
Chemical control is difficult as the disease remains in the soil for years. Use a club-root dip when planting.
Green control is best achieved by growing plants in sterilized compost

Foot and root rots affect a number of plants such as peas, beans tomatoes, cucumbers and bedding petunias. The roots turn black and the base of the stems rot.
Chemical control is not practical.
Green control is the most affective: raise plants in sterilized compost, avoid repeat plantings in the same area each year, and destroy diseased plants.

Storage rots affect bulbs and corms in storage, as well as stored onions. Soft patches appear with fungal growth on the surface.
Chemical control by dusting non-edible bulbs, tubers and corms with a fungicide before storing.
Green control is effective. Make sure that the bulbs are dry before storing them, and keep in a cool but frost-free, airy place. Check every few weeks for any soft bulbs and remove and destroy any found.

CHEMICAL CONTROL

Non-edible bulbs, corms and tubers should be dusted with a fungicide before storing to prevent rot.

BIOLOGICAL CONTROL

Bulbs, corms and tubers should be hung up in netting where air can circulate freely.

Blackleg

PHYSIOLOGICAL AND OTHER PROBLEMS

Some problems which appear to be caused by pests or disease have a physiological cause, such as wind chill or sun scorch. Others are caused accidentally by weedkillers, or deficiencies in the soil.

IDENTIFICATION

Cold damage is most on evergreens that are not completely hardy. Leaves are blackened or brown, puckered or withered. Prune out the damaged areas and many plants will outgrow limited damage.

Iron and manganese deficiencies are likely on chalky soils. Symptoms are similar: yellowing leaves, especially at the edges. Apply sequestered iron or trace elements for high soil pH in a chelated formulation.

Fasciated stems can be caused by injury or genetic quirk. The stems are flattened and appear fused together.

Nitrogen deficiency shows itself in pale green leaves which are sometimes mottled or yellowed. Growth is slow. Feed with high-nitrogen fertilizer.

Potassium deficiency shows itself in prematurely autumnal leaves. The leaves may roll inwards. Apply a sulphate of potash or fertilizer high in potassium.

Sun scorch happens behind unshaded glass in a greenhouse or where the temperature is very high. Brown patches on the upper surface of the leaves is the first indication, the edges may brown and become brittle. Improve shading for the plant in hot weather, and improve ventilation.

Weedkiller damage depends on the type of weedkiller used. Selective hormone weedkillers for lawn use will cause distorted growth if they drift onto ornamental plants. Contact weedkillers usually cause pale or bleached areas on foliage. There is nothing you can do except be more careful.

Viruses come in many forms, causing different symptoms. The leaves have a mottled pattern, yellowish stripes, and the plant is stunted. Not all viruses are regarded as undesirable — some striped flowers and variegated leaves, caused by virus infections, are considered attractive. Generally, all plants affected by a virus should be pulled up and destroyed as soon as possible.

Cold damage

Manganese deficiency

Iron deficiency

Fasciated stem

Nitrogen deficiency

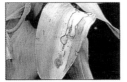
Sun scorch

Virus infection

SOWING IN POTS AND TRAYS

Tender bedding plants must be started off indoors or in the greenhouse. Sow in trays if you need a lot of plants, or in pots to save space. Many hardy plants such as rock plants and hardy border perennials can be sown in pots and trays, but they can be put out in cold frames to germinate.

SOWING IN POTS

1 For border perennials, rock plants, house plants and shrubs, sow in pots. Use a rounded presser to firm compost.

2 Sprinkle seeds evenly, using the sand technique if seed is very fine. Stand pot in a bowl of water to moisten the compost, then remove and let it drain.

3 Insert a label then cover with glass or put pot in a propagator if warmth is needed for germination.

4 Alpines and shrubs don't need much warmth so put them in a cold frame. Plunging the pots in sand reduces the risk of the compost drying out.

SOWING FINE SEED

1 If the seed is fine and difficult to handle, mix it with a small amount of silver sand to make spreading easier.

2 Sprinkle the mixture between your finger and thumb, as if sprinkling salt over your food.

SOWING IN TRAYS

1 Fill the tray loosely with sterilized seed compost. Level with the rim, then press down with a piece of wood. Leave a gap of 12mm (0.5in) below the rim. Water the tray before sowing or the seeds will be washed away.

2 Sprinkle seeds thinly over the surface. Large seeds can be spaced individually. Medium-sized seeds can be put in a folded piece of paper, then tap it with a finger to disperse seeds.

3 Sift more compost over the top, if instructions say you should do so.

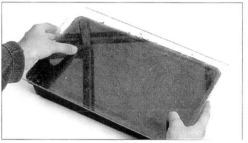

4 To keep the compost moist either place in a sealed plastic bag or cover with glass.

5 Each day, turn the glass over, or the bag inside out, to reduce condensation drips.

6 Once the seeds germinate, remove the glass or bag. Covering the seeds for too long could encourage disease through high humidity.

PRICKING OUT

As soon as seedlings are large enough to handle, prick them out into pots or trays of potting compost to give the seedlings enough space to grow healthily.

PRICKING OUT INTO TRAYS

1 Fill tray with sterilized compost. Level and firm the compost to 12mm (0.5in) below the rim.

2 Use a dibber to loosen the compost and lift out each seedling with as much compost as possible attached.

3 Use a dibber to make a hole deep enough to take the roots. Hold the seedling by a seed leaf. Firm compost gently around roots. Space seedlings 2–5cm (1–2in) apart.

4 Water thoroughly after transplanting and shade from direct sunlight for a couple of days.

PRICKING OUT INTO MODULES

Using preformed trays or modules will ensure even spacing of seedlings.

TRANSPLANTATION INTO POTS

1 Some plants such as cyclamen, tomatoes and dahlias are best pricked out into individual pots, instead of trays. This gives them more space to grow. Place them in small 8–10cm (3–4in) pots.

2 Once watered, keep the pots out of direct sunlight for a couple of days. Square pots are space saving.

PLUGS AND POT-READY PLANTS

1 Seedlings are often sold in 'plugs', separate blocks of compost. It is possible to do this yourself using trays made for this purpose. Sow one or two seeds in each cell and thin if necessary.

2 Transfer the seedlings into pots or trays as normal. Young plants are sometimes sold by nurseries in larger plugs, these should be potted up separately.

Sowing in cells saves time pricking out. This is suitable for most bedding plants and many vegetables that are started off in the greenhouse.

BORECOLE DWARF GREEN CURLED H

SOWING HARDY ANNUALS

Hardy annuals are undemanding plants that can be sown directly into the ground. Thin them out and water well in dry weather and you will produce masses of flowers with little effort.

SOWING IN ROWS

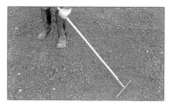

1 Make sure that the area is free of weeds and large lumps of earth, then rake level. Fine soil is needed to germinate seeds.

2 Mark out with sand or grit the areas in which each annual is to grow.

3 Make shallow drills in the soil according to the instructions, and plant in alternate directions to soften the effect.

4 Sow seeds as evenly as possible along the drill. Large seeds can be sown individually.

5 Label each section, rake the soil to cover the seeds.

6 Water well until seeds germinate and are established.

Hardy annuals are the easiest of all flowers to grow. They can be sown where they will flower, bloom quickly, and are usually bright and cheerful. These are godetias.

SOWING BROADCAST

1 Packets of mixed annuals and groups of one type can be sown broadcast (scattered randomly). At the seedling stage it is difficult to tell weeds from annuals. Scatter as evenly as possible.

2 Rake the seeds in to distribute and bury them, raking in different directions.

THINNING

Thin seedlings while young to prevent overcrowding. Hold down the soil on either side of the plant you want to keep, whilst pulling out unwanted plants. Space seedlings at distances recommended on the packet. Water after thinning if weather is dry.

SOWING ALPINES AND SHRUBS

Alpine, tree and shrub seeds often need to undergo a period of cold weather, Many prefer to be sown in the autumn and overwintered in a cold frame.

SOWING SLOW-GERMINATING PERENNIALS

1 Fill a small pot with a loam-based seed compost and firm gently.

2 Sow the seed thickly as germination is poor, but do not let the seeds touch each other.

3 Cover the seeds with potting compost, then sprinkle grit or coarse sand over the surface to discourage algae growth.

4 Plunge the pots up to their rims in a cold frame to prevent moisture loss. Cover with a sheet of glass if mice are attracted to the seeds.

PRICKING OUT

Label the pots. Keep the pots watered. Seedlings will usually germinate in the spring and during the summer. Prick them out and grow on in pots or in rows in a nursery bed (see opposite).

Left Aubretias are particularly easy alpines to raise from seed, and they flower quickly. They do not always grow true to type from seed.

BIENNIALS AND PERENNIALS

1 An easy way to raise biennials and border perennials is to sow them in a seed bed in late spring or early summer.

2 Take out shallow drills in rows about 23cm (9in) apart and sow seeds thinly. Water gently, then rake soil over the seeds.

3 Thin the seedlings out, if necessary and plant in another area where they can grow on until the autumn. Rake in garden fertilizer.

4 Space seedlings 15–23cm (6–9in) apart to allow room for growth. Water well.

5 Wallflowers need the growing tip removed every few weeks after transplanting, to encourage bushier plants. Put biennials in their flowering position in the autumn. Leave border perennials until the following spring.

SOFTWOOD AND GREENWOOD CUTTINGS

Softwood and greenwood cuttings root quickly and can be taken from fuchias and pelargoniums. Greenwood cuttings come from the soft tip of the stem after the first spurt of growth has slowed down.

KEEPING CUTTING FRESH

Softwood cuttings soon wilt, so put them in a polythene bag until they are to be used.

TAKING SOFTWOOD CUTTINGS

1 Many shrubs and pelargoniums (geraniums) can be propagated from soft new shoots. Do not cut below the third leaf from the tip.

2 Trim off the lowest pair of leaves. Trim the base of the stem, cutting straight across the stem just below a leaf joint.

3 Dip the cut tip of each cutting into rooting powder containing a fungicide.

4 Use a dibber to make a hole in a pot of compost for the cutting.

5 Either insert the cuttings around the edges of the pot or put into individual pots. Once watered, place in a humid propagator (or cover with polythene), keep in a warm light place out of direct sunlight.

TAKING GREENWOOD CUTTINGS

1 Take cuttings once the new growth has slowed down in early summer. For most shrubs, a 10cm (4in) long cutting from the shoot is adequate.

2 Place cuttings in a polythene bag or bowl of water to prevent wilting.

3 Shorten the length of each cutting to 8cm (3in), cutting straight across the stem.

4 Trim leaves from the bottom half of the cutting, using a sharp knife.

5 Dip the cut ends into a rooting hormone to speed up the rooting process.

6 Insert cuttings around the edge of a pot, water with fungicide and allow to drain.

7 Place pot in a warm, humid propagator in light but out of direct sunlight. A polythene bag could be used as an alternative.

BASAL STEM CUTTINGS

Basal stem cuttings can be taken in spring from many herbaceous plants that produce new shoots at soil level. This method is good for propagating dahlias.

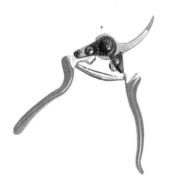

TAKING DELPHINIUM CUTTINGS

1 Use the basal shoots of delphiniums and lupins to make new plants. Remove shoots when they are 8–10cm (3–4in) long.

2 Trim the cuttings with a sharp knife across the end, remove any low leaves. Dip the ends into a rooting hormone.

3 Insert cuttings, one to a pot or two or three around the edge of a pot, into a mixture of peat and sand or a rooting compost. Cover cuttings to provide a humid atmosphere.

Chrysanthemum

TAKING DAHLIA CUTTINGS

1 In late winter place tubers in boxes packing moist compost or peat around them. Keep in a warm light place.

2 When the shoots have grown to about 8cm (3in) long, cut them off close to the tuber.

3 Remove the lowest leaves from the cuttings, and trim straight across just below a leaf joint with a sharp knife.

4 Dip the cut ends into a rooting hormone and insert several cuttings into each pot. Keep moist and pot up when they have rooted.

TAKING CHRYSANTHEMUM CUTTINGS

1 Cut off young shoots about 3–5cm(1–2in) long. Pull off lowest leaves and trim the end with a knife.

2 Insert cuttings around the edge of a pot. They will often root without rooting hormone, but using one will speed up rooting.

3 Cover with an inflated polythene bag. Check regularly, turning the bag to avoid condensation dripping onto leaves. Remove any rotted leaves.

SEMI-RIPE CUTTINGS

Semi-ripe cuttings are a good way to propagate many shrubs. Mid and late summer are the ideal time to take them. Cuttings will form roots in a month or two.

TAKING SEMI-RIPE CUTTINGS

1 Take cuttings of 5–10cm (2–4in) long from shoots that are nearly fully grown. The tip may be soft but the wood at the base should be hardening.

2 Strip the lower leaves from each cutting them trim the length if necessary.

3 Dip the cut end into rooting hormone.

4 Semi-ripe cuttings taken in summer will root in open ground if well watered, but will do better in a cold frame.

5 Firm cuttings to remove air pockets that could cause the cuttings or new roots to dry out.

6 Water with a fungicide added to prevent rot. Water often in dry weather.

7 Label each row to identify cuttings if you take several at the same time.

SOME SHRUBS TO PROPAGATE

The following shrubs root easily from semi-ripe cuttings. There are many others, so be prepared to experiment if your favourite shrub is not in this listing.

Abelia
Buddleia (butterfly bush)
Camelia
Ceanothus (Californian
   lilac)
Chaenomeles (quince)
Choisya (Mexican orange
   blossom)
Cistus (sun rose)
Cotoneaster
Daphne
Deutzia
Elaegnus
Escallonia
Euonymus
Forsythia
Fuchsia
Griselinia
Hebe
Helianthemum (rock rose)
Hibiscus
Hydrangea
Ligustrum (privet)
Philadelphus (mock orange)
Pieris
Potentilla
Pyracantha (firethorn)
Rhododendron
Ribes (flowering currant)
Rose
Rosemary
Santolina (cotton lavender)
Syringa (lilac)
Viburnum
Weigela

Santolina

Euonymus

Weigela

SPECIAL CUTTINGS

Some shrubs, such as clematis, sometimes root better if you use special techniques.

INTERNODAL CLEMATIS CUTTINGS

1 Take internodal cuttings to raise a lot of clematis, rather than layering which produces a smaller number of plants.

2 Make cuttings by severing them from the stem *between* leaf joints. Leave 2–5cm (1–2in) of stem below the leaves, with a short stem above leaf joint.

3 Remove one of the leaves, leaving a short stump. Leave the other leaf as a 'handle'.

4 Insert in the compost in the usual way. Pot up the rooted plants individually and grow on for a season before planting out.

HEEL CUTTINGS

1 Some shrubs root better if the cutting is taken with a 'heel' of old wood— a slither of bark.

2 Remove the cutting by pulling downwards so that a piece of stem bark comes away with the cutting.

3 Trim the cutting and insert into compost as usual.

4 Insert cutting, as usual, and put pot in a cold frame or cover with a polythene bag.

Right Juniperus cuttings usually root better if taken with a heel. Make them in early autumn.

Above Cuttings are one of the ways that azaleas can be propagated, they can be taken with or without a heel.

Left Evergreen elaeagnus root easily from cuttings taken in late summer or early autumn. A cutting with a heel can help rooting.

HARDWOOD CUTTINGS

Take hardwood cuttings in late autumn or when shrubs are dormant. Most are easy to root and need less looking after, than other cuttings, as they are left in the ground.

TAKING SEMI-RIPE CUTTINGS

1 Choose shoots grown in the summer, which are firm. Avoid weak and old shoots. Cut off shoots with secateurs, these can be divided up into shorter lengths later.

2 Pull off any dying leaves that remain on the shoot, then cut into sections about 15–23cm (6–9in) long.

3 So that you remember which end is the top, make a sloping cut above the top bud and a horizontal one underneath.

4 Choose a sheltered but not dry part of the garden and make a V-shaped slit trench.

SINGLE STEM CUTTINGS

If you are taking cuttings of trees or fruit bushes that you want to grow with a single stem, insert the cutting so the tip is just covered.

5 To stop water from rotting the base of the cuttings, sprinkle grit or coarse sand along the base of the trench.

6 Insert cuttings vertically 10cm (4in) apart, with only 2–5cm (1–2in) above ground.

Cornus alba and its varieties are grown mainly for their attractive coloured winter stems. They are very easy to propagate from hardwood cuttings.

ROOTING HORMONES

Rooting hormones—which can be powders or liquids— are most useful for plants that are difficult to root. They can be used on all stem cuttings. They are nor intended for use on leaf or root cuttings.

Most of the hormones will be taken up through the cut base of the cutting, not through the bark or stem, so only dip the cut surface into the powder or liquid.

If using a powder, dip the tip of the cutting into water first so that the powder adheres to the cutting easily.

Rooting hormones can be formed from different chemicals, suited to hardwood or softwood—most sold to amateurs are all-purpose.

Many contain fungicide, which reduces the risk of rot.

Most rooting hormones used by amateurs come as powders.

Some hormones are dissolved in water or solvents, but those sold to amateurs are usually in gel form.

PLANTS TO TRY

Most deciduous (leaf-shedding) shrubs can be propagated from hardwood cuttings. Popular ones include:

Cotoneaster
Dogwood (*Cornus alba*)
Flowering currant (*Ribes sanguineum*)
Rose (below)
Winter-flowering viburnum

Poplar and willow trees root readily from cuttings.

LAYERING

Layering is an ideal way to propagate shrubs and some house plants. You will usually have a larger plant than from cuttings. Air layering is a good technique if you have a leggy plant bare at the base. Simple layering is best for shrubs in the garden, serpentine layering is good for clematis or honyesuckle.

AFTERCARE

• Water thoroughly and prevent soil drying before the plant has rooted.
• Sever the stem from its parent in autumn or spring.
• After severing, pinch out the growing tip to get a bushy plant.
• Lift and replant if well-rooted; if not leave for a year.

PLANTS TO TRY

Most shrubs and some trees can be layered if there are suitable low-growing shoots, these include:
 Corylus avellana 'Contorta'
 Hamamelis (witch hazel)
 Magnolia x soulangeana
 Magnolia stellata
 Rhododendron (opposite)
 Syringa vulgaris (lilac)
 Viburnum

SIMPLE LAYERING

1 Choose a young, low-growing branch which be bent down easily. Trim leaves and sideshoots off the branch where it meets the soil.

2 Make a hole 10–15cm (4–6in) deep sloping towards the patent plant.

3 Hold the stem in contact with the soil using a peg of bent wire. Ensure that the end of the stem lies vertically against the back of the hole.

4 Return the excavated soil to bury the stem and firm well.

AIR LAYERING

1 Trim off any leaves growing where you want to make a layer. Make a polythene sleeve to go around the stem. Secure the bottom of the sleeve using tape or plastic covered wire.

2 Holding out the sleeve out of the way, use a sharp knife to make a slanting upward cut, half-way through, about 2.5cm (1in) long.

3 Brush a little hormone rooting powder or liquid into the cut, pack with sphagnum moss to keep cut open.

4 Pull the sleeve over the cut area and pack it with moist sphagnum moss. Tie at the top with more tape or wire.

AFTERCARE

• Care for the parent plant normally, do not remove the layered section until you can see roots.
• Once plenty of roots have formed, cut through the stem below the layered area. Tease out some roots when you pot it up.

PLANTS TO TRY

Air layering is commonly used for leggy indoor plants, but it can be used for garden trees or shrubs.
Indoors
Ficus elastica (rubber plant)
Dracaena
Outdoors
Hamamelis (witch hazel)
Magnolia
Rhododendron (below)
Syringa (lilac)

SERPENTINE LAYERING

Strip the leaves from a healthy shoot at points where the stem will be buried, leaving several intact. Make a slanting cut at each joint almost half-way through. Insert a piece of matchstick into the cut to keep it open. Pin down with wire, cover with soil, keep moist.

Plants to try Serpentine layering is suitable for climbers and trailers with long stems that can be pegged down into the ground such as:
Clematis (opposite)
Lonicera (honeysuckle)
Parthenocissus (Boston ivy)

LEAF CUTTINGS

Leaf cuttings can be fun to root, and are ideal for propagating house-plants such as African voilets (*Saintpaulia*) and Cape primroses (*Streptocarpus*).

LEAF PETIOLE CUTTINGS

1 African violets can be propagated from leaf cuttings taken with the stalk (petiole) attached. Choose young healthy leaves.

2 Trim the stalk, insert into a pot of cuttings compost, vermiculite or perlite, so the leaf blade just touches the compost.

3 Cover with the top half of a plastic drinks bottle or an inflated plastic bag. Label and keep in a warm light place.

4 Keep the compost damp but not wet. Remove condensation. Pot up the plantlet as soon as it is growing well.

LEAF SECTION CUTTINGS

1 Cape primrose leaves can be cut into sections 5–8cm (2–3in) wide, with a sharp knife.

2 Push cut section vertically into a tray of compost. Keep the side nearest the leaf stalk downwards, bury one-third of cutting.

3 Keep compost moist and warm, out of direct sunlight. Pot up plantlets individually

African violets are particularly easy to root from leaf cuttings (see leaf petiole cuttings).

LEAF BLADE CUTTINGS

1 *Begonia rex* produce new plants from the leaf blade (lamina). Mature leaves should be used, keeping part of the stem. Cut across the main veins underneath.

2 Place leaf on a tray of compost, pushing the stalk in helps hold the leaf in place. Use a piece of bent wire to hold the veins down onto the compost.

3 It is also possible to hold down the leaf with small stones.

4 Label, keep tray in a warm place. When small plants develop, separate them carefully and pot up individually.

67

DIVISION

Division is one of the easiest and quickest methods of propagation. Herbaceous plants benefit from division once they have formed a mature clump of growth.

DIVIDING HERBACEOUS PLANTS

1 Divide large clumps as the shoots emerge in spring using a fork to lift the clump.

2 Use two forks back to back to divide the clump into smaller pieces.

3 Replant without further division unless you wish to have smaller plants. To make smaller plants pull or cut the clump apart. Remove any dead plant material.

4 Rake in a garden fertilizer before replanting the smaller pieces into prepared ground.

DIVIDING FLAG IRISES

1 Divide rhizomatous flag irises after flowering, by lifting with a fork and shaking off the soil.

2 Replant the current season's growth, discard the old part of the rhizome.

3 Trim the leaves to 5–8cm (2–3in) to reduce the water loss whilst new roots grow.

DIVIDING AQUATIC PLANTS

1 To remove the plant from a basket, cut roots flush. Using a spade divide the clump into smaller pieces.

2 Aquatic rushes and irises have very tough roots and a sharp knife may be needed to cut through them. Replant the pieces in fresh compost, placing a new liner in the basket if it is to be re-used.

DIVIDING BEGONIA TUBERS

1 Start off tubers in late winter or early spring, in trays of compost. When shoots can be seen, cut tubers into pieces each one having a shoot or bud.

2 Dust the cut surfaces with fungicide, then pot up individually in small pots.

DIVIDING DAHLIA TUBERS

Division is a good way to produce only two or three extra plants. Divide the tubers in late spring with a sharp knife. Each piece should have buds or new shoots growing and a piece of old stem. Another method starts the tubers off in boxes or trays. When the growth is a few centimetres high, cut through the tuber, making sure that each piece has a shoot. Dust cut surfaces with a fungicide then pot up. Replant outside when the weather if good.

4 Replant spreading the roots either side. Cover the roots with soil, leave the top of the rhizome exposed.

ROOT CUTTINGS

Root cuttings are usually taken in winter when there is not much outdoor propagation to be done. Border plants and alpines root readily with this method.

DIVIDING HERBACEOUS PLANTS

1 Lift the parent plant with a fork to expose the roots.

2 If the plant has fleshy, thick roots cut some off close to the main stem or root.

3 Cut each root, into 5cm (2in) pieces, cutting horizontally across the top and with a sloping cut at the bottom.

4 Insert the cuttings into pots of gritty compost. The top of the cuttings should be flush with the top of the compost.

5 Sprinkle a thin layer of grit over the surface, label and keep in a cold frame or cool greenhouse.

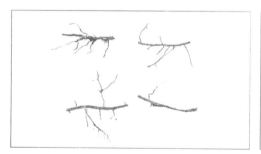

6 Plants with finer roots should be cut into 5–8cm (2–3in) lengths.

7 Lay the cuttings flat on the compost in a tray, cover with compost and store as above.

PLANTS TO TRY

Take root cuttings when the plant is dormant—preferably in early winter.

Perennials to try include acanthus, echinops, gaillardias and border phlox.

Some alpines as well as a few trees, can be raised from root cuttings

Romneya coulteri is an imposing shrub with flowers about 10cm (4in) across on a plant 1.2–1.8m (4–6ft) tall. It can be propagated from root cuttings taken in mid winter, about 7.5cm (3in) in length.

PRUNING 1

Most shrubs require minimal pruning to remove dead or diseased shoots. Some established shrubs benefit from pruning as it can encourage better-flowering or more compact plants

PRUNING FOR COLOURED STEMS

1 Shrubs such as the Dogwood need to be pruned annually or every second year to encourage new stems, like these shown here.

2 Prune in early spring cutting back each stem to an outward facing bud 5cm (2in) from the stump of hard wood.

3 Although the pruning looks severe, new shoots will soon appear.

PRUNING GREY-LEAVED SHRUBS

1 Prune small grey-leaved shrubs in early spring to prevent them getting straggly.

2 Cut close to the base, to where new shoots can be seen.

3 After pruning the plant will look like this but new shoots will soon grow to form a compact shrub.

PRUNING THE WHITEWASH BRAMBLE

1 This shrub is grown for its decorative winter stems that arise directly from the ground. Prune these annually in late winter or early spring.

2 Pruning is simple. Cut off all stems close to the ground, wearing gloves for protection.

3 New shoots grow quickly and these will be more attractive than the old canes.

PRUNING HEATHERS

1 Prune heathers by clipping them with shears to keep them compact and neat.

2 Trim the shoots back after flowering. Prune winter-flowering heathers in spring taking care not to cut into old wood.

Heathers become woody with age. Keep them in shape by clipping the dead heads off after flowering.

PRUNING 2

Shrubs such as buddleias need pruning every year and brooms benefit too from pruning. Cistus don't need routine pruning, but growth will be stimulated and more flowers produced if it is pruned.

PRUNING DECIDUOUS SUCKER-ING SHRUBS

Shrubs such as *Kerria japonica* and *Leycesteria formosa* will be improved by pruning every spring. Prune the flowered stems back to half their original length, to where there is a new shoot after flowering.

Remove about one-third of all stems to within 5–8cm (2–3in) of the ground. Cut back hard any diseased, damaged, or weak shoots.

PRUNING TO A FRAME-WORK

1 Plants that flowered the previous year on shoots produced that year need pruning every spring to keep them compact.

2 Cut back all shoots in spring to within two buds of the previous year's growth.

3 Although the pruning seems harsh, new shoots will grow rapidly and flower later.

REDUCING NEW GROWTH BY HALF

1 Shrubs such as broom and genista, will flower well without pruning but become straggly, with a bare base. Pruning to keep the plants compact is best done when the plant is young.

2 Prune back all green shoots by half the length of the light green growth. Do not cut back old, dark wood.

PRUNING SLOW-GROWING SUMMER-FLOWERING SHRUBS

1 Slow-growing shrubs that flower on sideshoots produced the previous year, grow well without pruning. You can keep them shapely and stimulate more sideshoots by pruning after flowering has finished.

2 Cut back the new growth— which is soft and pale—by about two-thirds, cutting to a leaf joint or a new shoot.

PRUNING 3

Climbers need careful pruning to restrict their height and spread, and to keep them flowering well towards the base.

PRUNING A RAMBLER ROSE

1 Cut out any very old, dead or diseased shoots to the base using long-handled pruners, after flowering.

2 Prune each main shoot of all sideshoots to between two and four pairs of leaves from the main stem.

PRUNING A CLIMBING ROSE

1 Cut out any dead shoots and one or two very old main stems can be cut to the base.

2 Grow new shoots by cutting one or two thick shoots back to 30cm (12in).

3 Reduce the length of all sideshoots to about 15cm (6in).

PRUNING CLEMATIS

1 If your clematis flowers from mid or late summer, prune severely in late winter or early spring, before new growth commences.

2 New shoots produced will flower later in the year.

3 If your clematis flowers in early to mid summer, you must prune more selectively. Before new growth begins, cut back about a third of the stems to about 30cm (12in) above ground.

4 To restrict the plant size and grow new sideshoots, prune back the remaining long branches to a pair of strong buds.

5 If your clematis has small blooms and flowers in spring or early summer, prune only to restrict size, after flowering.

Right Most clematis that flower on old wood require minimal pruning. Those that flower on current growth will become bare of flowers at the base unless pruned annually.

RUSTIC ARCHES AND PERGOLAS

An arch or pergola made from rustic timber is fairly simple to construct and looks good with climbing plants. The bark can be left on or if stripped, the wood will be easier to work with.

Rustic poles can be used to make an attractive support for climbing plants. The same basic joints are used.

A RUSTIC PERGOLA

1 A pergola should be first be planned on paper to ensure it suits the size of your garden.

2 The simplest way to fix horizontal poles to the uprights is to make a notch in the top of each upright, to fit the horizontal pole.

3 For a long pergola, saw two opposing and matching notches as shown. The join must occur over an upright pole. Fix with rustproof nails.

4 Notch the cross-pieces with a V-shape first, then adjust with a chisel before nailing.

A RUSTIC ARCH

2 Assemble the pieces to your own design using a series of basic, strong joints.

1 Before cutting any timber. sketch your design onto paper. A basic design is shown here but it can be modified to suit your needs. Remember to allow about 60cm (2ft) extra on uprights to sink into the ground.

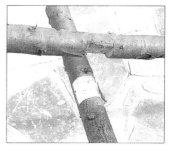

3 Where two pieces cross, mark the position and cut halving joints in each one.

4 Wood glue, in addition to rustproof nails, can be used to improve joint strength.

Opposite Clematis are often grown against a wall, but are good for arches.

5 Bird's mouth joints are used for joining some of the pieces. Mark the pieces, then cut out a V-shape about 2.5cm (1in) deep. Saw the other piece to fit and nail diagonally through the joint.

6 Assemble the sides on the ground first, and make the top separately. Hold the uprights in the prepared holes with wooden struts first of all while you drill and then screw the top into position.

FENCES

Every garden has a boundary, and unless it's secure your garden is at risk. Walls and fences do more than just contain people and animals, they can look attractive and provide the vertical spaces needed for your climbing plants.

ERECTING A PANEL FENCE

1 Panel fences are easy to erect if you use post spikes. Just use a special tool to protect the top, then drive into the ground.

2 Spikes must be absolutely vertical, so keep checking with a spirit-level.

3 Once the post spike is in the ground then the post itself can be inserted. Check again that it is vertical.

4 Lay the panel on the ground in position. Mark the next point for a post spike.

5 Drive the spike in, vertically. Do not leave in position or the panel will be difficult to fix.

6 Nail panel brackets to the post already in position, and on to the next post to be erected at the correct height.

7 Insert panel, and while someone holds it in position erect the next post. Nail through the brackets into the panel.

8 Check the panel is horizontal before and after nailing.

9 Finish off the post by nailing a post cap to the top, which prevents water soaking into the timber.

Right There are other fence designs to try. Here, vertical boards have been nailed either side of the horizontal bars, so that they overlap slightly.

WALLS

Tall boundary walls do not make a good DIY project unless you have bricklaying experience. A low garden wall like this one is suitable as an internal divider as well as a low boundary, and makes a simple bricklaying job with which to start.

MORTAR AND CONCRETE MIXES

For foundations for walls, drives or pre-cast paving

1 part cement
2.5 parts sharp sand*
3.5 parts aggregate*
* Instead of using separate aggregate and sand, you can use 5 parts of combined aggregate to every 1 part cement.

Bedding mortar (to bed and joint concrete/brick paving)

1 part cement
5 parts sharp sand

Masonry mortar (for brickwork)

1 part cement
3 parts soft sand

All parts are by volume. In hot climates, setting retardants may be needed; in cold climates, a form of antifreeze may be required.

BUILDING A LOW BRICK WALL

1 All walls need a foundation. Remove a trench 30cm (12in) deep and put in hardcore. Place pegs as a guide for the concrete. Check levels of the pegs.

2 Pour in the concrete, and level off with the pegs. Tamp the concrete level and remove air pockets with a piece of wood.

3 Leave the concrete to harden for a few days, then lay the first course of bricks. It is vital to form a small pier at each end—and at intervals along the wall if it is long— as shown.

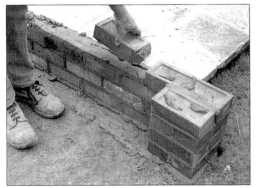

4 Continue to lay courses, first laying a ribbon of mortar on top of the previous row, 'buttering' one end of each brick, as shown.

5 Use a spirit level regularly, strike off excess mortar from the sides of the wall as you work.

6 Use the handle of the trowel to firm and adjust the level of each brick as it is laid.

7 Finish off the wall with coping, and pier caps. This makes the wall look better and protects the brickwork from moisture.

Bricks are a 'sympathetic' building material for paths and walls, integrating house and garden. A raised bed like this is a straightforward project to try, even if you have no previous experience.

SURFACES AND PATHS 1

Along with the lawn, hard surfaces such as paving create the backbone of the garden. Plants add the shape and form, but paving has a profound effect on the visual impact of a garden, so it's important to take care to get it looking good.

LAYING PAVING SLABS

1 Try to prepare proper foundations for paths or patios. The depth of hardcore depends on the weight the paving has to support: 5–10cm (2–4in) for foot traffic, 15cm (6in) for vehicles.

2 Compact the ground either by treading it, tamping it or by using a flat-plate vibrator like this, good for a large area. They can easily be hired.

3 Add the hardcore, checking the depth with a steel rule and a straight edge.

4 Compact the hardcore with a sledge-hammer or club, to break down large pieces

5 Bed the slabs with blobs of mortar (1 part cement to 5 parts sharp sand) one in each corner, one in the centre.

6 Position the slab as accurately as possible, and lower it down from one side.

7 Tap it into position with the handle of a mallet or hammer, check levels with a spirit-level. A slight slope is needed for a large area to allow water to drain away.

8 Place the spirit level across other slabs to check all levels are the same.

9 Paving slabs are designed to either fit flush or have mortar joints. Use spacers to make an even gap for mortar.

10 Fill the joints with a small pointing trowel, recessing the mortar slightly.

LAYING BRICK PAVING

1 Here the bricks are shown bedded on mortar, the base is prepared as for paving slabs but an even layer of mortar is spread across the area being laid. Lay the sides first to make it easier to check levels. The bricks can also be laid on sand.

2 Lay several rows of bricks in your pattern, pressing them into the mortar. Tamp down on a piece of wood, to ensure they are level.

3 To mortar the joints brush dry mortar mix into the gaps. Press down with a piece of wood to remove air pockets.

4 Water with a watering can fitted with a fine rose. Do not flood the area. Clean mortar stains with a damp cloth before they dry.

Right Bricks and plants look good together, as these tumbling petunias testify.

SURFACES AND PATHS 2

Paths and other hard surface areas can be the dominant part of the garden design, so mix materials and surfaces together: the stepping-stone path pictured opposite makes an imposing focal point but is practical in that it protects the lawn too.

LAYING PAVERS

1 Clay pavers look like bricks but are thinner and fit together without mortar joints.
After preparing a sub-base of 5–10cm(2–4in) compacted hardcore, mortar in position a firm edge to work from. Check levels and adjust if necessary.

2 Lay a 5cm (2in) bed of sand. Ensure that the pavers will be level with the edging when laid on the sand. Use battens as a height gauge, to enable a third piece of wood to level the sand.

3 As you lay the pavers in the required pattern, check that they butt up against each other and to the edging.

4 Hiring a flat-plate vibrator is the easiest way to settle the pavers into the sand. Tamping over a piece of wood will also be effective.

5 Brush sand over the pavers to fill the joints. Vibrating or tamping the pavers again may require more sand to be brushed into the joints.

LAYING STEPPING STONES

1 Pace out the area to indicate where each stone should be when you walk with a normal stride.

2 Lay the stones on the lawn, stand back to check that they look right visually.

3 Walk over the stones once more before you set them into the lawn, to make sure the spacing is comfortable..

A stepping-stone path can take the eye across to another focal point, protecting the lawn and your shoes.

4 Cut around the edge of each stone with a spade, deep enough to be able to remove a slice of grass, slightly deeper than the stepping-stone.

5 Slice beneath the grass with a spade, then lift out the piece of turf.

6 Use a little sand to level the base and bring the stone to the right height. Check the level and set just below the surrounding grass.

SURFACES AND PATHS 3

A large area of plain paving can look boring so think about creating an interesting effect by mixing materials. Crazy-paving can give a garden an old-fashioned feel especially if you choose natural stone or a sympathetic substitute.

LAYING CRAZY PAVING

1 Always lay the pieces dry first. Lay large pieces with a straight edges first, at the sides. You can fill in with smaller pieces once these are in place.

2 Once the pieces have been arranged loosely, start to bed them on a mortar mix (1 part cement to 5 parts sharp sand).

MIXING MATERIALS

Do not be afraid to mix materials: railway sleepers and bricks or clay pavers look good together, gravel softens the harshness of rectangular paving slabs, and rows of bricks break up areas of concrete.

3 Use a piece of board across the width of the paving and tamp to create a level finish.

4 Finish off by mortaring between the joints, using a small pointing trowel. You can add a cement dye to match the stone colour.

GARDENING BASICS

Right
Combining pavers with a range of pebbles creates an unusual surface.

INTRODUCING PEBBLES

1 Beach pebbles can be used to make a paved area more interesting, or to fill in gaps created when you lay a curved path. Create a bed of mortar, then lay the stones as closely as you can.

2 Use a stout piece of wood, laid across the adjoining slabs, to ensure that the tops of the pebbles are flush with the paving. Tap the wood with a hammer to bed them in evenly.

EDGINGS

LAYING A TERRACOTTA EDGE

A smart edge will put that finishing touch to a path, bed or border and will prevent wear and tear at the lawn edges.

1 Excavate a shallow trench deep enough to take the edging. The design being laid is the rope pattern.

2 Chisel off any mortar or rubble protruding beneath the path so the edging can be laid flush with the path.

3 Tap each piece down with the handle of a hammer, checking levels visually.

4 Back fill with soil, compact it to stabilize each piece. Add more soil and compact again.

5 Use a long spirit level to ensure that the edging is straight, adjusting height if necessary.

FIXING A WOODEN EDGE

1 Unwind the roll, and cut to size through the strands of wire with pliers or wire-cutters.

2 Dig out a trench at the right depth to allow the edging to sit in place.

3 Join pieces by wiring together in position.Check the level and height, then back fill with soil and compact it.

4 Lay a long piece of wood across the top of the edging, and knock it firmly into place with a club hammer, ensuring the top is level.

LAYING A LAWN EDGING STRIP

1 Use a spade to form a slit trench along the edge of the lawn, keeping it as vertical as possible.

2 Unroll the strip and cut it to size. Lay it loosely in the trench to estimate the length.

3 Back fill with soil, firming it without pressing so hard that you distort the shape of the edging.

4 Finish off by tapping it level with the handle of a hammer over a piece of wood. Make sure the edging is not above the lawn level, or the mower may be damaged.

A brick edging gives a smart finish to a path or lawn.

FLOWERS & FOLIAGE

No matter how well designed a garden is, with features like patios, pergolas and ponds, it is the flowers and foliage that make a garden such a pleasant place to relax in. In the following pages you will find plenty of advice on how to get the very best from your ornamental plants, as well as how to create features such as ponds, rock gardens and lawns.

Opposite
Be flexible in the way you approach your planting. In this border there is a happy mixture of annuals and shrubby plants together with herbaceous plants.

INTRODUCTION

Flowers and foliage are the flesh that clothes the skeleton of the hard landscaping. They give the garden shape by softening harsh outlines, adding colour and providing plenty of textures.

The plants used and the way they are arranged are a personal choice. Planting 'rules' should only ever be treated as guidelines which you can then interpret to suit your taste and garden layout.

Above Spring would not be spring without daffodils in their many varieties.

If starting from scratch, make sure that the garden framework is right before you begin planting. It is easier to undertake major construction work before the garden is planted. If lots of plants are needed, it is worth propagating your own.

Make the lawns after the hard landscaping, or improve existing grass. Lawns form the largest percentage of ground-cover in most gardens. Getting this area right will have an enormous

Above Use annuals with traditional border plants to create a 'cottage garden' atmosphere.

Left Tubs of colour help to bring life to an otherwise green area. The lavatera in the border is a good choice because it flowers for many months.

Left Few trees or shrubs have a long flowering season, so make the most of foliage. Golden *Sambucus racemosa* contrasts with a purple variety of *Cotinus coggygria*.

Above Hanging baskets add colour and height to a dull spot.

Below Pelargoniums are traditional summer bedding plants.

impact on the overall impression of the garden.

When you plant beds and borders, balance your long-term aims with immediate impact. Plants herbaceous perennials and shrubs first, as they take at least a year to start growing well, and fill in the gaps with plenty of bedding plants and bulbs for instant colour.

Make sure you get the best from your greenhouse, which can become an interesting year-round hobby in itself.

IMPROVING A COLD OR WINDY GARDEN

FLOWERS & FOLIAGE

An exposed or cold garden is problematic. If you choose suitable plants and use shelter belts and windbreaks, you can still enjoy the benefits of a beautiful garden.

PLANTING CONIFERS

Conifers are best bought as small pot-grown plants, which will keep the cost down and species suitable for growing against a wall will soon grow tall.

ARTIFICIAL WINDBREAKS

Moulded plastic windbreak nets will give protection for five to ten years and are useful while hedges and living screens are becoming established. Nail or staple the netting to stout posts 1.8m (6ft) apart.

Plastic webbing lasts for a similar time and is useful for vegetable or fruit gardens where appearance is not so important. Stretch each strand tight, then staple to the posts.

PLANTING A SHELTER BELT

A living shelter belt filters the wind and reduces its velocity, so that the plants are protected.

AVOIDING TURBULENCE

When wind hits a solid object it creates turbulence, which will damage plants.

Hedges and screens of tall shrubs are efficient wind breaks, reducing the wind velocity and turbulence.

1 To improve the soil structure properly, fork in garden compost or manure into a 60cm (2ft) wide strip.

2 Break down any large clumps of earth before planting and sprinkle on fertilizer (use a slow-acting one in winter)

3 Garden lines ensure that the row of trees will be straight. Plant the trees 30–60cm (1–2ft) apart, staggered if the area is very windy.

4 Hedging plants are sold in bundles of bare-rooted plants. Keep the roots moist until you are ready to plant them out.

5 Remove the plants one at a time, digging a large hole and spreading out the roots.

6 Always firm the soil well to remove air pockets and to anchor the roots firmly.

7 Rake the soil level, then water thoroughly. Keep well watered for the first season.

SCREENS AND THICK HEDGES

If you need protection from the wind or sound proofing from traffic, plant a double hedge. Space the plants 60–90cm (2–3ft) apart, in two staggered rows.

If the site is very exposed, a shelter belt of trees will give more protection than a double hedge. Plant trees 1.2–1.8m (4–6ft) apart so they grow into each other.

AVOID FROST TRAPS

In sloping gardens, placing hedges at the highest level, with an opening at the lowest level lets the cold air flow downhill.

PLANTING AND GROWING SHRUBS 1

Shrubs form a permanent framework for the garden, giving it shape over the year. Use them as a border or in mixed borders, as a specimen or a focal point plant. Get them off to a good start and your shrubs will provide years of pleasure in return for the minimum of time and effort.

BALLED PLANTS

1 Some plants are sold with their roots wrapped in hessian or a plastic material. They are usually cheaper than container grown plants of the same size.

2 Prepare the ground as for container-grown plants, checking the depth of the hole as shown.

3 Untie the wrapper when the shrub is in position and at the right depth, sliding it out of the hole. Try not to disturb the ball of soil.

4 Replace the soil, firming it well to remove air pockets and stabilize the shrub.

5 Water thoroughly, then apply a mulch of chipped bark, garden compost to conserve moisture and suppress weeds.

CONTAINER-GROWN SHRUBS

1 Space the potted shrubs out on to the ground to assess their final position in the border. This makes adjustments easier.

2 Dig over the ground, remove weeds, and fork in well-rotted manure or garden compost.

3 Set the plant in the hole in its pot, checking that the new soil level will match the old soil mark on the stem. Use a cane to check the levels.

IMAGINATIVE PLANTING

Shrub borders are often large but a small border can be planted using dwarf shrubs. Choose a mixture of foliage and flowering shrubs, deciduous and evergreen, so there is plenty of interest all year round.

In small gardens a mixed border can be used with tall shrubs at the back and herbaceous plants at the front, with evergreen shrubs for winter interest.

Some shrubs make good focal point plants. Plant them either in containers, as isolated specimens or as a group in a lawn. Use a bright flowering shrub as a focal point to view across

the garden against a background of less colourful shrubs.

Foliage lasts much longer than flowers and in a dull or shady area of the garden,

yellow leaves can be almost as bright as blooms. Group foliage shrubs together for an attractive picture throughout the summer.

PLANTING EVERGREENS

Shield from cold and drying winds until they are rooted into the soil. Make a shelter out of a sheet of polythene fixed to canes.

SPACING SHRUBS

After five to ten years most shrubs will become overcrowded so plant shrubs with final spacings in mind. Fill gaps with cheap, quick-growing shrubs.

1 If roots are tightly wound around the sides of the pot, tease some of them out to encourage them to grow into the surrounding soil quickly.

2 Replace the soil and firm it in well to remove any air pockets that could cause the roots to dry out.

3 If the soil is poor, apply a fertilizer around the plant avoiding the stem. Water well and apply a thick mulch of garden compost or chipped bark.

Established shrubs need little routine care, but weeding, feeding and mulching will keep them looking good. If a shrub has been planted in the wrong place, or has outgrown the area, it may be possible to move it to another part of the garden.

MOVING AN ESTABLISHED SHRUB

1 Quite large shrubs can be moved with care. Move deciduous shrubs when they are dormant and evergreens in the autumn or spring.

2 Dig a trench all around the shrub, forking around the roots to loosen them.

3 Use a fork to remove more soil if the shrub is large, being careful not to damage the roots.

4 When the root ball is a manageable size, use a spade to cut underneath it, working around the plant evenly.

5 Make sure the new hole is large enough to take the shrub. Roll up a piece of hessian or plastic sheeting and position against the root ball. Tilt the plant back and push the hessian underneath it, rocking the root ball over it.

6 Tie the hessian around the root ball. Lifting the shrub is likely to need two pairs of hands. Only small shrubs can be lifted easily by one person.

7 Use a barrow or trolley to move the shrub to its new home if necessary. Remove the wrapping material carefully. After filling in the hole and firming, water well and keep watered for several months in dry weather.

WEEDING

1 If annual weeds are a problem, you can use some contact weedkillers if you protect the stems and leaves. Use a dribble bar on the watering can to prevent spray drift.

2 Some weedkillers can be used with care around established shrubs to prevent weed seedlings emerging.

3 Hoeing and hand-weeding works well provided you do not let perennial weeds get established.

4 A mulch of garden compost or chipped bark will control weeds and cover bare soil.

5 Established shrubs do not usually need annual feeding, but young shrubs benefit from a dose of general fertilizer in the spring. If a shrub is not thriving, apply a little fertilizer.

6 Acid-loving shrubs can thrive in alkaline soils if they are treated with a chelated iron twice a year.

PLANTING GROUND-COVER SHRUBS

1 Ground-cover shrubs will suppress weeds after a few years growth. Planting through garden matting is simple and effective. Remove weeds first, then tuck in the edges of the matting into the ground to secure it. This method does not suit all colonizing plants as the matting can suppress the plants as well as the weeds.

2 Cut in a cross shape in the sheet to plant shrubs.

4 The matting will be concealed when the plants grow, but can be covered with chipped bark initially.

3 Plant the shrubs through the slit: a trowel can be used with small plants.

PLANTING CLIMBERS AND TRAILERS 1

Climbers need special care as they are often planted in dry areas, in the 'rain shadow' of walls, fences or trees. Take extra care when planting climbers so they get a good start with support to train them.

AIM HIGH

Fix trellis above soil level as shoots need support from about 30cm (12in) or higher. Plan to fix the trellis with the base about 30–45cm (12–18in) above the ground. This will allow more height on which to secure the climber.

PLANTING A CLIMBER

1 Fix the support first. Then dig a large hole to take the root ball, 45cm (18in) away from the wall. Work compost into the base of the hole.

2 Position the plant so that it leans towards the wall at 45° angle, and check the level with surrounding soil with a cane or stick.

3 Tease out a few roots from the root ball, replace and firm the soil. Water well.

4 Untie any shoots fixed to the cane. Tie them to the wall support, spread them out widely, vertically and horizontally, so the plant will not be bare at the base.

FIXING A BOUGHT TRELLIS

1 Expandable wooden trellises are ideal for lightweight plants such as large-flowered clematis, but unsuitable for vigorous climbers or wall shrubs. Expand the trellis to the required size, then mark fixing positions on the wall. Drill and plug the wall, allowing a gap for spacers.

2 Use small scraps of wood to hold the trellis away from the wall. Fix with rustproof screws.

PLANTING TIPS

Your climber will grow quickly if you add as much compost as you can, before planting. Adding moisture-retaining material is important, as the area used for planting climbers is usually drier than other positions in the garden.

To keep the ground moist, mulch the ground after planting with chipped bark or a similar material. Aim for a 5cm (2in) minimum depth of mulch.

PLASTIC TRELLISES

Plastic-covered metal trellises for clematis and other climbers that are not too vigorous usually come with spacer and fixing screws. If fixing to a brick wall, drill holes with a masonry drill use a wall plug the correct size.

PLANTING A TRAILER

1 Prostrate or low-growing plants will tend to tumble over the edge of a raised bed easier if they are planted at an angle. Set the root ball at an angle of 45°, growing towards the edge of the wall.

2 Trailers such as ground ivy will grow in all directions if not trained. Plant close to the edge of the bed, then direct as many shoots as possible down the front. Pinch out shoots growing inwards.

PLANTING CLIMBERS AND TRAILERS 2

Even if your patio is wall-to-wall paved, there are ways to plant climbers to soften the brickwork, without fixing trellis. Use self-clinging climbers, or support with wires or wall ties.

FIXING WITHOUT A SUPPORT

Lead-headed nails
Useful for fixing small climbers to old walls with soft mortar. Drive them in with a hammer, then fold the soft flap over to hold the shoot.
Epoxy resin ties A plastic tie you 'glue' by mixing a special putty with a hardener and pressing to the wall.

PLANTING IN PAVING

1 Lift one or two paving slabs next to the wall. Chisel away any mortar and remove the sub-base for the paving.

2 Once soil is found, add garden compost and slow-release fertilizer. Fork together, mixing it thoroughly. If the area is small, use a small border fork to mix together.

3 Plant the climber as described in the next section. The soil can be covered with fine gravel or beach pebbles to make it more attractive on a patio.

PLANTING A CLIMBER IN A CONTAINER

1 A container can be sited on top of paving. Use a large container as wall shrubs and climbers need space.

2 Place a layer of rubble or broken clay pots in the base to help water drain freely, then fill with a loam based compost.

3 Plant firmly and water well. Train to the support. Plant small ivies or annual trailers to cascade over the front of the container for summer colour.

SECURING CLIMBERS AND WALL SHRUBS

1 Old walls may have a soft lime-based mortar, so vine eyes (metal tags with a hole through which you can fix a wire) can be knocked in. House mortar will be too hard, so drill and plug the wall before inserting screw-type eyes. Stretch galvanized wire between the eyes 30–45cm (12–18in) apart. Twiners like clematis need vertical wires to form a mesh.

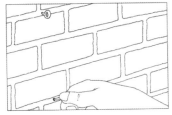

2 Tie shoots loosely to the wires, with twine or plastic leaving space for growth.

Right
Climbers such as *Lonicera periclymenum*, a honeysuckle, are vigorous climbers quickly covering a wall or fence.

PLANTING TREES 1

Trees should always be planted with care. You have only one chance to get them off to a good start, so choose your tree and a suitable position with care, then plant and stake it carefully.

PLANTING A TREE IN A LAWN

1 Mark out the edge of the circular bed 90cm–1.2m (3–4ft) across. Push the spade in vertically, then at a shallow angle.

2 Remove the top 30cm (12in) of soil, then fork over the rest thoroughly working in compost or manure.

3 Insert the stake before you plant then hammer it in.

4 If planting a container-grown tree, tease out some of the roots before planting.

5 Put the roots in the soil, lay a cane across the hole to check the soil levels.

BARE-ROOTED TREES

Bare-rooted trees should be planted while they are still dormant— between late autumn and early spring. Spread the roots out widely, checking that the soil level on the stem is the same as the surrounding soil.

6 Return the soil and tread in firmly to remove air pockets. If the soil is poor, rake in a slow-release fertilizer.

7 Water well, then apply a mulch at least 5cm (2in) thick to keep down weeds and conserve moisture.

HOW TO APPLY A TREE TIE

1 Select a tree tie that has a buffer to separate the stake from the tree itself.

2 Loop the tie around the tree, push the free end through the spacer.

3 Push the end through the tie around the stake. Leave the end long as the tie will need adjusting as the trunk grows.

4 To prevent the tie slipping, nail it in position. Staking is needed only for three or four years.

POPULAR STAKES

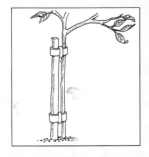

High stakes are best for trees which have long thin stems.
Low stakes suit most trees as they allow the stem to flex in the wind.
Angled stakes are good if adding a stake after the tree has been planted. Insert at an angle to miss the root ball.

Plant a tree in your lawn to suit the size of your garden. Where space is restricted, plant a small conifer.

PLANTING TREES 2

After planting, make sure your trees grow into an attractive shape, reduce competition from weeds and protect them from animals.

WIND PROTECTION

Evergreen trees and shrubs will benefit from wind protection in the first autumn and winter. Fix windbreak netting around canes but leave the top open. Remove in the spring.

FORMATIVE TRAINING

1 If you want a multi-stemmed tree, buy one with shoots along the trunk. Prune only the shoots that cross others or are badly positioned. Do this only once.

2 If you want a tree with a clear trunk, cut back all the shoots above the branching head to 10–15cm (4–6in). When the tree is dormant, cut these back to the stem.

3 If you want a tree with a dominant central leading shoot, prune back all other shoots to the stem leaving the dominant, most upright shoot to continue growing.

4 Some trees are best with a rounded, branching head. Remove lower shoots to make a clear stem. Remove the tip of the leading shoot when the tree has reached its final height.

CONSERVING MOISTURE AND CONTROLLING WEEDS

1 Thorough watering will help the tree to become established more quickly. Insert a pot close to the roots and water will penetrate the roots easier.

2 A mulch will conserve moisture, keep down weeds and look attractive. Lay at least 5cm (2in) depth to be effective.

3 Mulching sheets are not as attractive, but just as effective at controlling weeds and retaining moisture.

USING A TREE GUARD

1 If animals strip off the tree bark in your garden, provide guards for new trees. Those available are only suitable for trees with clear stems. Start at the bottom of the stem and wind the guard around as you work upwards.

2 Wire -netting can be used for conifers. Insert four canes around the plant and secure small-wire netting to this. Secure to the canes with galvanised wire.

GROWING BULBS 1

Bulbs, corms and tubers can be used to good effect in borders, in grass, formal beds and the home. Bulbs are available in the spring for summer flowering, so bulb planting is not just for the autumn.

PLANTING IN A BORDER

1 Dig a hole large enough to take a group of bulbs. Fork in compost or manure if the soil is poor.

2 Bulbs suitable for a border need good drainage. Add a layer of grit or coarse sand before planting.

3 Space out the bulbs, planting at a depth which allows twice their own depth of soil.

4 To deter slugs and improve drainage, sprinkle more grit around them.

5 If planting summer-flowering bulbs, mark their position to avoid planting others in the same spot.

Left Crocuses can grow in pots and bowls indoors, window boxes, beds and borders to bring colour when few other plants are flowering. They can even be planted in the lawn.

PLANTING IN GRASS

1 Use an edging iron to cut a straight line into the grass where you want to plant.

2 Use a spade to slice beneath the grass, then fold back the turf for planting.

3 Fork over the compacted ground to loosen it. Add fertilizer at the same time.

4 Bulbs, corms and tubers look best if scattered randomly as this gives a natural effect.

5 Large bulbs need planting with a trowel in twice their own depth of soil. Small bulbs can be pressed into the soil.

6 Fold back the turf flaps and firm carefully. Check the lawn level and adjust with extra soil if necessary.

7 Large bulbs can also be planted with a bulb planter instead of lifting the turf.

8 Most bulb planters are designed to release the core of soil easily.

9 Crumble some soil from the bottom of the core to cover the bulb. Press the plug of grass back into the hole.

GARDENING BASICS

111

GROWING BULBS 2

For indoors in early spring, try growing hyacinths in a glass.

HYACINTHS IN GLASSES

1 Above Buy good sized bulbs. Fill the glass with water so that the bulb base is just clear of the water. Keep the glass in a cold, dark place. Top up with water whenever necessary.

2 Below When the bud is emerging and beginning to show colour, move the bulb to a light, warm place to flower.

PLANTING HYACINTHS IN A BOWL

1 Part fill a bowl with bulb fibre, them put three or five bulbs in place so that a third of the bulb will be visible above the compost.

2 Water, then place the bulbs in a cool, shady place outdoors. Protect the bulbs with a plastic bag then cover with grit, sand or peat.

3 When the shoots reach 2.5–5cm (1–2in) tall, bring them into a light, cool place indoors. When the buds emerge move them to a warm area.

AFTER FLOWERING

1 Never force bulbs into a second year, plant them out in the garden and they may bloom another year. Discard bulbs forced in glasses or on pebbles as they do not do well after this treatment.

2 Let the bulb leaves die down naturally and only cut them off when they begin to wither. Do not bend or tie the leaves as next years flowering could be reduced.

3 Where bulbs grow in a lawn, do not cut the grass for at least six weeks after flowering. Wait until the leaves turn yellow then cut them off with shears before mowing.

DIVIDING BULBS 'IN THE GREEN'

Some bulbs are sold 'in the green', with the leaves on. Lift an overcrowded clump with a fork and separate it. Replant the smaller bulbs where they are, larger bulbs can be moved elsewhere. Water well.

DIVIDING OVER-CROWDED CLUMPS

1 Poor flowering could be caused by overcrowding. Lift, divide and replant the clumps of bulbs. Do this when the plant is dormant, but before the leaves die down completely, so it is easier to see where the clumps are.

2 Separate the clump into smaller pieces and replant some of the larger bulbs in the same way. Discard surplus bulbs or replant elsewhere.

LIFTING AND STORING

1 Some bulbs are best lifted and stored after flowering, to protect them from frost. Use a fork to carefully lift the bulbs. Keep the large bulbs and discard smaller ones. Place the bulbs to be saved on a wire rack for a few days.

2 Shake the bulbs in a bag of fungicide, remove them with care and store in paper bags in a cool dry place.

GROWING HERBACEOUS PLANTS 1

FLOWERS & FOLIAGE

Herbaceous borders are less popular than they used to be, but they can be used in an original and imaginative way, even in small gardens.

1 Prepare the ground well, adding compost and raking the ground level, before planting. Space the plants out on the ground before planting. Try to visualize the mature size of each plant before finally deciding on the plant positions. Ground-cover plants are best planted in bold groups and perennials in groups of three or five of each plant for a good effect.

PLANTING HERBACEOUS PLANTS

2 Water all plants an hour before planting.

3 Plant with a trowel or spade if the plant is large, working your way across the border.

4 Return the soil and firm well to remove air pockets.

5 Always water thoroughly unless the weather is wet.

6 Keep root-wrapped plants moist in a cool, shady place until ready to plant out.

7 Remove wrapping and spread the roots out widely in the hole. Water well.

114

HERBACEOUS PLANTS IN GRAVEL

If you have a gravel garden, try planting bold perennials like verbascum, acanthus, euphorbia or fennel.

GROUND-COVER

Many border perennials make good ground-cover plants, suppress weeds and look attractive.

Some die down in winter but are very pretty for the summer. For evergreen ground-cover try bergenias or epimediums.

ONE-SIDED HERBACEOUS BORDER

Herbaceous borders are designed to be viewed from one side, the tallest plants at the back and smaller ones at the front. This is a good choice for a narrow garden where an island bed is not possible. A width of 1.2m (4ft) is ideal for access to attend all plants. If possible, leave a narrow access path at the back.

ISLAND BEDS

These can be more interesting when there is space. Place the tallest plants in the middle and the smaller radiating towards the edges.

PLANTING AN INVASIVE PLANT

Some grasses and herbaceous plants can be very invasive. Plant them in a large bucket or pot to restrict their spread.

Make drainage holes in the base then sink into the ground so that the rim is level with the surrounding soil.

Put potting compost in the base of the container so that the root ball is at the right level. Firm well, add more compost around the sides and top up the container so that it is hidden.

GROWING HERBACEOUS PLANTS 2

FLOWERS & FOLIAGE

Most herbaceous plants will grow for years without attention, but they will eventually need dividing and replanting. Some benefit from staking, especially in exposed gardens.

DIVIDING AND REPLANTING

1 Loosen the clump with a spade or fork, and lift it onto the soil surface.

DIVIDING FOR PROPAGATION

If propagating more plants, pull the pieces apart by hand in small sections with a shoot and root. Pot them up or grow them on in another piece of ground before replanting.

2 Plants with fibrous roots should be divided with two forks placed back to back.

3 To maintain the plant's vigour, discard the centre of the old plant. Replant only the young pieces from around the edge.

4 Plants with thick fleshy roots may need a spade to chop it into smaller pieces. Divide the crowns with a sharp knife carefully then replant groups of two or three pieces.

5 Small plants can be lifted with a hand fork and pulled apart by hand, or separated with two hand forks.

STAKING PERENNIALS

1 Natural supports such as twiggy sticks are hidden when the plant grows through them. Insert sticks when the plants are just a few centimetres (inches) high, and new shoots will grow through them. If the plant is low growing, bend the tops of the sticks over as shown.

COMPACT FOLIAGE

Plants with tall flower spikes are vulnerable to wind damage, such as delphiniums, and should be staked with individual canes. Start tying the stem to the cane once the plant is 20–25cm(8–10in) tall.

2 Other supports are expensive but last for many years. Styles and sizes vary but they can be clipped together. Insert them before the plant reaches the height of the support.

CUTTING BACK

1 Some plants produce a second smaller flowering late in the season if they are dead-headed immediately after flowering. Cut the shoots off close to the base with secateurs or shears.

2 Dead-heading plants will make them look tidier. Some look better if they are cut back to ground level after flowering. New foliage will probably grow.

3 Cut back the dead flowered stems at the end of the season. The borders will look tidier and rotting plant material will not encourage overwintering pests and diseases.

KEEPING BORDERS BRIGHT

Shrubs, herbaceous and mixed borders, will look better if a few minutes are spent each week tidying them up. Feeding and watering are not essential, but the display will be more brilliant if you give the plants a boost.

FEEDING AND MULCHING

1 Feed your border plants annually, and shrubs when ever they need a boost. Roses, which are demanding feeders should be fed annually. Sprinkle the fertilizer around the edge of the plants, not over the leaves. Apply it in spring or early summer.

2 Hoe or rake the fertilizer into the top 2.5cm (1in) of soil, remove any that falls on leaves.

3 Water the ground to dissolve the fertilizer, if rain is not forecast.

4 For plants that seem sickly and are not thriving, a foliar feed can be tried. Apply when the sun has moved off the plant by drenching with a fine spray.

5 Mulching helps to suppress weeds and conserve moisture. It also improves the look of the soil. Apply in a layer 5cm (2in) thick to be effective.

SPECIAL NEEDS

Chalky soil will make some plants look yellow. Lime haters such as camellias need to be watered with a chelated iron (Sequestrene) at least once a year. Mix it with water, then apply following the instructions.

As the season progresses, borders can look untidy. Keep the plants watered and fed, and the ground weeded for a smart border like this.

WEEDING

1 Keep the hoe moving around the plants on a dry day, taking the tops off and leaving them to wilt and die.

2 Deep-rooted perennial weeds will regrow if you chop them off at soil level. Dig down and remove the roots completely.

DEAD-HEADING SHRUBS

Many herbaceous plants look better if dead-headed, but large-flowered shrubs such as lilacs also benefit. Take care to remove only the dead flower and not any buds.

END-OF-SEASON CLEAR-UP

1 Cut down the tops of herbaceous plants at the end of the season, unless they are hardy. Gather all the dead stems with a spring-tined lawn rake, and put on the compost heap. Leaving them on the ground will attract disease and slugs.

2 Pick fallen leaves off low ground-cover and rock plants as they block out light and encourage diseases.

PLANT SUPPORTS

Good supports will be hidden once plants have grown, and can make all the difference to whole ranges of plants—from herbaceous perennials to climbers and vegetables such as tomatoes and runner beans.

SUPPORTING CANES

1 This method is good for runner beans and sweet peas. Insert the canes in angled pairs, then slide a cane through the V formed at the top and tie firmly.

2 A wigwam of canes can be used for runner beans, sweet peas and climbers. Use three to five canes pushed into the ground at an angle and tie firmly.

3 Wigwam cane holders are easy to use. Canes push through the holes in the plastic ring which holds them firmly in place.

PLASTIC CANE GRIPS

Plastic grips can be used to hold the ridge of canes together. One design has two holes for the pairs of canes to be inserted, a horizontal cane is threaded through a plastic loop, which when pulled holds them firmly in place.

Above Metal plants supports are good for border plants with fragile stems. Place the supports early so the plants can grow through them.

SUPPORTING HERBACEOUS PLANTS

1 Twiggy sticks can be used as plant supports if inserted early so the plants can grow up through them.

2 Bend over the twiggy sticks if the plants are small so that they meet in the centre.

4 Chrysanthemums can be supported by the type shown above or net stretched between four canes. Raise the support as the season progresses.

3 Insert three or four canes around the clump and secure with twine or string.

5 Plastic-coated metal supports are more expensive but last for many years. They come in various sizes and and can be linked together.

6 Sometimes it is only the tall flower spikes which need support. Use single canes and tie the stem to the cane as it grows.

CANE SUPPORTS FOR GROWING BAGS

Tall plants grown in growing bags were difficult to support before the advent of proprietary cane supports. The one illustrated has three legs that are assembled using a base clip. When the support has been pushed through the growing bag from the bottom a retaining ring is pushed over the top of the cane clamp. The cane can then be pushed into the clamp.

SUPPORT FOR WALL SHRUBS AND CLIMBERS

Trellis or support wires are the best wall support for climbers. Wall fixers are an alternative to drilling walls, a popular make uses an epoxy bonder that you mix with adhesive in your hand until it turns the right colour. This is used to fix the plastic tie to the wall. After five minutes it will be dry enough to be able to tie the plant, but it is better to wait half a day if possible.

FLOWERS & FOLIAGE

GETTING THROUGH WINTER

Many plants can be saved from the winter cold if they are protected adequately. Frost-tender plants will succumb to frosts no matter where you live, plants that tolerate some frost in one area may be killed off in another area. Take into account the type of winters you experience and protect plants if in doubt.

LIFTING DAHLIAS

1 Lift dahlia tubers, with a fork, once the frost has blackened the foliage.

2 Stand the tubers upside down in a dry frost-free place. This will help moisture to drain from the hollow stems, and reduce the risk of rotting later.

3 Once the tubers are dry, pack them in boxes of peat, or other insulating material, and keep in a frost-proof place for the winter. Label the tubers individually if storing more than one variety.

PROTECTING VULNERABLE SHRUBS

1 Protect valuable shrubs of borderline hardiness with a winter wrap. Make a frame of canes, cover with polythene or layers of horticultural fleece to make a form of tent.

2 Protect tender wall shrubs with a shield of conifer branches.

ALPINES

Alpines grow in cold winter areas, but are prone to waterlogging. You can protect vulnerable alpines with a sheet of glass held in a wire frame, or on bricks, above the plants.

STORING TENDER BULBS

1 Lift gladioli and vulnerable bulbs before there are penetrating frosts. Use a fork to remove them and dry them off before storing. Bulblets or cormlets formed around the bases, should be stored separately.

2 Dust the bulbs with a fungicide—or dip them into a fungicidal solution, then leave to dry again.

3 Pack in paper (not plastic) bags, or nets, and keep in a frost-free place. Don't forget to label them.

Summer Bedding

When you buy your summer bedding plants or raise them yourself, plant them with imagination as well as care. Do not plant them out until all danger of frost has passed and make sure they have been hardened off. Be guided by your local parks department, if in doubt when to plant.

PLANTING IN DRIFTS

1 Plant in drifts for a bold effect. Bold splashes of colour look better than mixed plants together. Mark out a basic pattern before you plant.

2 Water the trays half an hour before planting, to ensure the compost is thoroughly moist.

3 Remove plants carefully and lay them on the soil to set the spacing. Adjust the space according to each plant's needs.

4 Dig a hole with a trowel and plant deeper than the depth of the seed tray. Firm in place to reduce the risk of the roots drying out.

5 Water well and continue to water in dry weather until the plants become established.

TIPS FOR BRIGHT BEDDING SCHEMES

Dot plants, sometimes called spot plants, are used to give height to a bed of low-growing plants. These can be other flowering plants or silver leaved foliage plants. Fuchsias are sometimes used, but try any plant that is bold and contrasts well with others.

Carpet bedding (below) uses flowering and foliage plants to create geometric, abstract, or theme designs in a formal way. You can try this in a small garden with dwarf bedding plants like lobelia, alyssum and French marigolds.

Island beds look good planted with a formal design, with a tall feature in the centre.
Informal grouping (below) appeals to gardeners who dislike formality. Interplant two, three or four plants so that they grow into each other.

Bedding plants don't have to be bold or even used in a formal bed. Here they are in a predominately white scheme in front of shrubs.

SPRING BEDDING

Clear summer bedding, as soon as it has finished, and replant for a spring display.

PLANTING SPRING BEDDING PLANTS

1 Lift the remains of the summer bedding, then fork over the ground. If necessary, apply bonemeal.

2 Remove all weeds, rake in the fertilizer if used, and level the ground ready for planting.

3 **Above** Water plants well half an hour before lifting.

4 **Above right** Lift with as much soil as possible, firming it into a ball around the roots.

5 **Right** Plant with a trowel checking that the spacing looks right as you go.

MIXED BEDDING SCHEMES

If planting more than one kind of bedding plant, allow plenty of space when you plant the first type. Then lay out the second choice to check spacing.

Fully plant a small area at a time, otherwise it will be difficult to avoid treading on young plants.

BULBS

Bulbs interplanted with spring bedding plants look good and extend the period of interest.

Plant the bulbs between the young plants as you go along, to avoid having to step on them.

A Lawn from Seed

Sowing a lawn is cheaper than making one from turf and will establish quickly if sown at the right time— in spring or early autumn. Regular watering will be needed if sowing takes place in the summer.

PREPARING THE GROUND

1 Level the ground, by raking down from the top of the levelling pegs. Check the level of the pegs with a spirit level.

2 Firm the soil by treading it to remove air pockets. Shuffle your feet over the area, first one way, then the next.

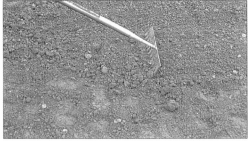

THE RIGHT TYPE OF SEED

Different seed mixtures are suitable for different tasks. Hard-wearing seed will contain ryegrass, decorative lawn seed will not. Lawns with ryegrass can look good and wear well.

These trial plots show how cultivation is as important as the seed. The left plots are a ryegrass mix, the plots on the right are without ryegrass. The top plots have been treated with weedkiller, but the bottom ones have not.

3 Rake the soil to a fine, crumbly structure. Leave for a couple of weeks to allow any weed seedlings to germinate, then hoe or use a weed-killer, safe for replanting in a few days. Rake once more.

SOWING GRASS SEED

1 Mark out the area into 1m (1yd) strips with pegs and string. Divide each strip into 1m (1yd) sections, using canes as guides.

2 Use a small container to measure out the amount of seed for 1 square metre (1 square yard). Apply to one square at a time, in alternate directions.

3 It is worth hiring a seed distributor if the area to sow is large. Once it has been calibrated to release the correct amount of seed, simply push the distributor over the ground.

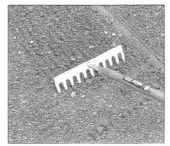

4 Rake the surface lightly, and in dry weather, use a lawn sprinkler to keep seeds moist.

Nothing sets off beds of flowers as well as a smart well groomed lawn.

A Lawn from Turf

FOLIAGE & FLOWERS

For an 'instant result' use turf to give you a usable lawn in a couple of months. You can lay turf at most times of the year if you avoid frozen ground and water in dry weather. Spring and early autumn are good times. Prepare the ground as for sowing seed.

LAYING TURF

1 Lay the first row against a straight edge. Butt each turf close against the previous piece.

2 Stagger each row like brick-work. Kneel on a plank to avoid damaging the turves.

3 Roll the plank forward as you lay further rows.

4 Tamp the turf down with the back of a rake or garden roller, to remove any air.

5 Brush sieved sandy soil or a mixture of peat and sand into the joints, to bind them together.

CREATING A CURVED EDGE

Peg down a hosepipe or rope with bent wire to create a curved edge. Use this as a guide to trim with an edging iron. Keep the grass moist in dry weather and until it is well established.

6 Use an edging iron to trim the edges if needed. Stand on a plank of wood to keep the edge straight.

130

MARKING OUT AN OVAL BED

1 Getting the proportions right is trial and error, start by marking out a rectangle.

2 Use string to check that the diagonals are the same length. Place pegs centrally along each side and stretch string between them.

Above Make beds and borders look smart by ensuring a neat edge. Take special care when cutting out curved beds.

3 Cut a piece of string half the length of the oval, between the top and bottom pegs. Use a side peg as a pivot to indicate where to insert other pegs.

4 Cut a piece of string twice the distance between one of these pegs and the top or bottom of the oval, whichever is furthest away. Make a loop from the string.

5 Drape a loop over the two inner pegs then mark a line on the grass in sand, keeping the string taut. Cut an outline of the oval with an edging iron, lift the turf with a spade.

ROUTINE LAWN CARE

Lawns are often the largest and dominant feature of the garden throughout the year. A neglected lawn can mar your garden, but one that is well-cared for will set off all the other features.

SPRING LAWN CARE

1 Use a mechanical spreader, as above, to feed your lawn easily. Spreading by hand requires the area to be divided into squares.

2 If the lawn is full of weeds, apply lawn weedkiller in mid or late spring. Use a dribble bar and mark off the areas treated to avoid over-dosing.

3 For a few weeds, spot treatment may be used. Brush or dab on a selective lawn weedkiller.

4 Rake or brush off debris. These will not harm the lawn but may provide a seed bed for weeds to grow in.

5 Trimming the edges makes the lawn look better. Long-handled shears are slow but make a neat job. An electric edge trimmer or line trimmer will do the job quickly.

6 Bare areas should be reseeded. Loosen the surface, sprinkle on patch seed. Water well and cover with plastic until the seeds germinate.

AUTUMN LAWN CARE

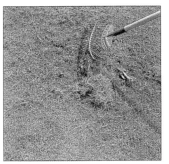

1 Rake the lawn to remove the 'thatch' of dead grass and old clippings, and moss.

2 A powered lawn rake will make the job much easier on a large lawn. A powered slitter, like this, will aerated a large lawn.

3 After raking, aerate the lawn. A tool that removes cores of soil is ideal but on small lawns, a fork will do.

4 Brush sand into the holes if your lawn soil is heavy clay. If your soil is sandy, brush in peat instead.

5 If the lawn is in poor condition, apply an autumn lawn feed. Do not use spring or summer feed as the fresh growth will be killed off by frost.

6 Use a moss killer for autumn use, if it is a problem. Lawn sand is unsuitable for this time of year, as it contains fertilizer.

7 Straighten uneven edges with an edging iron against a straight edge of timber. Do not do this too often as the lawn reduces in size each time.

DEALING WITH LAWN PROBLEMS

Bumps and hollows make mowing difficult, and broken edges leave the lawn unsightly. These can be repaired leaving it good as new.

REDUCING WEAR

Protect an area from concentrated wear, by pegging down a piece of mesh or netting. The grass will grow through it but the netting will protect wear on the actual surface.

BUMPS AND HOLLOWS

1 Use an edging iron or a spade to cut a cross through the centre of the area. Extend the cuts beyond the bump or hollow.

2 Use a spade to slice through the soil beneath the grass, so that you can lift it up to roll it back.

3 Roll back the four cut pieces to expose the soil beneath.

4 Remove soil if there is a bump, or top up if there is a hollow.

5 Level the soil as evenly as you can, then roll back the turf. If the level is not good, then lift the affected part and adjust.

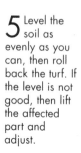

6 Firm the grass with the back of a spade, or tread it in by standing on a plank. Trickle fine soil into the joints, then water well.

134

REPAIRING A BROKEN EDGE

1 Use an edging iron or a spade to cut a rectangle around the affected area.

2 Push a spade under the grass, starting at the edge and keeping the slice of grass as even as possible.

3 Reverse the turf so the broken edge is on the inside.

4 Fill the hole with sifted soil, then sow grass seed.

5 Brush sifted soil into the joints to help them knit.

6 After watering, cover the reseeded patch until the seed has germinated.

FLOWERS & FOLIAGE

On a sunny site, even a small rock garden will enable you to grow a large collection of plants in a small space. With an island bed you can make a rock garden in your lawn, or build one in a corner of your garden.

MAKING A ROCK GARDEN

1 Choose a sunny site—sloping if possible but it can be made on flat ground by building a mound. Remove all weeds.

2 Lay a layer of hardcore as a foundation to aid drainage. Tip garden soil over this to a depth of 15–30cm (6–12in).

3 Cover the low mound of soil with inverted turves, to provide a base for the special soil mix.

4 Alpine plants prefer a mix of equal parts soil, coarse grit and peat. This suits most plants.

5 Mix the three ingredients well, turning them until they are blended together.

6 Mark out the area you want the final rock garden to occupy with string and pile the soil mixture to the height of the second layer of rocks.

7 Remove the string, then lay the rocks at ground level. Add more soil to to the back and sides to stabilize the rocks.

8 Add the second layer of rocks, keeping the grain of the rock (strata) in the same direction. Use a pole or crowbar to lever them into place.

9 Manipulate rocks with rollers or levers as they can be very heavy.

10 Add soil as each layer is built up, this will increase the height for the next row.

11 Make the sides slope and build towards a flattish summit with a nice rock laid on top.

12 Finish off with a layer of coarse sand or horticultural grit.

13 The rock garden will look much better if it is sited in a corner, with a backdrop of plants such as dwarf conifers.

ROCK GARDENS 2: PLANTING AND CARE

A rock garden can soon look neglected unless you plant carefully, avoiding vigorous plants. Trim back plants and make sure weeds are kept under control.

2 Water the plants and let them drain before planting. Knock them out of their pots, holding your hand over the root ball.

3 Use a narrow blade trowel to dig a larger hole then the root ball.

4 Pour gritty soil around the roots, making sure the crown is not too deep.

PLANTING A ROCK GARDEN

1 Space out the plants in their pots before you begin to plant. This lets you visualize the overall effect and makes it easier to alter plant positions.

5 After firming, trickle more grit around the plant, avoiding touching the leaves.

6 Firm and level the grit to create a pleasing finish.

FLOWERS & FOLIAGE

KEEPING THE PLANTS LOOKING GOOD

1 Always remove weeds when they are small, or they will smother small alpines.

2 **Right** Perennial weeds growing between rocks will be difficult to remove. Try applying a translocated weedkiller which will kill the roots and the leaves. Be very careful not to touch plants you wish to keep.

3 Slugs and snails will be deterred by coarse grit or chippings. Sprinkle pellets around vulnerable plants.

STONE CHIPPING DRESSINGS

A dressing of stone chippings will need to be topped up or renewed eventually. They get washed away and the soil works its way through. Make sure you place some beneath the collar of each plant so the leaves are kept off the wet soil.

CUTTING BACK

In the spring, cut off any dead shoots killed during the winter. Many alpines will remain more compact and vigorous if the dead flowering shoots are cut off with shears.

PLANTING IN WALLS AND PAVING CREVICES

Make the most of all available planting spaces by packing a dry wall with interesting alpines and planting between the paving too,

PLANTING IN PAVING

1 Chisel out a few crevices if your crazy paving is mortared to a depth of at least 5cm (2in).

2 Ready made crevices should be cleared of old soil and filled with loam-based compost.

3 Use small plants or seedlings and tease most of the compost away to make insertion easier.

4 Trickle more compost around the roots after planting.

5 Firm gently with your fingers to remove air pockets.

6 Water carefully with a fine mist from a compression sprayer. This will not wash the compost away. Water regularly until they are established.

7 Sowing alpine seeds directly into the crevices is worth trying. Sprinkle a few seeds onto compost, cover with more compost and water as before.

PLANTING A DRY STONE WALL

1 Plant small seedlings or cuttings in the crevices, even small spaces can be planted this way.

2 Press moist compost into the space to cover the roots with a pencil or dibber to avoid air pockets.

3 If the compost falls out press a few small stones into the space to hold it in.

4 Keep the plants and compost moist by spraying with a fine mist. Once established, they will not need regular watering.

5 Try sowing a few alpines directly into the wall, by mixing with compost in your hand.

6 Moisten the seed/compost mix and press into a suitable crevice. Choose robust alpines such as aubrieta.

Many alpines can be grown in crevices in the side of a dry stone wall, but even if the wall is mortared you can create a similar effect by planting vigorous trailers like aubrieta to spill over the edge.

A GARDEN FOR WILDLIFE

If you love wildlife, modify your garden to encourage birds and butterflies. Wild flowers can be looked upon as food sources for wildlife instead of as weeds —many are as pretty as cultivated plants.

SOWING AND PLANTING WILD FLOWERS

1 The easiest method to produce a wild flower meadow, is to sow a special mixture on prepared ground. The wild flowers will find it easier to become established if you start from scratch.

2 Specialist nurseries sell wild flower plants. Buy these to save time and trouble.

LONG GRASS AND WILD FLOWERS

Leave part of the lawn unmown and unweeded, to add 'texture' in a large lawn. This will look acceptable in a small lawn if you leave the grass long around a tree in a corner. Cut with shears in the autumn when the flowers have finished blooming.

3 Plant the seedlings as soon as possible after unpacking, and plant according to needs.

NURSERY-BED WILD FLOWERS

To plant wild flowers in an established lawn or a wild area, sow the seeds like cultivated plants and grow in a nursery bed until large enough to plant out.

You can buy wild flower seed mixtures that are every bit as bright as highly bred plants— and attract wildlife too.

MAKING A MINI-POND

Make a mini-pool to encourage pondlife, if you don't have a proper pond.

You can make one out of a half barrel or plastic tub, sinking it into the soil or leaving it above ground.

Make sure that the container is level and leave the top just above soil level to reduce the risk of soil falling in. The

barrel can be lined with a pond liner if it leaks, or repair it with sealing mastic.

You can make a mini-pool for birds and animals to drink from with an old dustbin lid. Sink it flush with the ground, and mask the edge with stones or plants. Keep it topped up with water throughout the summer.

143

WINDOWBOXES

Make a really bold box with a single-colour or single-subject planting, or make it subdued and have foliage predominating. Don't leave your windowboxes empty at the end of the autumn—this is the time to plant them up with spring bulbs.

PLANTING A SUMMER WINDOWBOX

1 Place a layer of broken clay pots over the drainage holes. If you don't have any of these, use coarsely chipped bark.

2 Partly fill the box with good compost. Use loam-based compost, as it is less prone to drying out and starvation. Adding water-absorbing crystals (see Planting a Hanging Basket) will help conserve moisture.

3 Buy pot-grown plants although costing more, they make better plants more quickly. Space the plants whilst still in their pots. Adjust if necessary. Space foliage plants along the box— one will look like a mistake.

4 Make sure that the plants have been watered first, then knock them out of their pots and plant. Trickle compost between them to fill any gaps. Firm gently. Water thoroughly and place in position.

PLANTING A SPRING WINDOWBOX

1 Bulbs need less feeding than summer plants. You can re-use some of the old summer compost and mix it with fresh compost. Wash out the box with garden disinfectant first.

2 Place pieces of broken clay pots or coarsely chipped bark over the holes to allow for drainage.

3 Add just enough compost to cover the bottom few centimetres (inches).

4 Place larger bulbs, such as daffodils, at this deeper level.

5 Add more compost so that the larger bulbs are almost covered. Then plant smaller bulbs such as scillas or crocuses between them. Cover with more compost.

6 For winter flowering, pansies or forget-me-nots, can be planted before finally topping up with compost. The bulbs will grow through them.

HANGING BASKETS

While you are planting out your windowboxes, be sure to plant a few hanging baskets too— they're challenging but make a real welcome at the front door.

PLANTING A HANGING BASKET

1 Line a basket with damp sphagnum moss, to where the first plants will be placed.

2 You can add water-absorbing crystals to the compost to aid moisture retention in hot weather.

3 Add compost to the level of the moss. Insert seedlings through the mesh, trying to keep compost around the roots.

4 Add more compost, plant another layer, then fill to just below the rim. Put a bold plant in the centre of a mixed basket.

5 Fill in any gaps. Water well. Do not hang up immediately. Keep in a sheltered place for a week to let plants settle.

PLANTING A HALF-BASKET

1 Line with moss and plant as described for a normal basket. Propping the basket on small pots will be helpful.

2 Plant the top last, then hang on a wall in a porch or sheltered spot until established. Move to its final position after a week or two.

BASKET LINERS

Moss makes an attractive liner, but many proprietary liners are available. Although less attractive, once the plants bush out, you will hardly notice them. Choose one which allows side planting unless you only want to plant the top.

Once the plants are fully established, take the basket outside. They are usually hung from chains on a bracket which can be fixed to a fence post.

TUBS AND TROUGHS

Tubs and troughs will add colour to dull parts of the patio, and bring life to a balcony. Try planting a permanent container with a selection of year-round interest plants such as alpines.

1 Place pieces of broken clay post, or coarsely chipped bark o cover the holes.

2 If weight is a problem, use a peat-based compost, otherwise use a loam-based compost.

3 Place a tall, bold plant in the centre, as a focal point, in both perennial and summer displays.

4 Plant some trailers around the edge to take the eye downwards. Small-leaved ivies are good but you could use a flowering trailer for a summer display.

5 Top up the container with compost after planting and water well. A dressing of chipped bark or cocoa shells will improve the appearance.

MOVING TUBS

Reconstituted stone and concrete tubs and urns are very heavy. Always get help to move them.

Right A decorative tub can enhance the display of flowers. Don't spoil the effect with too many trailers. This one is planted with geraniums, a fuchsia, and *Helichrysum petiolatum*.

FLOWERS & FOLIAGE

PLANTING AN ALPINE TROUGH

1 Choose pot-grown plants and an attractive trough. Lay broken clay pots at the bottom and top up with gritty loam-based compost. Space out the plants.

2 Remove plants and some of the compost around the root ball if necessary. Plant the alpines at the same depth as they were originally planted.

3 To improve the appearance of the planted trough, sprinkle some stone chippings or fine gravel over the compost.

Right A sink garden looks better if small rocks are placed among the alpines.

PLANTING A BARREL

1 If you have a large area to dig such as a vegetable plot, or a new garden to cultivate, divide it into two equal areas. Then you can dig to one end.

2 Plant three clematis (or other climbers) at a slight inward angle.

3 Insert three canes so they cross at the top. Tie together with twine or use a cane holder.

4 Tie the plants to the canes. Once they reach the top, they will become self-supporting

TREES AND SHRUBS IN TUBS

Give your patio a touch of distinction by growing a few trees and shrubs in large pots. They are easy to look after and many look attractive all year round.

PLANTING A TREE

1 Right Choose a large container—at least 30cm (12in) in diameter. Make sure it is frost-proof. Insert a drainage layer before adding loam-based compost, which has the weight to support a tree in windy weather. Fill so that the top of the root ball is 2.5–5cm (1–2) below the rim.

2 Left Remove the tree from its container and stand it on the new compost. Trickle more around the sides.

3 A tree will offer a lot of wind resistance, so ram the compost firmly around the root ball to ensure stability.

PLANTING SHRUBS

1 Single specimen shrubs can be planted but a collection of dwarf shrubs with contrasting or colourful foliage will be attractive for a longer period. Stand the plants in a group first to see how they look together.

Right Groups of shrubs can be as effective as one shrub.

TREES IN TUBS

If the base of the tree looks bare plant it with shade loving plants such as ivies, spring bulbs or sow some quick and easy hardy annuals until the tree is established.

A SUITABLE COMPOST

Use a loam-based compost for trees and shrubs. If you are growing lime hating shrubs they will need an ericaceous mix. This will be more acidic then other types of compost.

2 Plant firmly, ensuring they are at their original depth in the compost.

3 Cover visible compost with a mulch of gravel, cocoa shells or expanded clay granules.

CARING FOR PLANTS IN CONTAINERS

If you look after your containers, they will reward you with healthy growth and a good show. Neglecting feeding and watering will bring disappointing results. The benefits of care and attention can be seen and enjoyed.

FEEDING YOUR PLANTS

1 If you can't remember to feed regularly, try placing a sachet of slow-release fertilizer beneath each plant.

2 Slow-release fertilizer can be added to the compost, releasing its nutrients when the weather is warm.

WATERING YOUR PLANTS

1 An automatic watering system is ideal for containers close together on a patio. Run a small drip tube from the main supply pipe, adjust the flow rate.

2 A hosepipe is the easiest way to water a lot of containers. Fit an outside tap and run piping to parts of the garden so a hose can be attached.

3 Use a lance attachment fitted to a hose, compression sprayer, or basket pump to water hanging baskets.

4 An alternative to a lance, is to tie the end of a hose to a garden cane. This holds the hose rigid so you can hold it up to a basket.

3 Soluble and liquid fertilizers are quick-acting and produce rapid results. Feed regularly at the rate recommended.

4 Remember to feed trees and shrubs, as the compost must sustain a lot of growth over a long period. Sprinkle slow-release fertilizer over the surface in spring and then fork it in.

ROUTINE CARE

1 Many summer bedding plants cease flowering early if you allow the flowers to set seed. Dead-head plants with large flowers, they will look tidier and will flower for longer.

2 Give summer bedding plants a health check once a week. Remove yellowing leaves and those affected by disease or pests, unless you can control them by sprays.

3 Control pests and diseases promptly as close planting can cause the problems to spread quickly. Systemic insecticides and fungicides are the most effective.

MAKING A POND

Old-fashioned concrete ponds used to be difficult to construct, but with modern liners and pre-formed pool, making a pond is a job you can complete in a weekend.

A PRE-FORMED POND

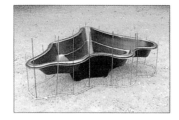

1 Insert canes around the edge and lay rope around them to transfer the shape to the ground.

2 Dig out the shape as carefully as possible. Check on the shape by laying the pond in the hole regularly. Making the hole a few centimetres (9inches) larger than the actual pond, will make backfilling easier later.

3 Lay wood across the hole to check the level and measure down from this.

4 Put the pool in the hole and check that it is level.

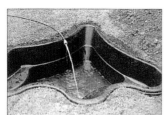

5 Run water into the pool, as the level rises, pack fine soil around the edge.

6 Pack soil with wood, firmly beneath the shelves to avoid causing stresses within the moulding. Check the level as you fill and pack.

MARGINAL SHELVES

Waterlilies prefer the deeper water in the centre, most aquatic plants grow in shallow water. A marginal shelf will let you grow many kinds of plants.

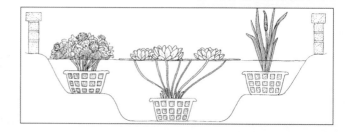

A LINER POND

1 Use a length of hosepipe to mark out the shape or your pond. If doing the job in winter, run hot water through the hose to make it more supple.

2 Dig out soil to the right depth. Leave a shallow ledge 23cm (9in) wide half-way down the total depth of the pool. Remove grass from the edge deep enough for the thickness of the paving and the mortar.

3 Make sure that the edge of the pond is level. Space pegs 90–120cm (3–4ft) apart around the edge. Go around the pool with a spirit-level.

4 Put a layer of sand 12mm (0.5in) on the bottom and the marginal shelves, and the sides if possible. If the soil is very stony, use a polyester mat instead of sand.

5 Drape the liner loosely in the hole, making sure that there is enough overlap all around. Hold the edges in place with a few bricks. Run in water from a hosepipe.

6 Lift the bricks from around the edge and let the liner move a little as the liner fills up with water. There will be creases, remove these by stretching and adjusting the liner.

7 Once filled, cut off surplus liner, leaving a flap of about 15cm (6in) all way round. This will be covered and held in place by the mortar and paving.

8 Bed a paved edge on a mortar bed of three parts sand to one part cement. Crazy-paving or rectangular slabs can be used around the edge of an irregular shape like this.

STOCKING THE POND

The best time to stock the pond with plants is mid spring to early summer. Do not put any tender floating aquatics in until there is no risk of frost. Add fish at any time, but wait for a few weeks if the pond is recently planted.

PLANTING A WATERLILY

1 Although you can plant waterlilies in special planting baskets, an old washing-up bowl holds more compost and has room for expansion.

2 Always add oxygenating plants. These can be planted around the edges or in their own containers.

3 Cover the compost surface with gravel to help anchor the plants down, It will also reduce the chance of fish stirring up mud in the water.

4 If early in the season, the waterlilies will have short stems, so sit the container on bricks. Once the stems have grown, remove the bricks and sit the container at the bottom of the pond.

PLANTING MARGINAL AQUATICS

1 Buy a special planting basket, and line it with turf, or a special liner, to hold in the compost.

2 Put the plant in the container, adding compost in the bottom if the plant is small. Add more compost free of fertilizer.

3 Cover with gravel to anchor the plant and keep the compost in place.

4 Gently lower the basket into the water so that it sits on one of the marginal shelves. Make sure that the top of the basket is covered with water.

ADDING FISH

2 Release the fish by opening the bag and letting them swim free. Do not keep the fish for too long in the bag as they may be starved of oxygen.

1 Float the bag on the surface for a couple of hours so that the temperatures equalize. Never release fish straight into the pond when you get them home.

FLOATING PLANTS
Some aquatics float, and only need placing on the surface.

POND MAINTENANCE

You will need to spend a couple of hours in the spring and autumn to keep the water sparkling and the plants healthy. If you stock fish, be prepared to keep a small area free of ice in freezing weather.

CLEANING THE POND

1 Thoroughly clean the pond after two or three years. The pond pump will empty most of the water. Use a bucket to finish emptying the water.

2 Once the water level is low, the fish will be easier to catch. Keep them in containers filled with the old pond water. Cover with netting to stop them jumping out.

3 Remove all plants, scrub off the dirt and mud, then rinse with a hose. Scoop out the dirty water with a bucket.

4 Refill with tap water, which contains chlorine harmful to fish, so keep the fish away for a few days before returning them.

5 Take the opportunity to divide and repot overcrowded plants.

6 Pull or cut each plant apart to make several smaller pieces.

7 Repot each portion. Remember to cover the surface of the compost or pot with gravel before replacing in the pond.

SPRING AND SUMMER POND CARE

1 Algae will usually disappear once the larger plants are growing well, absorbing nutrients and shading the water, but chemical controls are available and you should follow the instructions very carefully.

2 Reduce blanket weed, by twisting it around a cane or stick. This algae can also be controlled with an algicide.

AUTUMN POND CARE

1 Rake out leaves before they sink and start to rot. You can use a lawn rake but be careful if you have a pond liner.

3 Trim off dying leaves from marginal plants or those on the edge of the pond, to reduce the amount of vegetation that may rot during the winter.

2 Rake out some of the plants which have become overgrown.

4 Cover the pond with netting to stop more leaves falling in. Once leaf fall has passed, remove the netting.

WINTER POND CARE

1 Float tennis balls on the pond surface if frost is forecast. The balls will provide small ice-free areas. This method is only for short cold spells.

2 To release toxic gases built up in a frozen pond, stand a pan of hot water on the ice. Tie a string to the handle so that you can retrieve it, if it sinks.

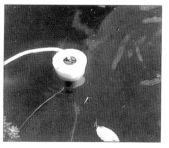

3 Use a pond heater to keep it ice-free. It costs no more than a large light bulb to run. There are mains and low-voltage versions.

GREENHOUSE BASICS

A basic greenhouse is simply a protective shell which you need to equip to display the plants well and provide extra growing space. Adding an automatic ventilator opener should be regarded as an essential, not an optional extra.

INSTALLING AN AUTOMATIC VENTILATOR

1 Automatic ventilators are quick and easy to install. Follow the instructions carefully as products vary. This one is first fixed to the centre of the manual ventilator.

2 The other end of the bracket is bolted to the frame.

HIGH VENTILATORS

If you buy a greenhouse with a high manual ventilator, difficult to reach, make sure that an easy-winder is also supplied.

3 Finally, the opener will need adjusting so that it opens and closes at the right temperature.

FIXING A SHELF

1 Shelves are invaluable as they provide extra growing space. Aluminium greenhouse shelves come in kits that you assemble yourself. They should be supplied with brackets that bolt together and fix to the frame.

2 Assemble all brackets for the shelves first, and use a spirit-level to check they are all level.

3 Bolt the shelf to the bracket, using the nuts and bolts supplied.

4 End pieces are available to make a better finish and reduce the dangers from sharp metal corners.

ASSEMBLING AN INTEGRATED BENCH

1 Fitted benches come with most metal greenhouses as an optional extra. They are worth buying as they will suit the size of the greenhouse. Follow the instructions, but they will probably bolt to the existing frame.

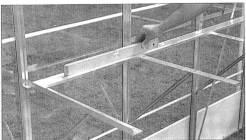

2 Check the levels of each length of surface. Adjust at this stage, before you finish assembling the surface.

GETTING THE BEST FROM YOUR GREENHOUSE

The greenhouse can be used to propagate many garden plants, tomatoes, cucumbers and other vegetables.

In winter you need to insulate to keep it warm; in summer you'll need to ventilate and shade it to keep it cool.

THERMAL SCREENS

A thermal screen will conserve heat if you pull it across at night. Hang it on wires that run along the eaves. Just push it to one end in the morning, and pull it across at night.

If you want to reduce costs by heating just part of the greenhouse, separate it vertically with plastic sheeting. You may be able to buy a special kit.

INSULATING A GREENHOUSE

1 In a metal greenhouse, buy clips that you insert first, then hold the polythene in place either by snapping or pushing in a cap. Adhesive tape can seal the overlaps.

2 In a timber-framed greenhouse, pin the insulation to the glazing bars with drawing pins.

3 Always insulate the ventilators separately so that they can be opened. Ventilation is important in an insulated greenhouse to avoid diseases caused by high humidity.

SHADING A GREENHOUSE

1 Paint-on shading is a cheap and easy way to reduce the scorching effects of the summer sun.

2 To save time if the greenhouse is large, spray it on. Avoid the spray drifting over the glazing bars.

3 At the end of the summer, remove the shading with a duster or cloth when its dry.

4 Internal shading is not as effective but is better than none. Fix plastic net to the inside of the glazing bars, with clips used for insulation.

EXTERIOR ROLLER BLINDS

These are very effective, and more flexible than a paint-on wash as you can remove or apply shading to suit the weather.

HOW TO MAKE A CAPILLARY BENCH

1 To make a capillary bench fix a length of plastic gutter to the edge and lay a sheet of polythene over the bench.

2 Cut a length of capillary matting, available from garden centres, to size leaving one edge to fold into the gutter. Top up the gutter with water by hand.

WATERING THE GREENHOUSE

Watering is the most demanding aspect of greenhouse gardening—it is a daily chore for much of the year. You can make life much easier if you install an automatic watering system.

INSTALLING A CAPILLARY BENCH

Lay capillary matting over the whole bench. Cut matting to size, do not leave any trailing over the edge, as it may drain water away.

You can make your own reservoir using a ball valve, but it is easier to buy one designed for the job which can be connected to the mains. If this is not possible, buy one designed for use with a bag (the hose connector will be a different size).

Use the matting as a wick to draw water from the reservoir to the bench matting.

HAND-WATERING

1 Press your finger into the surface to judge if the moisture level is adequate.

2 Alternatively, use a moisture indicator in a few pots as a guide.

OVERHEAD SPRAYING

If you prefer a spray system, buy one that can be suspended from the roof. Nozzles are screwed into the tubing at intervals. Some can spray on both sides or just one side of the greenhouse.

IMPROVISING

You can improvise reservoirs. This system uses a length of plastic gutter as a reservoir, into which one end of the matting is inserted. Keep the gutter topped up with water by hand, from a cistern, or dip fed by a water bag.

Bottom picture Capillary benches are not suitable for seedling and cuttings which need to be watered by hand.

3 Plants in large pots are best watered without a rose on the can, using a finger on the end to reduce the flow.

4 Water seedlings with a rose on the can, facing upwards when they are small so that the water falls more gently.

F
L
O
W
E
R
S

&

F
O
L
I
A
G
E

DISPLAYING AND CARING FOR GREENHOUSE PLANTS

Arranging your pots attractively, will keep your greenhouse looking good. Feed, water them, and maintain the correct humidity.

MAKING THE MOST OF SHELVES

Shelves are good for trays of seedlings in spring and to display pot plants during the summer. Take care not to shade the plants below too much.

HANGING SHELVES

Shelves can be fixed from either the roof glazing bars or by brackets to the side glazing bars. Choose a suitable type.

POT PLANTS

Try growing pot plants in a group by growing them, in their pots, in the greenhouse border rather than on shelving.

STAGING DISPLAYS

1 Build your displays in different heights to make a striking show. Pots can be stood upon empty pots... use trailers at the front to cascade over the edge.

2 Tiered staging makes the most of usable space. Use the bottom shelves for resting plants or as storage.

3 Self-watering containers can be used for display in the greenhouse. Plant a large tub with bold feature plants or one striking plant such as this aubergine.

Although this is larger than most greenhouses, the same kind of display can be achieved on a more modest scale.

CLIMBERS

On a lean-to-greenhouse, paint the back wall white to reflect light and as a background for wall shrubs and climbers. Plant in the border and train them up wires fixed to the back wall.

CREATING THE RIGHT ATMOSPHERE

1 Fit one automatic ventilator so the temperature never becomes too high. Open more ventilators or open the door to keep the greenhouse cool.

2 Plants prefer humid atmospheres so when the temperature is hot, damp down the paths with a watering-can to increase humidity.

COLD FRAMES

Cold frames are invaluable for overwintering vulnerable plants, if you don't have a greenhouse. They can also be used as an overflow in late spring or for hardening off seedlings before you plant them out. To get the best from your frame, insulate it against severe frosts.

ERECTING A COLD FRAME FROM A KIT

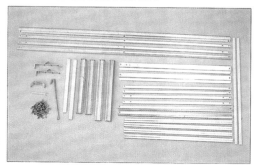

1 Aluminium kits are easy to make, they come with all that you will need, including glass. Check that all the parts are there when you open the box.

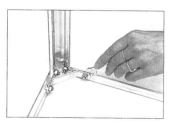

2 Bolt the frame together on the order suggested.

3 When the main frame is completed, insert the glass. It is held in place with clips or glazing strips. Slide or fix on the tops, making sure they lift or slide easily.

INSULATING A COLD FRAME

1 Glass and aluminium frames will be colder than brick-walled ones. For more protection, insulate the sides with expanded polystyrene.

2 Cut the sides, allowing for the thickness at each end. Push into place so that they are a tight fit. If loose, wedge pieces of card in at one end to hold them in position.

TYPES OF COLD FRAME

Aluminium frames are widely available in kit form and easy to make. They are glazed to the ground, letting in more light. They quickly loose heat through the sides unless you insulate them in the winter.

Wooden frames do come as kits but are more expensive and less widely available. You can make your own and make it blend in with the garden better than a metal one can.

Brick-walled frames are seldom used by amateurs as they are more difficult to construct. They do protect plants better than thin -walled frames.

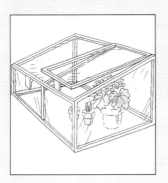  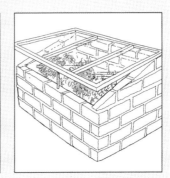

INSULATING AND VENTILATION

1 Never insulate the top of a frame permanently, unless using bubble polythene, as the plants need light. On very cold nights a covering can be used but needs removing the next day.

2 Good ventilation is essential in warm weather, even in the winter. Sliding tops are useful as they are less prone to wind damage.

3 Lifting tops sometimes have an adjustable device. A simple wedge can be made with notches so that you can open the top by different amounts as the plants are hardened off.

FRUIT & VEGETABLES

The kitchen garden holds its own special charm; a bed of ripening vegetables, clusters of tomatoes catching the sun, and crisp rows of salad crops all look as good as they taste. Add a few decorative herbs and some cordon fruits, and this part of the garden will compare well with the ornamental area.

Opposite
The produce of the kitchen can look good as well as taste good. Apples like these 'Sunset' look particularly appetizing.

INTRODUCTION

Fruit, vegetables and herbs are rewarding to grow. The results of your hard work are enjoyed on your dinner plate. Many herbs are highly ornamental and worth growing in the flower garden even if of no culinary use.

The kitchen garden is particularly labour-intensive, and the difference between a mediocre and bumper crop can be accounted for by the amount of care and attention it has received. Many of the tips in the following pages will help you to achieve better or bigger crops, and extend the harvesting season.

An early start can produce crops weeks ahead of the normal time, yielding home-grown produce at a time when it is more expensive in the shops. Cloches, floating cloches and horticultural fleece are among techniques described and there are hints

Above Marrows and courgettes need space, but a single plant is useful.

Left 'Doyenne du Comice' is grown as a tree but can be trained as a cordon or espalier.

Left Kitchen gardens were dedicated to fruit, vegetables and herbs in the past, but don't despair if space is limited. A worthwhile collection can be grown even in a small plot.

Left Crops of strawberries are within everyone's reach.

Below Enjoy apples like these 'Idared'.

for extending the season into late autumn plus ideas for storing what you can't eat fresh.

There are tips on extra crops you can harvest once the main harvest has been collected.

Growing vegetables can be fun too, and even though you can't feed a family from a few windowboxes or containers on the patio, it is rewarding to harvest early potatoes from a growing bag, or pick pretty red-leaved lettuces from a windowbox.

A crop of onions is easy to grow from seed. Grow plenty to store for winter use.

You will find plenty of ideas for growing herbs and vegetables in containers in the greenhouse and outdoors.

Fruit trees are not only for orchards, they can be trained to grow against a wall or fence, and there are fruit trees which take up little space and look pretty too.

To avoid repeated descriptions of routine tasks such as sowing, thinning, feeding and picking, the key cultivation tasks are summarized for vegetables and fruit in extensive tables.

F R U I T & V E G E T A B L E S

GROWING VEGETABLES AND HERBS

Make your kitchen garden as attractive and productive as possible through careful planning. If space is limited, try growing some of the more decorative vegetables and herbs in flower beds.

CHOOSING A SITE

Most fruits and vegetables need a sunny site to do well. Place fruit trees so they do not cast a shadow over the vegetables and plant herbs in a sunny place.

There's always space to grow a few herbs. Many make pretty container plants.

DISPLAYING HERBS

Many herbs are leafy and dull and a herb garden is a good way to display them. If it has a geometric shape, then it will be a feature even in winter. If you have the space, make it complex and ornate with a centrepiece such as a birdbath or sundial.

If you do not have space for a formal herb garden, a 'chequer-board' garden makes an interesting feature for a large patio.

Herbs are easy to integrate with flowers. Plants like thyme, shown here, and chives, make good edging for flower beds.

Most herbs do well in containers, and compact ornamental herbs are ideal.

Many herbs are decorative enough to grow in the flower border. Place tall ones at the back and use low-growing herbs as an edging.

WAYS WITH VEGETABLES

The conventional method of growing vegetables is in long rows.

Above A basketful of courgettes is just one of the regular delights for anyone who can find space for vegetables.

Opposite The kitchen garden can look attractive and be productive. The 1.2m (4ft) bed system has been used in this plot.

This is a convenient way to grow them, and if kept weeded, can look attractive too.

The 1.2m (4ft) bed system is popular with organic gardeners as the beds are wide enough for cultivation to be carried out easily from the paths on each side. This means you do not need to walk on the soil which can compact it. Mulching can prevent the need for digging. Spacing may need to be adjusted to allow room to walk between the rows.

A large range of vegetables can even be grown in containers—such as peas and potatoes.

Some vegetables are decorative enough to be among flowers, if you don't mind gaps once you begin to harvest them.

GROUNDWORK

A vegetable plot needs digging at least once a year, and deep digging is beneficial for some crops. Spend time thinking about crop rotation and planning what to plant where.

CATCH CROPS AND INTERCROPS

To make the best use of available space, grow quick-maturing crops between slower-growing ones. If you plant lettuces in the ground between sweet corn plants, they will keep the ground free of weeds and should be ready before the sweet corn casts too much shade. Radish seed mixed with parsnip seed, allows you to crop the radishes before the slower parsnips need all the space.

Catch cropping enables you to sneak in a quick crop in cleared ground. Early potatoes might allow you to plant a lettuce crop.

DOUBLE DIGGING

1 Start by digging out a trench 60cm (2ft) wide and barrowing the soil to the other end of the trench.

2 Fork over the bottom of the trench.

3 Spread a layer of manure or compost over the forked area.

4 Dig out the next trench, throwing the soil forward to fill the excavation left by the previous one. Fill the last trench with soil put to one side.

CROP ROTATION

By rotating the position of various types of crop you can reduce the risk of certain pests and diseases in the soil, and you can group crops with similar needs in terms of soil fertility and its pH level.

There are several variations, some people use a four-year rotation, but a three-year rotation is fine for a small garden or allotment.

One part is kept for perennial crops, the rest is divided up into three parts. Each year the crops are rotated within these three areas as shown.

GROUP A
Grow: aubergines, beetroot, carrots, celeriac, celery, courgettes, cucumber, garlic, leeks, marrows, onions, parsnips, peppers, potatoes, pumpkins, salsify, scorzonera, shallots, tomatoes.
Dig and feed: double dig, add manure, feed crops.

GROUP B
Grow: broad beans, chicory, French beans, lettuce, peas, runner beans, spinach, Swiss chard, sweet corn.
Dig and feed: single dig, apply fertilizer at start of the season, before sowing.

GROUP C
Grow: broccoli, Brussel sprouts, cabbages, cauliflowers, kale, kohl rabi, turnips, radishes, swedes.
Dig and feed: single dig, add lime if needed to bring the pH of the soil to 6.5–7.0. Apply a general fertilizer in the spring, and a supplement if needed during the season.

GROUP D
Grow: any crops that need to remain in the same piece of ground, such as asparagus, globe artichokes, rhubarb or Jerusalem artichokes.

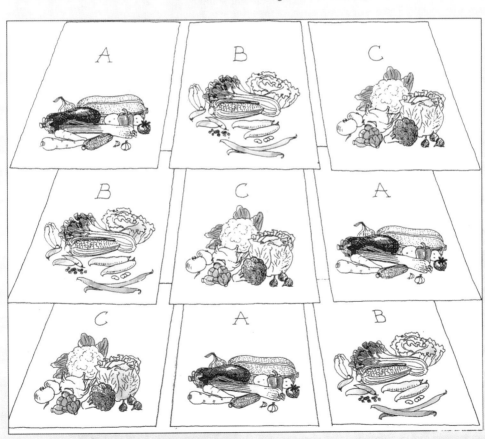

MANURES AND FERTILIZERS

Fruit and vegetables need plenty of feeding for good crops. Synthetic fertilizers are good for a short-term boost, but adding humus improves the soil structure as well as feeding the plants. This almost always leads to better crops than those grown only by the use of artificial fertilizers.

ADDING FERTILIZERS

1 A hopper is the most efficient way to distribute fertilizer to an allotment or large kitchen garden. Calculate the rate, then fill and simply push along the rows.

2 If applying by hand, measure the amount required for a square metre or yard. A small container can be marked with the quantity for easy spreading.

3 Mark off the area with strings stretched 1m (1yd) apart to divide the area into metre or yard squares.

4 Pour the fertilizer into your free hand and scatter as evenly as possible over the area. For each small square, use the container to scoop up the right quantity each time.

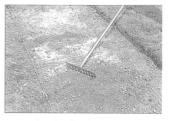

5 Rake the fertilizer into the surface before sowing or planting.

6 Some plants need a boost while growing. Cabbages benefit from nitrogenous fertilizer. Sprinkle it around the individual plants, keeping it off the leaves, then hoe or water in.

7 Most fruit trees will benefit from a general garden fertilizer in the spring. Sprinkle it around the base of the tree tree, keeping it off the trunk, then hoe it in.

MAKING GARDEN COMPOST

1 Compost bins are useful but you can save money in the kitchen garden by making a heap like this. Start with a thick layer of waste vegetable matter, 1m (1yd) square.

2 Tread the heap to compact the material when it is 30cm (1ft) deep, then sprinkle on sulphate of ammonia or a compost accelerator.

3 Continue to add garden or kitchen waste, with grass cuttings (not if weedkiller has recently been used on the lawn).

4 Continue to build up the heap in layers like this, and water if possible when the weather is dry.

5 After several months, depending on the time of year and the weather, the compost will be ready for use. Use any unrotted compost from around the edge to form the base for a new heap.

Cloches are the next best thing to a greenhouse or cold frame, and indispensable if you want fresh vegetables early or late in the season, when they are more expensive in the shops.

3 Right Plant out early vegetables that are hardy, such as broad beans or the hardiest of lettuces, once the ground has warmed up for a week or two. Make as much use of the space in a large cloche by sowing radishes or carrots either side of lettuces.

WARMING THE SOIL

1 In spring, put cloches in a couple of weeks before sowing to warm the ground.

2 Pay attention to the end pieces, or the cloche will become a wind tunnel. Ends can be a sheet of glass, but proprietary cloches have specially designed ends. Make sure the cloche is secured with pegs.

4 Right Tent cloches are less expensive, but as good for warming up the ground and protecting seedlings.

TUNNEL CLOCHES

1 Plastic tunnel cloches are useful for starting off early vegetable seedlings.

2 Make sure the plastic is secured with wires or strong wind will damage them.

3 Secure both ends firmly to resist the wind and pull the plastic taut.

FLEECY FILMS

1 Horticultural fleece will protect your crops from a degree or two of frost. Once the seedlings have been sown, pull over the fleece and secure with bricks.

2 Lay the fleece over the area so there is room for the crops to grow, but cover the edges with soil so no gaps are left. Water normally.

FLOATING CLOCHES

Protective netting give some protection against wind and hail and exclude many pests. They provide a little frost protection. Peel back the netting to weed or thin seedlings, replacing it later.
Perforated plastic film (right) will protect seedlings like other floating cloches and are long-lasting.

WHEN TO USE FLOATING CLOCHES

Floating cloches are used in the spring, but they can be useful for autumn protection too. Liquids will penetrate them, so you can water and apply liquid feeds through them. To weed or feed with non-liquid fertilizer, peel back the material and put it back when finished.

Many vegetables can be left under the cloche until they mature but not any which need pollinating, such as dwarf beans.

4 Use soil to hold down the edges of the cloche to stop the wind lifting them.

5 Use a soil thermometer to test if the soil is more than 7°C (45°F) for germination.

6 Either remove the cloche for sowing or planting or pull up the plastic on one side.

AN EARLY START 2

Many vegetables can be started off in pots or trays so that they are already growing well when you plant them out. You will be able to harvest them many weeks before those sown in open ground

Right Cabbages can be sown outdoors but also in pots indoors for an early start.

STARTING OFF SHALLOTS AND GARLIC

1 Start off large shallots in pots in a greenhouse or frame, in early winter. Plant so that the base of the bulb just sits in the loam-based compost or soil.

2 Keep moist. They will grow better in gentle warmth. Try to keep them growing slowly and in good light. Put in the garden 15–20cm (6–8in) apart in early spring.

3 Garlic is best planted in the garden in the autumn. They can be put into modules like these in mid or late winter, covered with 2.5cm (1in) of compost, planted out in the spring.

AN EARLY ROW OF PEAS

1 Sow peas in a piece of guttering lined with garden soil. Cover with more soil, put in the greenhouse in good light until they are 8cm (3in) tall.

2 Dig a wide drill the depth of the guttering. Use a garden line to make sure you keep the drill straight.

3 Slide the compost out of the length of gutter and into the drill. Firm the soil around the new row of peas, then cover with cloches to advance growth.

EARLY RUNNER BEANS

1 Eight weeks before the last frost is likely, sow runner bean seeds in pots, three to a pot. You can thin to two plants later.

2 Cover the seeds with 5cm (2in) of compost. Place in a light position in a frost-free greenhouse and keep watered.

3 Harden them off two weeks before planting out in a cold frame. Plant out when safe to do so.

SOWING IN POTS

1 Vegetables sown in pots can be given a good start. This is useful for brassicas if you have club-root disease in the soil. The plants will be better able to resist the disease with sterilized compost.

2 If more than one seedling germinates, thin to just one in each pot.

3 Once hardened off, plant them in the garden.

SOWING IN MODULES

1 These are useful for many types of vegetables, such as lettuce, that are planted out while still small. Sow a couple of seeds in each.

2 If more than one seed germinates, thin to one seedling while still small.

3 Make sure the seedlings have been watered before planting out, and remove each one with its root ball intact. They will grow quickly if planted this way.

EXTENDING THE SEASON

Use your cloches at the end of the season as well as the beginning, and protect your vegetables for winter use.

WINTER PROTECTION

Right Some vegetables and herbs, such as parsley, will continue to crop for much longer if you cover the row with cloches before cold weather arrives. Be sure to cover each end, so that the cloche does not become a wind tunnel.

PROTECT FROM FROST

1 In mild areas both beetroot and celeriac can be left in the ground for winter use if the soil is well drained. Protect from severe frosts with a layer of straw 15cm (6in) deep.

2 In cold areas, lift the vegetables, twist off the tops and store in moist sand in a frost-free place.

SOW WINTER SALADS

1 Extend fresh winter vegeta-bles, by sowing winter radishes and corn salad (lamb's lettuce) in late summer.

2 They can be sown in the open, but do better in a cold frame with a cloche.

3 Winter radishes are sown in late sum-mer. Lift the roots in late autumn to store in damp sand, in a cold dark place.

RIPEN LATE TOMATOES

Use cloches to ripen outdoor tomatoes at the end of the season. Lay straw on the ground, remove the supports and let the plants lie down on the straw.

Cover the row of cloches to speed the ripening process. Large barn cloches are best for this.

CORN SALAD

Sow corn salad (lamb's lettuce) in late summer. Harvest the leaves, a few at a time as needed.

ENCOURAGING FURTHER CROPPING

It may be possible for some crops to produce a bonus crop, even after harvesting.

EXTRA SPRING GREENS

Leave the stump after harvesting early cabbages. Make a cross-shaped cut i the stalk with a sharp knife. After a few weeks a cluster of small heads will have grown. Harvest these for a crop of spring greens.

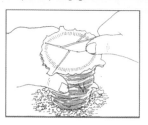

MORE CALABRESE

Cut as normal, but do not discard the plant. Leave it to grow smaller heads on side shoots.

Harvest the smaller heads on side shoots, after a few weeks.

CUT-AND-COME-AGAIN LETTUCE

1 Loose-leaf lettuce can be harvested in stages. Remove leaves from several plants in the row.

2 If a whole head is needed, try harvesting by cutting across the plant 2.5cm (1in) above the soil. The stump should resprout for a second harvest.

HARVESTING SPINACH

1 Harvest ordinary and New Zealand spinach a few leaves at a time. The tips of New Zealand spinach as well as the leaves, to prevent flowering and produce side shoots.

2 When harvesting whole spinach plants try cutting the leaves 2.5cm (1in) above ground, as they will often regrow and produce another crop of leaves.

PAK CHOI AND CHINESE CABBAGES

Harvest your pak choi while they are still young. Cut off the leaves 2.5cm (1in) above the soil. New leaves will be produced for a later crop.

Harvest Chinese cabbages by cutting them off 2.5cm (1in) above the ground, leaving a stump. New growth will appear within a few weeks.

By growing a selection of different lettuce varieties, you will be able to harvest over a longer period...especially if you stagger the sowings. Include some loose-leaf varieties that you can harvest as individual leaves, often over a period of several months.

SOWING VEGETABLES 1

Get your vegetables off to a good start by preparing the seed beds carefully

PREPARING THE GROUND

1 Break down clods of soil left after rough digging, to produce a fine surface for sowing.

2 If large lumps are difficult to break down, try treading on them to crumble them into smaller pieces.

3 Rake the soil level, gathering any large stones to one end.

4 Leave small stones, but remove large ones.

SOW WINTER SALADS

1 Always use a garden line to keep the rows straight. Wind the surplus around a peg keeping the line taut.

2 Use the corner of a hoe or rake to make a drill. Try to keep to the recommended depth on the packet.

3 Sprinkle the seeds thinly, and as evenly as possible. If this is difficult buy a seed dispenser.

Most gardeners sow vegetables in long rows, but use a 1.2m (4ft) bed system and you avoid treading on the ground to weed, cultivate and harvest, as you can reach the rows from both sides. If you mulch well, this can be the basis of a no-dig method of cultivation as the soil is not compacted.

The rows can be sown closer together with this method.

4 If dry, run water into the drill first to soak the soil. Water before sowing to reduce the chance of seeds being washed away.

5 Cover the seeds by shuffling your feet along the sides of the drill, pushing the soil back into the drills.

6 You may find it easier to rake the soil back into the drill, but be careful to rake in the direction of the drill and not across it.

SOWING VEGETABLES 2

Although most vegetables are best sown in conventional single rows, some can be sown broadcast, and others are best sown in multiple rows. Consider fluid sowing where you need to get tricky crops of to an early start.

Closer spacing is possible if you grow your vegetables in 1.2m (4ft) beds. Traditional row spacings allow for having to walk between the plants from routine cultivation.

SOWING MULTIPLE ROWS

1 Some seeds are usually sown in multiple rows close together. Take out a wide drill with a draw hoe.

2 Space the seed in the bottom of the drill. Large seeds like peas and beans can be spaced accurately by hand.

3 Push the soil back. Cover with mesh wire-netting if mice and birds are a problem until the seeds germinate

FLUID SOWING

1 Fluid sowing gets seeds off to a good start. Use it for parsnips and parsley. Sow thickly onto damp kitchen paper. Keep in a warm place.

2 Check daily and keep moist. As soon as roots emerge, wash them off the paper into a sieve. Don't wait for leaves to grow.

3 Mix wallpaper paste without fungicide, or use a kit from a garden centre. Stir the seeds into the paste to mix them well.

4 Take out the drill as you would normally, at the usual depth.

5 Place the paste in a plastic bag and cut off one corner. Do not make the hole too big. Twist the top of the bag and squeeze the paste along the drill. Cover with soil and water if dry.

SOWING BROADCAST

1 Some seeds can be sown broadcast. Scatter as evenly as possible on prepared ground.

2 Rake the seeds into the soil, in the opposite direction to when the ground was prepared, to distribute the seeds better.

THINNING AND TRANSPLANTING

Thin your vegetables while they are still small, so that you have a full row of well-spaced plants. Take special care with vegetables which need to be transplanted.

MULTIPLE SOWING

Some growers plant out vegetables in small clusters of seedlings, such as carrots, onions and leeks.

They are best grown in modules of four to six seeds in a cell.

Plant out intact, without separating them. You will not get exhibition quality crops but the overall weight is often good.

BEWARE CARROT FLY

Carrot flies lay their eggs around carrots when they are thinned. The smell of crushed leaves is thought to attract them.

Thin in the evening. Nip the surplus plants off at ground level, do not pull up.

Take the thinnings away with you, rather than leaving them on the ground.

THINNING

1 Thin as soon as seedlings are large enough to handle. Leave remaining seedlings twice as close as the final spacing to allow for losses.

2 When the seedlings are almost touching, thin to their final spacing. If there are gaps it may be possible to lift some of the thinnings carefully and transplant to make good the gaps.

TRANSPLANTING

1 When transplanting from open ground, water thoroughly an hour before, if the weather is dry.

2 Loosen the soil if plants are close together, or lift with a hand fork so that each seedling has a ball of soil attached.

3 Plant out with a trowel, firming the soil as you go. Use the blade of the trowel to press the soil around the roots.

4 The handle of the trowel can be used instead but the trowel will get dirty and unpleasant to use.

PLANTING OUT FROM MODULES, TRAYS AND POTS

1 The compost must be moist before removing the seedlings from the trays. To remove them, squeeze out from the base, while gently pulling at the top.

2 A plant grown in a pot will come out cleanly if you invert the pot. Hold the plant between your fingers and shake gently. Tapping the bottom of the pot will remove any stuck plants.

3 Plant the seedlings with a trowel, at their final spacing, then firm the soil gently and water in well.

PLANTING BRASSICAS

1 If club root is a problem, grow your brassica seedlings in pots of sterilized compost and plant out when they're growing strongly. This will not eliminate the disease but the plants get off to a good start and the effects will be minimized.

2 Brassicas are also attacked by cabbage root fly, the larvae burrow into the roots and stems. Place a proprietary or improvised brassica collar around each seedling, making sure that it lies flat on the soil. This will deter the flies.

STAKING AND SUPPORTING

Runner and climbing French beans, tall peas and tomatoes all need some form of support, which should be inserted when the plants are small.

GROWING BAG SUPPORTS

This is just of one the types of support for canes in growing bags. They hold the canes upright in the shallow compost. They are expensive but will last for many years.

PEA STICKS

Save twiggy sticks from prunings or cut from a tree. Select the right height for the plant and push the stick into the ground between the peas when they are 5cm (2in) high. The peas support themselves by curling tendrils around the sticks.

NETTING

Nylon netting is a good support for both peas and beans. Stretch it between two posts or make a framework from battens or canes. Use a 10cm (4in) mesh and tie it on securely. Young beans may need to be threaded through to start them climbing.

BAMBOO CANES

1 A wigwam of canes is ideal for a few runner bean plants and will look attractive at the back of the border. Tie four to six canes together near the top or use a plastic holder which the canes are pushed through.

2 Runner beans will twine around the canes and be self-clinging. Start them off by winding them round the canes, keeping them off the soil where they are vulnerable to slug and snail damage.

3 For a long row of runner or climbing French beans, insert two rows of 2.4m (8ft) canes at a slight angle so they cross near the top.

4 Slide a horizontal cane along the top in the V formed by the crossed canes. Pull it downwards to wedge the canes, then tie them all together.

5 Individual canes are useful for tomatoes, but make sure that 30–60cm (1–2ft) of the cane is pushed into the ground, to support the weight of a fruiting plant.

ROUTINE CARE

Regular weeding, feeding and watering will bring out the best in your vegetables. The increased yields always make the effort worthwhile.

WEEDING

1 Regular hoeing is the best way to keep down the weeds. A Dutch hoe is the most efficient, but can be difficult to manoeuvre between close plants.

2 Hand-weeding is inevitable if the weeds grow close to the crops plants. Pull up the weed with one hand while holding the vegetable firmly to reduce root disturbance.

3 Pernicious weeds, such as thistles and bindweed, will break off if they are pulled and spread further. If you are careful, you can paint translocated weedkiller on to the leaves, killing the roots. Be careful not to touch the crop plants.

FEEDING

1 A balanced fertilizer should be applied before planting. Some vegetables benefit from a specific fertilizer as the season progresses. Sprinkle it along the rows at the recommended rate, keeping it off leaves.

2 Use liquid fertilizers to boost growth during the summer. Most plants will usually respond rapidly to a liquid feed at this time. Dilute according to instructions.

WATERING

Sprinkler The best way to water a vegetable garden is with a sprinkler that distributes the water over a wide area.

Seep hose (right) are effective for vegetables planted in rows.

Once one row has been watered thoroughly, move the hose to the next one.

SPECIAL TECHNIQUES 1

Some vegetables, such as chicory and endive, are more succulent and less bitter if you blanch them. Rhubarb is forced in the dark to provide tender young stems earlier than normal.

GROWING AND FORCING CHICORY

1 To produce chicons (blanched heads) for winter use, sow in late spring or early summer. Lift the roots from mid-autumn onwards, and leave them exposed for a couple of days to retard growth.

2 When the roots have dried, trim off the leaves 2.5–5cm (1–2in) above the top of the root. Store any spare roots in a box of sand, peat or dry soil, until you are ready to use them.

3 **Right** Trim the bottom of each root so that it fits a 15–23cm (6–9in) pot. Pack soil around the roots, so the shoulder of each root is just beneath the soil. Put a pot of the same size over the top, and cover the holes. Keep in a temperature of 10°C (50°F) for 3 weeks, keeping moist, and harvest when they are 15cm (6in) tall.

FORCING RHUBARB

1 To force rhubarb in the garden, place an old barrel or wooden box over a root in early to mid winter, or use wire netting and canes as shown.

2 A better crop will result if straw is piled into the cage to generate warmth. With a wooden box, pile manure over the top and around the sides.

3 A plastic dustbin with the bottom cut out can be used. Check growth after a couple of months, pulling stems when they are 25–30cm (10–12in) long.

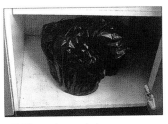

4 Roots can be forced indoors, but first lift a crown at least two years old and exposed to the cold for a few weeks. Put the crown in a black plastic sack and pack slightly moist peat or soil around the root or pot it up. If too wet, the soil will encourage fungus diseases. Secure the top with a twist-tie.

5 Place the sack in a warm place indoors until the forced stems are ready to harvest. Discard any roots or stems with fungus.

BLANCHING ENDIVE

Grow endive as lettuce, but blanch the leaves so they are not too bitter. Two weeks before harvesting, cover each plant with an old plate or blanching dish sold especially for the purpose.

Remove the cover only when you are ready to eat the endive. The covered area will be pale and less bitter.

Far right Rhubarb is so easy to grow that it is often taken for granted. It makes a decorative foliage plant and the forced stems are an early treat.

SPECIAL TECHNIQUES 2

FRUIT & VEGETABLES

Tomatoes can be grown well outdoors if you choose a suitable variety. In cold areas try raising tomatoes in grow bags or pots in a porch. If you have been put off growing potatoes because of the hard work earthing and lifting up, try growing them under black polythene.

POTATOES UNDER POLYTHENE

1 Roll out the polythene over the prepared ground. To prevent the polythene being blown away, pull soil over the edges to secure it in place.

2 Make slits in the polythene, spaced for the variety you intend to grow. Plants the tubers through the slits with a trowel

CHITTING

If you chit the tubers you will have have crop several weeks earlier.

Place the potatoes in trays in a frost-free place. The tubers are ready to plant when they are 2cm (3/4in) long.

3 Once the tops have died down, harvest the potatoes by lifting the polythene. Most of the potatoes will be lying on the surface ready to harvest.

EARTHING UP

Potatoes grown in the ground have to be earthed up to prevent the tubers being exposed to the light. This can cause them to turn green and become inedible.

Earth up in stages using a hoe to mound soil up each side of the plants.

OUTDOOR TOMATOES

1 Plant tall varieties that need staking 38–45cm (15–18in) apart, once hardened off.

2 Protect the plants with a barn cloche initially, to get them off to a good start.

GROWING BAGS AND POTS

Tomatoes do well in growing bags, using special supports makes staking easy. You can also grow bush types if you do not want to stake.

If a heavy crop is not essential, grow suitable varieties in pots.

3 When the plants are too tall for the cloches, remove them and stake immediately. Use one stake for each plant and push them well into the ground.

4 Keep the main stem tied to the support as it grows. Remove all sideshoots by pinching out the growing tips. Let the plant concentrate on the lower trusses of fruit.

5 Bush and dwarf tomatoes sprawl on the ground and do not need staking. Plant them 30–75cm (12–30in) apart. Cover with a floating cloche, if possible, until harvesting or they grow too tall.

SPECIAL TECHNIQUES 3

Traditional trench varieties of celery require blanching, but you can grow the self-blanching type in blocks and let them blanch each other. Carrots can be an easy crop to grow, but if carrot fly usually devastates your crop beat it with a simple barrier.

BEATING CARROT FLY

Erect a barrier of polythene or mesh netting around vulnerable seedlings, if carrot fly is a problem. Chemicals have limited success.

Make the barrier 60–90cm (2–3ft) high, beyond the height the fly normally reaches.

SELF-BLANCHING CELERY

1 Plant self-blanching varieties in blocks rather than rows. The inner plants are then protected by the outer ones. Plant celery 23cm (9in) apart to increase the blanching effect.

2 Harvest by lifting with a fork. You will have to discard more leaves from the heads on the outside of the block than in the inner part.

BLANCHING TRENCH CELERY

1 Trench varieties are usually planted in a trench to make blanching and watering easier. Fork in as much organic matter and manure, as possible.

2 Plant in rows 30cm (12in) apart, with 25cm (10in) between the plants.

3 Keep well watered. The trench can easily be flooded with water periodically in dry weather.

4 Some people earth up their celery with soil, but many gardeners prefer to blanch the stems with paper or drainpipes. Wrap corrugated cardboard or light paper loosely around the stems. Add more layers as the plants grow taller, overlapping the layers slightly.

Special Techniques 4

POLLINATING MARROWS AND COURGETTES

1 Marrows and courgettes are usually pollinated by insects, but hand pollination may be needed if the weather is cold or fruits are not forming. The female flower (left) has the small swelling, which is the embryonic fruit, behind the flower.

2 Pollinate marrows or courgettes with a fully open male flower, pressed against the female stigma.

3 A paintbrush can gather pollen from the male flower, then be brushed on to the stigma of the female.

4 Harvest courgettes while they are still young. The more you pick, the more fruits the plant will produce.

GROWING ONIONS FROM SETS

1 Make shallow drills 30cm (12in) apart. Space onion sets 15cm (6in) apart. Press firmly into the soil so the tips will protrude above the soil.

2 Cover the drills with soil so the tips of the onions are just visible. If birds pull at the onions, protect them until they form roots. Wire-netting or black cotton strung between pegs will deter the birds.

ENSURING SWEET CORN POLLINATION

1 Sweet-corn is wind-pollinated, and has male and female flowers. Male flowers are on top of the plant, females are below and form the cobs.

2 Block planting rather than in rows, will increase the chances of fertile cobs.

3 Press a fingernail into a kernel to test if it is ready to harvest. If milky liquid oozes out, the cob is ready. If the liquid looks watery, it is under-ripe.

Vegetables such as onions and courgettes are easy to grow, especially if you plant onion sets.

GREENHOUSE VEGETABLES 1: TOMATOES

Tomatoes are a popular greenhouse crop, and you should be able to harvest them over a long season. If you have a heated greenhouse start them early, if not, do not plant until you are sure there is no possibility of frost.

TOMATOES IN BORDERS

1 Right Try tomatoes in the greenhouse border for a couple of years. After that, replace the soil every two years, or use one of the other methods described. This will avoid problems from soil-borne pests and diseases. Plant 45cm (18in) apart from late winter in a heated greenhouse, or late spring in an unheated greenhouse. Tomatoes need regular feeding, use specially formulated liquid tomato feed for best results.

TOMATOES IN BORDERS

1 Ring culture is worth considering once the border ceases to be productive. Take out a trench and line with polythene to eliminate disease from the soil below.

2 Place fine gravel or coarse grit in the lined trench, and put special ring culture bottomless pots on top.

3 Fill the pots with good loam-based compost and plant the tomatoes. Water into the rings until roots are established, then water into the aggregate.

2 Although canes can be used for support, string is a more economical method.

3 As the plants grow, gently loop the string around the growing tip, to form a spiral.

4 Remove side and base-shoots while they are still small, by snapping off cleanly.

5 If fruits are failing to form shaking the plants each day and misting the flowers with water can help to spread the pollen.

6 Remove yellowing lower leaves. They are not needed and removing them will allow more light to reach the fruits.

7 Harvest the fruit when it is just ripe, and pick with the green calyx attached.

8 **Right** When six or seven sprays of fruit have set, remove the growing tip two leaves above the top spray of flowers, to allow these fruits to mature.

GROWING BAGS

1 These provide an alternative to a contaminated border, but careful watering and feeding are needed. Plant three tomatoes in a standard bag.

2 Cane supports can be pushed through the bottom of the bag into the border below, or strings can be suspended from the roof (see Tomatoes in Borders).

BUSH VARIETIES

The advice given above is for cordon or indeterminate varieties. Bush varieties are not normally grown in the greenhouse, but if they are, support will not be needed and sideshoots should not be pinched out.

GREENHOUSE VEGETABLES 2: AUBERGINES, CUCUMBERS, MELONS AND SWEET PEPPERS

All these vegetables are easy to grow in a greenhouse, and make a change from tomatoes. It is sometimes recommended that you avoid growing these different crops together, but in an amateur greenhouse, you can grow any combination of them.

Below Aubergines are decorative plants, and make a change from tomatoes in your greenhouse.

AUBERGINES

1 Aubergines can be grown in growing bags or 20cm (8in) pots with a loam-based compost. Pinch out the growing tip when the plant is 30cm (12in) tall.

2 Allow only one fruit to develop on each shoot. Remove other flowers and pinch out the growing tips, three leaves beyond the developing fruit.

3 The plants should be kept well watered and fed, and benefit from high humidity.

4 Fruits are heavy, so stake tall varieties. Purple fruits are usual although some are white. Harvest with at least 2.5cm (1in) of stalk attached.

CUCUMBERS

1 Bush varieties can be allowed to sprawl, but most greenhouse varieties are trained to wires or canes. Plant in growing bags or the border—two in a standard bag. One cane for each plant with wires stretched horizontally.

2 Tie the main stem to the cane. Pinch out the growing tip when it reaches the roof.

3 Many modern varieties produce only female flowers which have a small embryo fruit behind the petals.

4 Tie sideshoots to the wires. When tiny cucumbers grow, pinch out the shoots beyond two leaves after the fruit. Feed and water well, keep the air humid.

SWEET PEPPERS

Grow sweet peppers as described for aubergines, in pots or growing bags. Provide a stake, and pinch out the growing tip once the plants reach 60cm (2ft).

MELONS

1 Plant in a cool or heated greenhouse in late May, in growing bags or the border. Use a cane per plant, stretching wires horizontally across.

2 Tie the sideshoots to the wires. Pinch out the tip of the plant when it reaches 1.8m (6ft).

Pinch back all sideshoots on melon plants to two leaves beyond each flower. If necessary, pollinate by hand using a paintbrush. Thin to four fruits on each plant and support them in net slings.

PATIO VEGETABLES

You can grow a wide selection of vegetables in small spaces. Some are attractive enough in containers to make pleasant patio plants.

GROWING BAGS

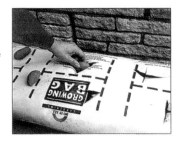

1 These can be used for many vegetables, even early potatoes. Do not open the bag in the usual way, cut slits to plant the tubers through—equivalent to planting beneath black polythene.

2 Keep the plants well watered and feed with a liquid fertilizer.

3 One growing bag can produce a good crop of potatoes and be fun in the process.

4 Spinach and self-blanching celery can be grown in this way. Sow directly into the bag or plant as seedlings.

5 Peas and dwarf French beans can be sown directly into the bag.

6 **Right** Lettuce, salad onions and tomatoes can crop well in growing bags.

WINDOW BOXES

2 Cut-and-come-again varieties of lettuce can be grown in windowboxes. Just pick enough leaves for one meal at a time, taking care not to strip any plant totally.

1 Miniature or tumbling varieties of tomatoes can be grown in windowboxes and even hanging baskets.

TUBS AND POTS

1 Some varieties of tomato can be planted in pots or tubs. Plant in late spring or early summer. protect from late frosts. Feed regularly using liquid feed or slow-release fertilizer in the compost.

2 Compact varieties supply a good crop of tomatoes.

3 Courgettes and bush cucumbers do well in tubs or large pots, and can look very attractive too.

HARVESTING AND STORING

Correct harvesting and storage will enable you to enjoy the fruits of your labour, throughout the winter months.

MAKING AN ONION ROPE

1 Onions can be stored in nets, but an onion rope is attractive if the onions have been harvested with their dried stems intact.

2 Tie onions to the rope wrapping twine around the neck of each onion and the rope.

3 Hang the ropes in a cool place where air circulates freely around them.

PROTECTING CAULIFLOWER CURDS

If left unprotected, cauliflower curds discolour in the summer light and are damaged by frost in winter. Fold over the leaves to protect them.

When the curd is almost mature, fold over leaves to protect it. Bend them so they do not break, and the head will last in good condition for longer.

In winter, tie the outer leaves with string to hold them over the curd. This is important with older varieties, new varieties have leaves that curl anyway.

PICKING BRUSSELS SPROUTS

Varieties bred for freezing have sprouts that mature at about the same time. Others usually mature in succession. Pick the lowest ones first, leaving the smaller ones at the top to mature. Snap off any yellowing leaves to reduce the risk of disease.

STORING CARROTS AND BEETROOT

1 Lift any crops which you are unable to use to stop them rotting in the ground.

2 Twist off leaves or the roots may rot.

3 In a large box, lay the roots on damp sand so they do not touch each other. Build up layer by layer, finish with 15cm (6in) of soil or sand. Store in a cool shed or outside as shown.

STORING POTATOES

1 Lift potatoes for storing after the foliage has died down.

2 Leave them on the surface for a couple of hours to dry.

3 Sort out the tubers, discarding the smallest, use up the middle-sized ones, and only store the largest. They must be kept frost-free, in paper sacks in a cool place. The potatoes must be dry before storing.

Below Store what you can for winter use.

STORING WINTER CABBAGES

Winter white cabbage and red cabbages are best harvested while in good condition, and stored in a cool, frost-free place. Strip off the coarse outer leaves before storing.

Store them in a well-ventilated, cool place, just above freezing. Place them on a slatted bench (straw

will help to protect them, but it's not essential) or hang them in nets.

VEGETABLE FACTS AT YOUR FINGERTIPS

This table is a quick reference guide for advice on how to grow common vegetables. Always check the seed packet or planting instructions for dates and spacings.

VEGETABLE	SOW	PLANT	HARVEST
ARTICHOKE, GLOBE	Mid/late spring	Spring	Early summer to mid autumn
ARTICHOKE, JERUSALEM	Plant tubers	Early/mid spring	Mid summer to following spring
ASPARAGUS	Early/mid spring	Spring	Late spring
AUBERGINE	Late winter/early spring	Early summer	Late summer/early autumn
BEAN, BROAD	Spring or early autumn	Sow *in situ*	Summer
BEAN, FRENCH	Late Spring/early summer	Sow *in situ*	Summer
BEAN, RUNNER	Late Spring/early summer	Early summer	Summer
BEETROOT	Late Spring to mid summer	Sow *in situ*	Summer and autumn
BROCCOLI, SPROUTING	Mid/late spring	Spring	Late winter to mid spring
BRUSSELS SPROUT	Late winter to mid spring	Spring	Late summer/early winter
CABBAGE, CHINESE	Late Spring to mid summer	Summer	Summer and autumn
CABBAGE, SPRING	Late summer	Autumn	Spring
CABBAGE, SUMMER/ AUTUMN	Early to late spring	Spring/summer	Summer/autumn

VEGETABLE	SOW	PLANT	HARVEST
CABBAGE, WINTER	Spring	Late spring/summer	Winter
CALABRESE	Late winter to late spring	Sow *in situ*	Early summer to mid autumn
CAPSICUM	Late winter to early spring	Early summer	Mid summer to mid autumn
CARROT	Early spring to early summer	Sow *in situ*	Mid summer to mid autumn
CAULIFLOWER, EARLY SUMMER	Autumn or late winter (under glass)	Spring	Early summer
CAULIFLOWER, SUMMER/AUTUMN	Mid to late spring	Early summer	Summer and autumn
CAULIFLOWER, WINTER	Late spring	Summer	Winter (mild areas) or spring
CELERIAC	Early/mid spring	Late spring	Early/mid autumn
CELERY	Early/mid spring	Late spring	Late summer to late autumn
CHICORY, FOR CHICONS	Late spring/early summer	Sow *in situ*	Winter
CHICORY, HEARTING TYPE	Summer	Sow *in situ*	Autumn
CORN SALAD (LAMB'S LETTUCE)	Spring to autumn	Sow *in situ*	Summer, autumn, winter
CUCUMBER, INDOOR	Late winter to late spring	Spring or early summer	Summer to mid autumn
CUCUMBER, OUTDOOR	Late spring/early summer	Late spring or early summer	Summer

VEGETABLE	SOW	PLANT	HARVEST
ENDIVE	Mid spring to mid summer	Sow *in situ*	Mid summer to late autumn
KALE	Mid or late spring	Late spring or early summer	Autumn and winter
KOHL RABI	Early spring to early summer	Sow *in situ*	Early summer to mid autumn
LEEK	Mid winter to mid spring	Late spring or early summer	Mid autumn to early spring
LETTUCE	Early spring to mid summer	Late spring to mid summer	Early summer to mid autumn
MARROW, PUMPKIN, SQUASH, COURGETTE	Mid or late spring	Late spring or early summer	Mid summer to mid autumn
MELON	Late winter/early	Late spring/early spring	Mid summer to mid autumn
ONION	Late winter to mid spring	Early/mid spring	Mid summer to mid autumn
ONION, JAPANESE	Mid summer to early autumn	Sow *in situ*	Early spring to mid summer
ONION, SPRING OR BUNCHING	Early spring to early autumn	Sow *in situ*	Late spring to late autumn
PARSNIP	Late winter to mid spring	Sow *in situ*	Mid autumn to late winter
PEA	Early spring to early summer	Sow *in situ*	Summer
POTATO	Plant tubers	Mid or late spring	Early summer to late summer

VEGETABLE	SOW	PLANT	HARVEST
RADISH	Early spring to early autumn	Sow *in situ*	Mid spring to late autumn
RADISH, WINTER	Mid summer to mid autumn	Sow *in situ*	Mid autumn to early winter
SALSIFY	Early to late spring	Sow *in situ*	Mid autumn to late winter
SCORZONERA	Mid/late spring	Sow *in situ*	Mid autumn to early spring
SHALLOT	Plant sets (bulbs)	Late winter to mid spring	Mid summer to early autumn
SPINACH	Late winter to mid summer	Sow *in situ*	Late spring to mid autumn
SPINACH, NEW ZEALAND	Spring	Sow *in situ*	Mid summer to mid autumn
SWEDE	Late spring/early summer	Sow *in situ*	Mid autumn to early spring
SWEET CORN	Mid/late spring	Late spring/early summer	Late summer/early autumn
SWISS CHARD	Early spring to mid summer	Sow *in situ*	Mid summer to mid autumn
TOMATO, INDOOR	Mid winter to early spring	Early to late spring	Early summer to mid autumn
TOMATO, OUTDOOR	Early to mid spring	Late spring/early summer	Mid summer to mid autumn
TURNIP	Early spring to early summer	Sow *in situ*	Early summer to mid autumn

GROWING HERBS

Few gardeners have space for a formal herb garden, but a mini herb garden is possible in a small space. Some ornamental herbs can be grown in flower beds and borders.

MAKING A HERB WHEEL

1 A herb wheel is a feature which allows you to grow a small collection of herbs. An old cartwheel could have herbs planted between the spokes.

A brick version can be made using a circle with a diameter of 1.5m (5ft) or larger. If there is space, plant an upright rosemary in the centre.

2 Lay a circle of bricks on end or at an angle to create a dog-tooth effect. Adjust the diameter of the circle if necessary for a close fit. The bricks can be laid on a shallow mortar base. When set, mortar the bricks in place. Otherwise, compact the soil around each brick, checking levels with a spirit-level.

3 Lay lines of bricks as the 'spokes', leaving plenty of room for planting. If the bricks do not meet exactly in the centre, do not worry. Mask any gaps with a plant or ornament—or an attractive pot containing herbs.

4 Top up the soil between the spokes with a loam-based potting compost, or good garden soil.

5 Plant up your herb wheel with a collection of perennial herbs that you will use and that are ornamental.

6 Finish off, by covering surface with stone chippings or cocoa shells.

PLANNING FOR WINTER

1 Pot up a few herbs that are small enough and that will grow on indoors. Chives can be treated this way.

2 Plant up in 15–20cm (6–8in) pots, water well and keep by a light window.

3 Lift some mint before it dies back in autumn. Pot up in and keep on a light window-sill.

219

HERBS IN CONTAINERS

Containers offer plenty of scope when space is limited, or if you want herbs by the back door or on a patio.

GROWING BAGS

1 Mint does well in a growing bag, and this ensures that it does not invade the rest of the garden. Different mints can be grown together in one bag, four at a time, and can be harvested as you need.

2 Growing bags are suitable for many low-growing annual herbs.

PLANTING A BARREL OR TUB

1 Use a large container for shrubby herbs such as bay. Drainage holes should be clear and use a loam-based compost.

2 If the plant is small for the container, plant a decorative edging of a compact herb such as golden thyme.

PLANTING A HERB POT

1 Herb pots look attractive, but always bear in mind the ultimate size and spread of each herb. Put small herbs in the planting pockets. Fill the pot with compost to that level, add the roots, then add more compost. Plant an attractive shallow-rooting herb in the top.

2 A herb pot like this is a very decorative feature, so harvest just a few leaves at a time, to avoid spoiling the effect.

WINDOWBOXES

Herbs can make attractive windowbox plants, using compact types such as marjorams, parsley and mints. Shrubby sage can be used but be prepared to replant every year or so.

Herbs are best harvested fresh, but many can be dried or preserved in other ways to enjoy when fresh herbs are not available.

COLLECTING FRESH HERBS

1 Herbs such as basil, tarragon and marjoram should have the growing tips used first. Harvest the larger leaves later.

2 Pick the outer leaves from parsley, sorrel, lovage and salad burnet first. More leaves will continue to grow.

3 Harvest leaves and sprigs from shrubby herbs, such as rosemary and thyme from areas that do not spoil the shape.

4 Harvest chives and Welsh onions by cutting them down to 4cm (1.5in) with scissors. More leaves will grow back.

Although most herbs are best used fresh, as soon as possible after picking, most can be dried or frozen.

AIR DRYING

1 Hang those herbs that can be cut as sprigs to dry in an airy place. Tie them in small bunches and they will be dry enough after a week.

2 Dry leaves on a wire rack. For small leaves, cover the rack with muslim or cheesecloth. Do not wash the leaves, but wipe off any dirt. Leave them in a dark place for a week.

3 Store in glass bottles (dark glass is best). Plastic and metal containers can affect the chemistry of some herbs. Label carefully.

FREEZING

1 Many herbs can be frozen. Chopped parsley, chives, and mint all freeze well. Use equal measures of water and chopped herbs. Whole leaves can be put into trays of water.

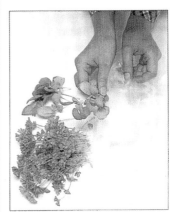

2 Whole sprigs can be put in the freezer and crumble easily when frozen. Blanch and dry first, if storing for a long time.

GROWING FRUIT

To grow a wide variety of fruit you do not need an orchard or very large garden Small apple trees grow in patio pots, strawberries grow well in containers on a balcony, and cordon trained apples and pears look good against a garden fence.

You will suffer poor crops if frost damages the blossom on tress like apples and pears. The latter are vulnerable as they flower earlier than apples. In a mixed kitchen garden, plant fruit trees so they do not cast shadows over the vegetables.

CHOOSING A SITE
Almost all fruits prefer a sunny site, avoiding frost pockets and cold air.

FRUITFUL IDEAS
If space is small, plant trained fruit trees, such as fans, cordons or espaliers,

against a wall or fence. They look decorative and take up little room.

Ballerina apple trees grow as a narrow column, even without pruning, and make an ornamental feature both in flower and fruit.

Some fruits can be grown well in tubs or pots on the patio where they will make a feature. Apple trees should have been grafted to a very dwarfing rootstock. Avoid vigorous trees such as pears.

You can even grow an apple as a decorative edging to a bed, perhaps in the kitchen garden. Step-over apples are single-armed espaliers.

The step-over method (left) makes an ornamental edging. 'Ballerina' apples (bottom of opposite page) grow into narrow columns.

Below It's easy to grow a wide range of fruit in the garden, including blackcurrants, strawberries and raspberries.

Even rampant fruits like blackberries, as well as hybrid berries, can be trained to look neat. They won't become overgrown, or be difficult to pick at harvest time, if they are trained to wires stretched between stout posts.

Apples pruned like cordons can be trained over a strong arch instead of against angled canes. Don't try hazardous thorned fruit.

PLANTING A FRUIT TREE OR BUSH 1

Fruit trees will be in the ground for a long time, so thorough ground preparation is vital. Plant with care.

PLANTING A CORDON OR ESPALIER

1 Fix the horizontal wires first, spacing them 30–45cm (12–18in) apart, and 10–15cm (4–6in) away from the fence or wall. Secure a cane at an angle of 45°, if planting a cordon.

2 Plant the tree with the stem 23cm (9in) away from the wall or fence. Place a cane across the hole to check levels. If planting a cordon, make sure that the stem can be tied to the cane.

PLANTING A FREE-STANDING TREE

1 Make a hole one-third larger than the width of the tree container. Add manure or compost and fork over so the plant does not sit on compacted ground.

2 Test the root ball for size and depth. Adjust soil levels if needed. If adding a stake, do this now, on one side of the hole, before you plant the tree.

3 Tease out some of the roots to encourage them to grow out. Return the soil, enriching it with compost, manure or slow-release fertilizer if necessary.

4 Tread the soil firmly with your feet to remove any air pockets.

5 Hoe the firmed soil to remove your footprints, and mulch the surface to conserve moisture and suppress weeds.

3 Mix a slow-release fertilizer into the soil. Rake level, firm with your feet and water well.

Below Every garden has some space for fruit—a cordon pear can be trained against a fence.

4 If planting a cordon, tie the stem to the oblique cane in several places to ensure it grows at the correct angle. Tie the main stem upright of an espalier, securing horizontal branches to the wires.

1 Prepare the ground as for trees, making the hole wider than the root ball. Use a cane to check levels.

2 Hoe and rake the ground to remove weeds and compressed footprints.

3 Cut back hard those bushes which grow on stems that sprout from a low base.

PLANTING A BARE-ROOTED TREE

Spread the roots out as widely as possible in the planting hole. Enlarge the hole if necessary.

PLANTING A FRUIT TREE 2

Trees need staking initially, but using an inappropriate tree tie can do more harm than good. In exposed gardens, or for very large trees, a different staking method may be used. The examples here are adequate for the majority of ordinary garden trees.

STAKING A FRUIT TREE

1 A low stake is better than a tall one, as the flexing of the stem in the wind can help to strengthen it. Insert the stake when planting, so at least 60cm (2ft) should be in the ground.

2 Use a proprietary tree tie as they are easy to adjust and have a spacer to hold the stem away from the tree.

ROOTSTOCKS

The rootstock determines the vigour and size of your fruit tree. Trained trees will almost certainly have been grafted on to an appropriate rootstock by the nursery. For bush and standard trees, you need to make sure that you select one with an appropriate rootstock.

The illustration shows the relative heights for an apple tree of the same age on different rootstocks. They indicate the space needed to grow them.

A dwarfing rootstock is useful for cherries and plums if you have a small garden. The cherry rootstock called 'Colt', for example, will

reduce the tree's size by about one-third (and it will crop sooner). Most plums sold in garden centres will have been grafted on to a dwarfing rootstock.

The rootstocks available vary in different countries, so if in doubt ask about the characteristics of the rootstock before you buy.

These are the likely heights of apples grown on different rootstocks. The more dwarfing the rootstock, the lighter the crop will be. The tree will fruit sooner and it may be possible to grow fruit in a garden that would otherwise be too small.

3 Make sure the tree is held firmly against the spacer.

4 Check ties every year, loosening when the trunk has expanded. Staking is needed for about the first three years.

5 Use a mulch, at least 5cm (2in) thick to suppress weeds and conserve moisture. Chipped bark is long-lasting and looks good.

6 Use a tree guard to protect the trunk if rabbits are a problem, stripping off the bark.

Above Most fruits trees benefit from initial staking, especially those grown on very dwarfing rootstocks. Always check the ties annually as they may need to be loosened to prevent the ties biting into the stem.

PRUNING TRAINED APPLES AND PEARS

Intensively trained apples and pears, grown as cordon and espaliers, must be pruned in summer and winter, to encourage cropping.

Opposite Apples and pears trained against a wall or fence can look very attractive. This is an espalier-trained pear: the pretty blossom will be followed by a heavy crop of tasty fruit.

PRUNING A CORDON

1 Shorten any long shoots grown since summer pruning, to 5cm (2in) on sideshoots.

2 Thin spurs to avoid overcrowding, while the plant is dormant. This is only done on established plants, not young ones.

3 Remove the weakest and most congested spurs first, leaving those remaining well spaced.

4 Once the main stem has reached the required height, prune the main stem back to within 12mm (0.5in) of the old wood.

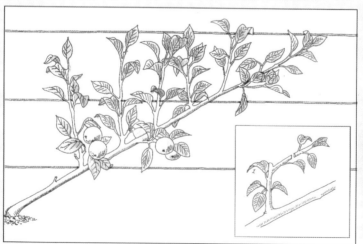

5 Prune sideshoots in late summer, once they are brown and woody at the base.

6 **Left** Prune to one leaf above the basal cluster of leaves, on all spurs.

PRUNING AN ESPALIER

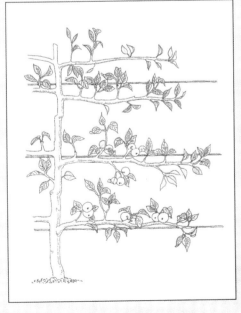

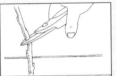

1 When the plant is dormant, thin out overcrowded spurs. This will only be needed on established espaliers.

2 In late summer, when this year's shoots are brown and woody, begin pruning. Cut back shoots over 23cm (9in) long, to three leaves above the basal cluster.

3 Cut sideshoots from spurs, back to one leaf above the basal cluster of leaves.

4 Cut back any secondary growth to one leaf from its base, in early autumn.

PRUNING A BUSH OR STANDARD APPLE OR PEAR TREE

The methods shown here are easy if pruning has been carried out regularly. They are suitable for bush and standard trees. If the flowers and fruit on your tree grow mainly in clusters along the shoots, follow the advice for spur pruning. If the fruit grows mainly on the tips of the shoots, follow the advice for pruning a tip bearer.

Bush apples are not difficult to prune and give a high yield.

BARK RINGING

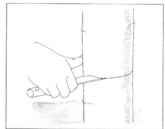

1 Bark ringing helps to reduce the vigour of a strong apple or pear, and may stimulate a poorly fruiting tree to produce a better crop. Make two cuts, deep enough to penetrate the bark and hard wood layer, in late spring.

SPUR PRUNING

1 While the tree is dormant, prune each branch in turn. Cut sideshoots to 2–6 buds.

2 Shorten the tip of the main shoot by one-third and one-quarter.

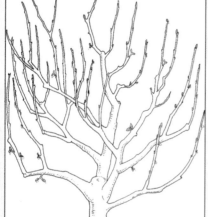

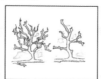

3 Thin spurs if needed. Cut out the weakest and remove others to leave spurs well-spaced and uncongested.

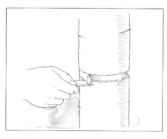

2 Remove the bark with the knife blade, around the tree.

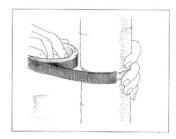

3 Wind waterproof tape around the wound to reduce the risk of disease. Remove when the wound heals.

PRUNING A TIP BEARER

1 Some apple trees bear fruit at the ends of their branches. Simple shorten those longer than 23cm (9in), cutting them back to five or six buds.

2 Thin out very vigorous shoots growing close together.

Cut out some crossing branches to keep the tree open and uncluttered.

NICKING AND NOTCHING

You can reduce the vigour of a shoot by removing a small crescent of bark and hard wood, just below a bud. This will restrict the growth of the shoot above. This process is called nicking.

If you want to stimulate a branch to grow out, perhaps to fill in a gap, make a similar cut just above the bud. This is known as notching.

Apples grown on dwarfing rootstocks will make compact bushes or small trees, like this 'Sunset'. Ask your garden centre for advice.

THINNING AND ROOT PRUNING

To grow large apples and pears, thin overcrowded spurs in winter and thin overcrowded fruits in summer. If your fruit tree is too vigorous, try root pruning.

ROOT PRUNING

2 Dig a trench around half the tree, using the guide line.

3 Use a fork to expose deeper roots.

1 Root pruning when the tree is dormant, may help reduce its vigour. Make an arc around half of the tree, inside the spread of branches. Root prune only one half of the tree each year.

4 Saw through large exposed roots. Leave small, fibrous roots undamaged. Fill in with soil and firm back.

THINNING SPURS

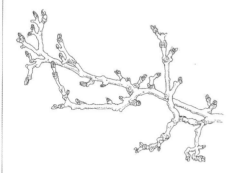

1 Thinning overcrowded spurs will help the trees to produce fewer but better fruits.

2 Remove weakest spurs to leave remaining ones well-spaced.

THINNING FRUIT

1 Leaving branches like this will result in fruits being small and of poor quality. Thin them out.

2 Surplus fruit can be removed with secateurs, leaving fruits 5–8cm (2–3in) apart.

FRUIT & VEGETABLES

235

PROTECTING YOUR FRUIT

Apples and pears are prone to pests and diseases, so spraying is advisable for an unblemished crop. Strike a balance by using some non-toxic controls and spraying when the chemicals will not harm beneficial insects.

GREASE BANDING

1 Winter moths climb the fruit trees in the autumn or early winter. A grease band will trap them and reduce the population.

Buy proprietary grease bands to make the job less messy. Cut off enough to go around the trunk with a short overlap.

2 Tie the bands into place at the top and bottom. Make sure that they are in close contact with the trunk.

3 Pull off the outer cover from the middle of the band, to expose the sticky greased surface. Check regularly and remove any debris which could act as a bridge over the grease.

PHEROMONE TRAPS

1 Pheromone traps work by attracting male insects to the scent of a female. They are available for codling moths and some other insects.

2 Place the pheromone on the sticky surface of the trap.

3 Hang the trap in the tree, so it can be checked regularly. Killing males will reduce the population as fewer females will be fertilized. Check traps twice a week, spraying when there are a lot of males around.

TERMS YOU MAY NEED TO KNOW

Sprays control pests should not be used when bees are pollinating the flowers. Make sure that you understand the following terms.
Bud burst is when tight buds are just expanding, **green cluster** when the flower buds are obvious, **pink bud** (white for pears) is when colour starts to show, and **petal fall** is when the petals of the first flowers start to drop.

Pink bud (apple)

Full flower

HOW TO GROW OUTDOOR GRAPES

There are several ways to grow outdoor grapes, but the Guyot system described here is one of the easiest.

FORMATIVE PRUNING

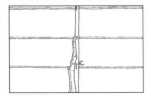

1 Prune the main shoot back to just three strong buds.

2 The first summer, let these shoots grow, tying them to grow vertically.

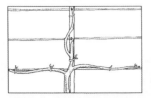

3 Next winter, lower the two strongest shoots and tie horizontally. Cut the upright shoot back to three buds. Next summer, tie in shoots growing vertically.

ESTABLISHED GUYOT PRUNING

1 Prune the central shoot back to three buds. Select two new shoots to shorten and tie in.

2 Cut out all other shoots. Bend over the young shoots and tie to the bottom wires.

3 New shoots grown on the bottom wire should be tied in to the other wires, so that they grow vertically.

4 Pinch out the growing tips to leaves above the top wire., and any sideshoots growing from shoots already carrying fruit.

Grapes can be very decorative fruit. This variety is 'Brandt'.

How to Grow Peaches and Nectarines

Peaches and nectarines are both treated in the same way. A fan-trained tree will give good results in all but mild areas. It is best to buy a ready-trained tree or consult a specialist book. The advice given here is for established bush and fan trees.

THINNING

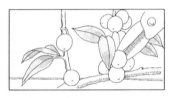

Peaches and nectarines may need thinning to produce a bigger crop. Snip off surplus fruit, to leave just one fruit per cluster.

PRUNING A BUSH TREE

1 In early summer, cut out any dead or diseased branches. If the tree is congested, cut out some older branches.

2 Cut back any dying branches on a tree that has been fruiting for several years. Don't do this to more than one-quarter of the branches overall.

PRUNING A FAN TREE

1 Disbud young shoots, so they grow every 15cm (6in), once leaves emerge in the spring. Leave the bud at the base of the shoot alone, to carry fruit next year.

2 After harvesting, prune each shoot that has borne fruit. These are shoots developed from a bud left to grow from the base during spring pruning.

3 Tie this replacement shoot to the cane that supported the fruited shoot that has just been removed.

How to Grow Currants

Blackcurrants are easy to grow and prune. Red and white currants are also easy fruit to grow, but they are trained and pruned in a different way.

PLANTING

1 Plant in well-prepared ground to which fertilizer has been added. Plant at the same depth.

2 Plant 1.2–1.5m (4–5ft) apart and firm the soil well around the roots.

3 Straight after planting, cut back all the stems on a blackcurrant to the first or second bud above the ground. this stimulates new shoots to grow.

4 For red and white currants, prune off any sideshoots growing within 10–15cm (4–6in) of the soil, to produce a clear stem.

5 Prune back the main shoot by half, to an outward-facing bud. The next winter, reduce the length of all main shoots grown from last years pruning by half.

PRUNING AN ESTABLISHED BUSH

1 Prune blackcurrant bushes over three years old annually, ideally after harvesting or in the autumn. Cut any badly placed branches back to their origin.

2 Prune established red and white currant bushes annually. Shorten the tips of leading shoots to encourage new growth.

3 Prune each sideshoot from these branches to just one bud.

RASPBERRIES, BLACKBERRIES AND HYBRID BERRIES

PLANTING RASPBERRIES

1 Plant raspberries 45cm (18in) apart in a shallow trench with compost or manure added. Spread out the roots.

2 Firm the ground. Cut back to 25cm (10in). In mid summer, cut back original stem just above ground level and tie in.

PRUNING AND TRAINING RASPBERRIES

1 Train to wires stretched between posts. Space the wires 30cm (1ft) apart.

2 Prune summer-flowering varieties after fruiting. Cut back to ground level, canes that have fruited. Prune autumn-fruiting plants during the winter, cutting all canes back to ground level.

PRUNING BLACKBERRIES AND HYBRID BERRIES

1 Train fruit to wires stretched between posts, to make pruning easier.

2 Prune established plants after fruiting or when dormant. Cut back to the ground all canes that have fruited. Tie in the new shoots, spreading them out.

PLANTING BLACKBERRIES AND HYBRID BERRIES

Plant bare-rooted plants when dormant, from late autumn to early spring. Space them 2.4–5cm (8–15ft) apart depending on the variety.

HOW TO TRAIN RASPBERRIES

A post and rail system (see above) is simple and effective, although there are several other methods.

Space the wires at heights of 75cm (2.5ft). 90cm (3ft) and 1.5cm (5ft). Tie in the new shoots each season when 90cm (3ft) tall. Space them 10cm (4in) apart.

At the end of the season the canes will be above the top wire. Bend them over and tie down to the top wire. In spring, cut back to leave the canes 15cm (6in) above the top wire.

HOW TO GROW GOOSEBERRIES

Plant, feed and mulch goose-
berries as for blackcurrants,
prune after planting.

FORMATIVE PRUNING

Prune back shoots, after
planting, by half to stimulate plenty of branching.

PRUNING AN ESTABLISHED BUSH

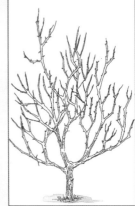

1 Prune bushes
over three
years old annual-
ly. In winter cut
the tips of all
main shoots back
by half of the
summer growth.

2 Prune each sideshoot
from these branches
back to 8cm (3in).

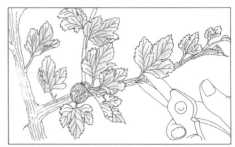

3 In early to mid summer cut
sideshoots back to five leaves
from their base. This will keep the
bush more open and reduce the risk
of diseases. Leave the main shoots
intact during summer pruning.

How to Grow Strawberries

Strawberries are very easy to grow, but always buy certified disease-free plants. If disease affects your plants, buy fresh plants. The method described is simple and reliable. Some varieties crop just once, while others produce several crops between early summer and mid autumn.

PLANTING

Strawberries need fertile soil so work plenty of compost or manure into the ground, removing all weeds before planting.

Rake in fertilizer, then plant 45cm (18in) apart, in rows 75cm (30in) apart.

The plants often arrive with bare roots. Spread the roots out on a mound, making sure that the crown is level with the surrounding surface, then return the soil.

Most plants are sold in pots. Water them an hour prior to planting out and plant at their original depth.

Remove flowers that appear during the first year. This allows the plants to get well established before bearing a crop of fruit.

ROUTINE CARE

1 The plants benefit from regular feeding. Sulphate of potash should be applied in early spring. If plants need a boost, apply sulphate of ammonia in mid spring.

2 Hoeing or hand weeding will keep down weeds.

3 Use special mats to keep the fruit clean. These must be in place as the fruits develop.

NEW PLANTS FROM RUNNERS

Spread out the runners in early to mid summer, and peg where there is a strong tuft of leaves into pots of compost plunged into the soil.

Pinch or cut off the runner just beyond the pegged-down point, but *do not sever the link with the parent plant*. Remove surplus runners not required.

Check after six weeks, and if the plant has rooted well, sever it from its parent.

4 It may be cheaper to lay a thick bed of straw around the plants.

HARVESTING AND STORING FRUIT

Fruit needs picking with special care if you plan to store or preserve it. Only pick perfect fruit—damaged or imperfect fruit should be used up when still fresh.

HOW TO STORE

These are some of the best ways to store some of the most popular fruits.

APPLES	Store wrapped; freeze as slices or purée; bottle as slices
APRICOTS	Freeze halved; bottle
BLACKBERRIES	Freeze whole; bottle
CHERRIES	Freeze after stoning (pitting); bottle
CURRANTS (BLACK, RED, WHITE)	Freeze whole; bottle
GOOSEBERRIES	Freeze whole or purée; bottle
PEACHES AND NECTARINES	Freeze after stoning (pitting); bottle
PEARS	Store wrapped
PLUMS	Freeze after stoning (pitting); bottle
RASPBERRIES	Freeze whole; bottle
STRAWBERRIES	Freeze whole or purée

PICKING AND STORING SOFT FRUIT

1 Pick strawberries carefully by the stalk to avoid bruising.

2 Pick raspberries as they become ripe. Pull them gently off the stalk, leaving the plug behind (pick with the stalk only if you will exhibit in a show.

3 Soft fruits freeze well. Remove stalks and hulls, then freeze the fruit whole, spread out on trays.

4 Once frozen, transfer the fruit to bags or boxes, and remove as much air as possible.

PICKING AND STORING APPLES AND PEARS

1 Apples and pears are ready for picking when the fruit comes away from the tree easily. Twist and remove the fruit with the stalk intact.

2 Bruised fruit does not store well. Line a basket with straw or paper and place the fruit in this as you harvest it.

3 Wrap each fruit individually in greaseproof paper, placing the fruit in the centre of a square of paper.

4 Fold two opposite corners over the fruit carefully.

5 Fold over the other two corners and place fruit in trays.

6 **Right** Keep in a well ventilated container in a cool but frost-free place.

FRUIT FACTS AT YOUR FINGERTIPS

Use this table as a quick reference guide for advice on the requirements and harvesting times for all the common fruits. The dates given are for popular varieties and methods of cultivation: these may vary for specific varieties and the weather. Always check the label or seek advice from the nurseryman about planting details, spacings and if pollinators are required.

NAME	SOIL AND SITE	HARVEST	REMARKS
APPLE	Any soil. Full sun. Avoid frost pockets	Late summer to late autumn	Regular pruning and spraying necessary for good crops
APRICOT	Well-drained soil, warm, sunny position. Frost protection	Mid and late summer	For small gardens choose a tree grafted on a very dwarfing rootstock
BLACKBERRY AND HYBRID BERRIES	Undemanding Avoid frost pockets	Mid summer to early autumn	Regular pruning and training are essential
BLACKCURRANT	Undemanding.	Mid and late summer	Annual pruning and feeding
BLUEBERRY	Only acid soils – pH 5.5 or less	Mid to late summer	Protection from birds may be necessary
CHERRY	Ordinary soil	Mid and late summer	To make cherry growing easy in a small garden, choose a self-fertile variety
FIG	Any soil, sunny position	Late summer and early autumn	It may be necessary to restrict root spread
GOOSEBERRY	Any soil. Best in full sun. Avoid frost pockets	Early and mid summer	Very prone to a form of mildew, so routine spraying may be necessary
GRAPE	Well-drained, fertile soil. Full sun	Early and mid autumn	Dessert grapes are best grown in a greenhouse

NAME	SOIL AND SITE	HARVEST	REMARKS
KIWI	Any soil, warm, sunny position	Mid autumn	Needs a male plant to pollinate the female fruiting variety
PEACH AND NECTARINE	Fertile soil, sunny position	Mid summer to early autumn depending on variety	Except in the warmest areas, best grown as a fan against a warm wall
PEAR	Fertile soil, sunny position	Early autumn to early winter	Will need a pollinator. Seek advice for your variety
PLUM, GAGE, DAMSON	Fertile soil, sunny position	Late summer to late autumn	Avoid early varieties in cold areas (blossom is often damaged by frost)
RASPBERRY	Fertile soil, sunny position	Mid summer to mid autumn	Prune and train annually
RED CURRANT AND WHITE CURRANT	Any soil if well-drained	Mid and late summer	Can be trained as a cordon
STRAWBERRY	Fertile soil in full sun	Early summer to autumn	Propagate new plants regularly

BIG IDEAS FOR SMALL GARDENS

WORKING OUT YOUR OWN DESIGN

You may be starting a garden from scratch, in which case you have the freedom to arrange the elements you want within it in almost any form, bearing in mind aspect, prevailing wind, views (both pleasing and ugly), and privacy. Alternatively, you may want to replan a garden that you have previously planted and arranged without originally giving a lot of thought to its overall design, or to redesign a garden you have inherited when moving house. If you have just taken over an established garden it would be wise to wait a year before planning it so that you can assess its present design and planting before you decide which factors you want to retain and which you would prefer to change.

Before working on a design it is best to make an accurate scale plan of the garden, even if this seems rather complicated. Also some thought needs to be given to what you want to use the garden for as well as how you want it to look. Once your garden plan has been drawn up you can use it to arrange the various areas that you require and plan the planting, bearing in mind some of the clever tricks that an expert uses to change the space visually, add excitement and deal with the problems encountered in your particular plot.

Making a plan to scale

Aspect

The direction your garden faces, together with the position of the house, surrounding walls, trees, and fences, affects the amount of sun or shade it gets. Use a compass to get an accurate position for north and mark this on your plan. Make a note of the sunny and shady areas at different times of the day. This will help you to position both structures and plants in your garden.

Views

You will want to show off a good view. Framing it with trees or shrubs will highlight it. At the same time an ugly view is best hidden. Mark this on your plan so that you remember to design in a concealing barrier.

Overlooked areas

Privacy can be provided by trees, pergolas and frameworks for climbing plants, so show the areas where the garden is overlooked on the plan.

Noise

An area thickly planted with evergreen shrubs or trees will help to deaden noise, so mark in the position of a busy road or other sources of noise.

The first thing you need to do when designing your garden is to measure the area accurately and make a detailed, scale plan of it. Omit anything you do not want to include in the new design but show the position of anything you want to keep, such as an old tree or specimen shrub. You will also need to show the positions of other fixtures, as these can influence your design. Mark the site of manholes, overhead cables (so that you don't plan a tree in their path) and underground drain lines and cables plus their depth (so that you don't cut through them when digging a pond or other excavations).

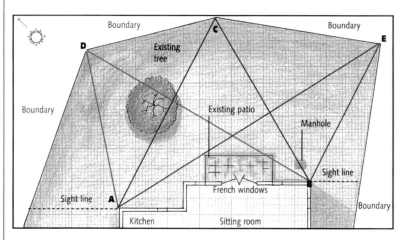

Stages in drawing a plan

1 Do a rough sketch on a large piece of paper first. A long tape, 30 m/100 ft will make measuring easier and more accurate. Start by marking in the area of the house, which should be included in the plan. Mark the positions of doors and windows. To measure the distance of the boundary at each side of the house use a sight line from the house. To do this, stand so that you can look directly along the house wall and with one eye line up a point on the boundary along the same line. Mark this spot with a cane and then take a measurement from the nearest house corner to this point. Then do the same on the opposite side.

2 Now move on to the garden. By using triangulation, positions can be plotted accurately. Measure from one house corner, **A**, to the end of the garden

to a point such as a boundary corner, **C**. Then measure the distance of **C** from the opposite house corner, **B**. Mark these two distances on the plan. Do the same from **A** and **B** to the opposite boundary corner **D** (or any other boundary corners). If the house and garden are wide you may need to measure from a number of points along the house to a range of boundary points – see lines from **A** and **B** to **D**, **C** and **E** on the plan, above.

3 Once the boundary distances are recorded, move on to those items in the garden that cannot be moved, such as manholes, oil tanks, and trees or shrubs that you wish to keep. Use triangulation as described in step 2 to plot the positions of each of these. Heating vents, rainwater barrels and garden tap positions also need to be shown. To avoid confusion you may find it easiest to use a different colour for

lines and measurements to each point. For large trees, you will also need to measure the approximate diameter of the trunk and radius of the canopy and mark these on the plan.

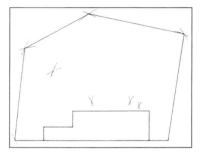

4 Now move on to making a proper scale plan. For this you will need a large piece of graph paper. First work out the scale you need to use to fit the complete garden onto the paper: a scale of 2.5 cm to 3 m or 1 in to 10 ft is a usually a good size. Note the scale used on the plan itself, and also show the north point. To mark each pair of measurements use compasses, set to each recorded scaled-down distance, and draw a short curve (see diagram, above). The point at which the curves from two measurements cross is the accurate position. Draw in the boundary lines by connecting these points. Mark the positions of the items such as manholes, trees, shrubs (see step 3) within the garden in the same way and show a rough circle for a tree or shrub canopy.

5 (See diagram, above right.) Mark on the plan the positions of any views to be accentuated or blocked out (making it clear which is which), any overlooked areas of the garden, any wet areas, slopes, and the main wind direction. All of this information is important in helping you design the garden.

6 When the plan is drawn in outline, arrange the elements you wish to include in the design. Use two sheets of tracing paper; one to show the basic structure and one for the planting. Design the basic structure first, then overlay the second sheet on top and position the planting on this.

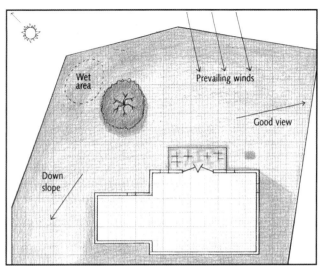

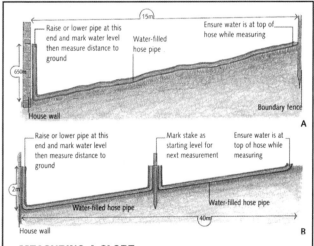

MEASURING A SLOPE

A simple way to measure a slope is to use the Egyptian method, which uses a garden hose (see diagram **A**). Lay one end of the hose, filled with water, at the top of the slope and run it down the slope, holding the second end in the air to avoid water loss and ensuring that the water remains in the pipe end at the higher level.

Gently lower the second end until you can see the water just reaching the top of the pipe. Measure the distance from this water level to the ground and this will give you the drop on the slope.

On a long slope you may need to take two or more measurements, then add them together (see diagram **B** for how to do this).

Designing the garden

Points to consider

The list below gives some of the factors you may wish to include in your design. Pick out those that you would like to incorporate and make your own check-list, grading it in order of priority. In a small garden you are unlikely to be able to fit in everything you would like to include, so less vital choices may have to disappear.

Lifestyle
- Areas for outdoor living/BBQ
- Children's play areas
- Pets
- Clothes line/airer

Structures and fittings
- Boundary wall, fence or hedge
- Patios and paths
- Lawns
- Gates
- Dustbin
- Coal bunker/wood shed
- Greenhouse/cold frame
- Lighting
- Rainwater tanks
- Compost bins
- Pergola/arbour
- Moving water feature/pond

Ornamental extras
- Pots/statues
- Sundial/bird table
- Decorative natural materials

Planting
- Ornamental plants
- Herbaceous border
- Rock or gravel garden
- Vegetables/ herbs/fruit
- Cutflowers
- Raised beds
- Trees
- Wild area
- Wildlife area to attract birds/mammals/ butterflies/bees

There are several points to consider before you put pencil to paper and plan your design, work out the materials you need to implement it and decide on the planting. First of all consider the style of the house – its period, shape and the materials used in its construction, so that house and garden will blend visually. Then think what style of garden you want to create – the following pages will give you some ideas and help you to decide what you prefer.

Formal gardens, with sides that form mirror images, match well with symmetrical houses, but even here most people opt for an easier, natural-looking informal style.

A wild garden with a naturally shaped pond, areas of long grass, fallen timber and wild flowers, will bring in the wildlife that help to keep pests at bay. This garden style appeals to the organic gardener. A wild garden can also be included as part of an informal garden.

The minimalist design of a Japanese garden, with its raked gravel, and carefully positioned sculptural plants and boulders, works well in a small space and is easily maintained. However, if you enjoy working in the garden, you may prefer the cottage-garden style with intermingled vegetables and flowers and plants spilling over paths.

A strong skeleton

When you look through the gardens that follow you will notice that they are based on a simple, strongly shaped skeleton, which ensures that the garden looks good at all times of the year, both when overflowing with greenery and flowers and when growth is more restricted. The pattern may be based on curves, geometric shapes or a mixture of both. A series of interlocking circles, or squares and rectangles, both provide a clean, distinctive background. Squares and rectangles can also be used very effectively across the diagonal.

Tricks of the trade

In a small rectangular garden a series of centrally positioned circles that decrease in size away from the house can increase the apparent size of the garden. Lines that run away from you can make an area appear longer.

A long narrow space looks more interesting if the length is broken up into a series of separate 'rooms'. Create a focal point with an eye-catching seat, urn or specimen tree or shrub. Provide interest at a range of levels by fixing structures for plants to grow up, such as trellis, arches, pergolas. A secret corner gives interest. Create privacy with a plant-covered arbour; provide shelter from the wind with trellis screens and climbers; frame a view with an archway or shrubs.

Creating a series of terraces is the best way of dealing with a sloping garden. This will require quite a lot of initial work but the resulting series of levels, held in place by retaining walls or banks and linked by steps or paths, can look very attractive. Use a small slope to make a rock garden.

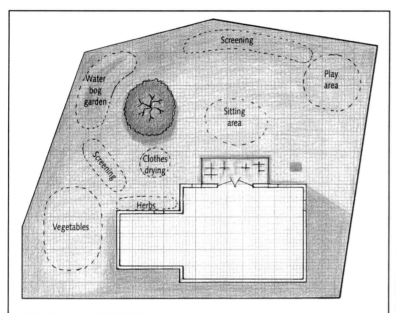

Water bog garden

Screening

Play area

Sitting area

Clothes drying

Screening

Herbs

Vegetables

THE STAGES OF DESIGN

1 Bearing in mind sunny and shady areas, wind, views, privacy, noise, and practicalities of access, roughly mark in areas for each of the uses you want to include in your design.

2 Now integrate the marked areas, using the basic pattern you have chosen of straight or curved lines or a mixture of both. You can, of course, use a number of overlays to try out a range of patterns. Once you are satisfied with the basic design, go over this in pen.

3 Place the planting sheet over the construction plan and, bearing in mind all the points mentioned in step 1 which will affect your choice of plants, plan the areas to be planted in more detail.

Time-saving considerations

As well as soil and situation, altitude, rainfall, and wind are contributory factors to what will grow well in your garden. Wherever your garden is situated there will be plants that flourish and others that will be hard to grow. Local garden centres are a good source for plants that thrive locally. Growing these will be much less time consuming than choosing unsuitable alternatives.

Terracing
When terracing it is important to remove the topsoil temporarily during construction, then level the subsoil before replacing the topsoil. If you do not do this the depth of topsoil will vary considerably at different points on each terrace.

A poorly drained garden shows up in constantly wet or puddled areas. Improving the condition of the soil will greatly improve drainage. Low-lying areas can be used for a pond, or bog garden. However, if the problem is severe, laying drains may be the only answer.

Budgeting
Constructing a garden from scratch can be expensive in terms of materials and hired labour. A loan may be needed if you want to complete the construction and planting in one go. If you can do much of the work yourselves the cost will be considerably reduced.

Alternatively draw up a work time schedule so that you can pay for the work in instalments. Start with the basic construction jobs of installing any electricity, forming the boundary, building a patio and making paths. As a second stage add areas of lawn and some of the key plants plus quick-growing climbers and annuals. The decorative features such as ponds, moving water features, arches, pergolas and arbours can be added later.

See also:
- *Form and shape, Chapter 6*
- *Identifying and improving soil, page 102*
- *Laying drains, page 103*
- *Electricity in the garden, page 112*

DESIGNS FOR SPECIFIC SHAPES AND AREAS

The shape and situation of a garden have a great bearing on the best type of design to create to ensure that it becomes interesting. Even the plainest and smallest garden is enhanced by a few surprises and a long, narrow strip always benefits from being divided into a series of garden 'rooms'.

In this chapter top garden designers have created innovative solutions to some common problems that arise due to a garden's shape, and factors such as land gradient or situation.

▲ **Before conversion** the garden had a flowerbed on the left-hand side, a pile of rubble in the centre, a lower area on the right where, possibly, an old shed or greenhouse stood and the space was outlined by a fence and walling.

Courtyard garden

This tiny garden, designed by Jean Goldberry, displays many interesting features. From the house a small pergola creates an arched entrance to the garden and a pathway leads off to the right to a circular terrace with a central statue. Then it turns left up to the main terrace shaded by a wisteria which clothes the pergola with long, falling streamers of lilac-blue flowers in late spring. The path then curves around to join up with the original terrace by the house, passing the central raised circular water feature on the left, where a low fountain splashes a collection of pebbles. Tall grasses echo the shape of the falling water. To the right of the path stepping stones, softened by ground-hugging plants, line up to lead off to the right to a spot that is discreetly hidden by shrubs.

THE GARDEN'S PROBLEMS	HOW THEY WERE SOLVED
Rubble in the centre of the garden.	This rubble, utilized for hardcore, created a base for the brick terrace.
The garden was not only small, but also flat and uninteresting.	A design was created to include a range of levels which would give the space more interesting contours.
Wind, mainly from the right-hand side, was a problem in this small space.	Trees were planted to provide shelter for the raised sitting area.
An unattractive view of a huge area of a neighbour's wall to the right.	The pergola over the sitting area was constructed to hide some of the wall and raising the terrace also helped.
The owner was very keen to have a water feature but was concerned about the safety of grandchildren when visiting.	A raised brick-edged water feature with a shallow layer of pebbles and a low geyser was constructed in the centre of the garden. The height makes it safe for small children.

▼ The planting scheme was cleverly arranged to give this tiny area depth, perspective and a lush feel.

DESIGNER'S PLANTING SCHEME

Key plants
1   Sorbus commixta 'Embley'
2   Rosmarinus officinalis 'Miss Jessup's Upright'
3   Cistus x purpureus
4   Cornus controversa 'Variegata'
5   Box, Buxus sempervirens clipped into a globe
6   Wisteria floribunda 'Macrobotrys'
7   Japanese fatsia, Fatsia japonica 'Variegata'
8   Crab apple, Malus 'Van Eseltine'
9   Juniper, Juniperus communis 'Hibernica'
10 Lavender, Lavandula x intermedia
11 Hebe 'Caledonia'
12 Yucca gloriosa

Decorative detail
13 Geranium psilostemon
14 Globe artichoke, Cynara scolymus
15 Miscanthus tinctoria 'Nanus Variegatus'
16 Geranium pratense 'Mrs Kendall Clark'
17 Penstemon 'Alice Hindley'
18 Astilboides tabularis

Plants for added colour
Morning glory, Ipomoea purpurea
Nemesia strumosa 'KLM'
Lobelia 'Riviera Blue Splash'
Larkspur, Consolida ajacis
Blue daisy, Felicia heterophylla 'Spring Marchen'
Antirrhinum – tall white variety in sunny spaces

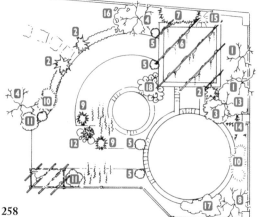

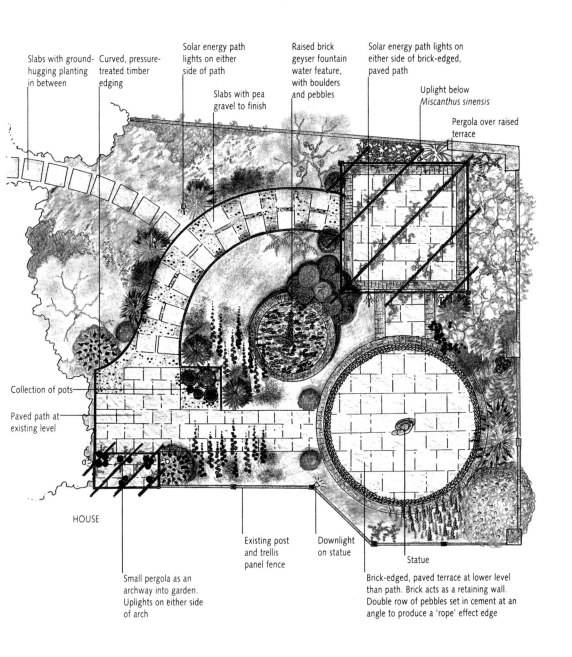

Slabs with ground-hugging planting in between

Curved, pressure-treated timber edging

Solar energy path lights on either side of path

Slabs with pea gravel to finish

Raised brick geyser fountain water feature, with boulders and pebbles

Solar energy path lights on either side of brick-edged, paved path

Uplight below *Miscanthus sinensis*

Pergola over raised terrace

Collection of pots

Paved path at existing level

HOUSE

Small pergola as an archway into garden. Uplights on either side of arch

Existing post and trellis panel fence

Downlight on statue

Statue

Brick-edged, paved terrace at lower level than path. Brick acts as a retaining wall. Double row of pebbles set in cement at an angle to produce a 'rope' effect edge

CONSTRUCTION

There is so much to look at in this tiny garden that it appears much larger than it really is. The clever use of a large variety of hard surface materials, helps to break up the space, as do the subtly changing levels.

Flagstones, of varying sizes, are used for the area next to the house with a step down to the brick-edged circular paved area, where pebbles are used as an edging. The path and square sitting-out area use the same materials but the curved path mixes gravel and paving with an edge of timber to hold the gravel in place. Slabs, edged by creeping plants, form a slightly different-looking walkway that leads away from the initial path and through the area to the left.

▲The view along the side of the house looking towards the circular terrace and statue, with the water feature on the left. The eye is drawn to this central grouping, which gives the courtyard depth and perspective. Sorbus trees at the back break the wind and provide late summer berries and autumn colour. In summer the garden becomes a haze of pinks, blues and lilacs.

PLANTING

Jean gave the seating area an oriental feel with wisteria on the pergola backed by bamboos and a variegated *Fatsia japonica*. She also used junipers to reflect yet soften the upright pergola posts. Junipers, still small in these pictures but which will grow to over 3 m/10 ft, are also planted to form a frame for the pots by the water feature.

KEY PLANTS

▲The magenta flowers, with their black centre, of this cranesbill, *Geranium psilostemon* form a brilliant area of colour. The leaves are pink tinted in spring, turning a rich red in autumn.

◄The leaves of *Miscanthus tinctoria* 'Nanus Variegatus' add highlights with their cream and bright green stripes. This dwarf clump-forming grass grows to 45 cm/18 in.

▲ The curving path that leads back towards the house uses paving edged with gravel to soften the effect and the slightly raised edging prevents soil spilling onto the path. Plants fall over the path's edge to soften the outline. The path can be seen leading off into the background in the centre top of the picture.

The pergola over the sitting area, and the smaller one used to form an archway, persuade the eye upwards and provide an area for climbing plants. The raised water feature introduces yet another level, while the mixed boulders and pebbles provide a contrasting and varied kind of hard surface.

Lighting creates a different look for the garden at night. A down-lighter, is used to pinpoint the statue in the centre of the circular terrace and solar energy path lights, indicate the start of the stepping-stone path and highlights the pergola-covered terrace. This lighting focuses the eye on nearby plants and makes the path safe to use at night.

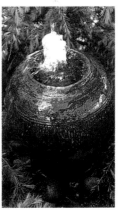

FOR EXTRA COLOUR

Rock roses display very decorative flowers and *Cistus* x *purpureus* is specially stunning. The decorative tissue-paper thin, magenta pink flowers are highlighted by yellow centres and evenly distributed splashes of dark purple-maroon. Plants of the Mediterranean region, cistus grow well in dry, well-drained soil and this hybrid will grow to about 1–1.2 m/3–4 ft in both height and spread. They also have a long flowering season. Flowers appear in late May and continue well into July.

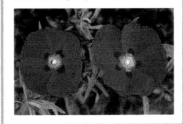

Special effects

A raised water feature The type of water feature, (top), with a raised brick edge allows you to sit on the rim of the pool and enjoy the water from close at hand. The low central geyser- like waterfall mimics the sound of a gurgling stream to create a relaxing atmosphere.

In the same way, water spills out of an upside-downpot, (above), to coat the container with a flowing golden glaze. Both these features provide an additional eye-catching focus in winter as well as summer for any area of the garden that lacks other interest.

▲ Forming a background to the circular terrace, a group of tall penstemon 'Alice Hindley' with their bell-shaped pale lilac flowers, frill-edged in a deeper tone, bloom right through from mid-summer to early autumn.

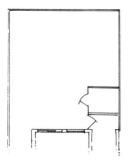

Square garden

A square garden has many advantages over long and short gardens. It does need to be visually shortened with horizontal divisions, nor does it need to be broken up with vertical or diagonal lines in any way. However, a strong defining central shape that brings the eye towards the garden's centre can transform the space, as is clearly shown in this garden designed by Jean Goldberry.

▲ **Before conversion** the garden shed and work-shop provided the main focal point and the plain geometric shape of the garden was clearly emphasized.

▼ **The planting scheme** was kept to two main areas over opposite corners of the garden, with pots on the terraces to provide extra colour.

THE GARDEN'S PROBLEMS

A downward slope from the end of the garden towards the house.

An ugly fence at the end of the garden.

The shape of the rectangular area of paving next to the house is harsh.

A large tree from next door overhangs the bottom of the garden on the left.

A side alley with uninteresting views of neighbouring houses.

HOW THEY WERE SOLVED

A raised patio was formed above the slope.

Raised beds in front of the fence hide it and are easy to maintain.

The terrace was curved to improve the shape, creating a path between the house and the shed.

A summer house was placed in this area as little would grow in this light.

Two wide wire arches were planted with the climbers clematis, sweet pea and a *Trachelospermum* to conceal the view.

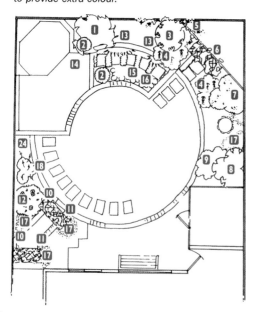

DESIGNER'S PLANTING SCHEME

Key plants
1 Bamboo, *Indocalamus latifolius*
2 Box, *Buxus sempervirens* 'Elegantissima'
3 *Choisya ternata* 'Sundance'
4 *Fuchsia* 'Tom Thumb'
5 *Clematis armandii*
6 *Rosa* 'Kathleen Harrop'
7 *Daphne odora* 'Aureomarginata'
8 *Viburnum davidii*
9 *Phlomis italica*
10 *Trachelospermum asiaticum* – over arches
11 *Clematis viticella* 'Alba Luxurians' – over arches
12 *Cistus purpureus*

Decorative detail
13 *Sisyrinchium striatum*
14 *Geranium cinereum* ssp. *subcaulescens* – between slabs

15 *Bergenia ciliata*
16 *Geranium pyrenaicum* 'Bill Wallace'
17 Bronze fennel, *Foeniculum vulgare*
18 *Erysimum* 'Bowles' Mauve'

Plants for added colour
Antirrhinum 'Black Prince'
Osteospermum 'Nairobi Purple'
Maurandya scandens in purple – in spaces on the fence
Petunia – trailing in deep purple, burgundy and red – in pots and baskets
Convolvulus 'Star of Yelta' – on fences and arches
Stock, *Matthiola* 'Giant Excelsior' in mixed colours

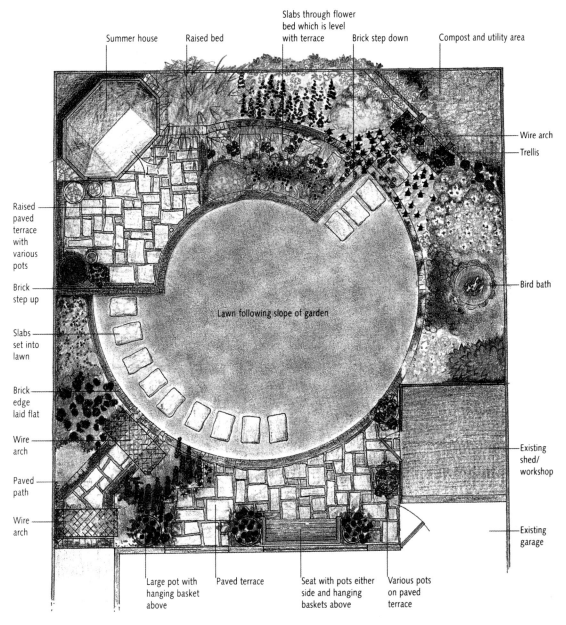

Summer house Raised bed Slabs through flower bed which is level with terrace Brick step down Compost and utility area

Wire arch

Trellis

Raised paved terrace with various pots

Brick step up

Slabs set into lawn

Brick edge laid flat

Wire arch

Paved path

Wire arch

Lawn following slope of garden

Bird bath

Existing shed/ workshop

Existing garage

Large pot with hanging basket above Paved terrace Seat with pots either side and hanging baskets above Various pots on paved terrace

HOUSE

263

CONSTRUCTION

The circular central lawn is outlined around its circumference with brick and paving to strengthen the simple, strong shape which is the key to the transformation of this plain square garden. The raised paved terrace at the end of the garden follows the curve and overlaps the lawn and, on the same higher leve, slabs run through the flower bed so that the raised bed behind is reached easily.

Slabs laid in the lawn follow the shape or lead through an archway into the neatly concealed compost area. Square trellis covers the fences to break up the harsh outlines and provide a framework for attaching climbers.

The summer house, positioned diagonally across a corner, is in an

▲ Positioning a summer house underneath the branches of a large tree, extending over the corner from next door, turns an unsuitable spot for plants into a decorative and enjoyable feature.

PLANTING

Jean used a range of grasses, bamboo, a clipped box and shrubs to provide a basic round-the-year evergreen structure. Striking rich pink and purple perennials and annuals provide some summer colour: petunias, the osteospermum 'Nairobi Purple', the fuchsias and the climbing *Maurandya scandens* amongst them.

KEY PLANTS

▲ A trellis and archway mask the compost area, entered through a wrought iron gate. These also provide a framework for honeysuckle and the evergreen *Clematis armandii* which has early, scented white flowers.

◀ A range of gold and cream-splashed ivies, *Hedera helix* cultivars, soften the edge of the raised stone bed, backed by the rich red, pink and purple flowers of the fuchsia 'Tom Thumb'.

◀ *From the end of the garden the view includes the plant-covered arches which straddle the path that curves round from the side of the house and help to hide the house next door.*

ideal position to view the garden, while the path from the side of the house, edged with bricks to define its route, is angled to reach the slab path around the lawn. With its wire arches covered in climbers, this creates a division between the terrace by the house and the flower bed on the left.

The terraced areas in front of the house and the summer house are broken up with pots of evergreens, for year-round interest, and colourful annuals.

▲ Plants with a range of leaf colours fill the raised bed by the arch. Creamy yellow spikes of *Sisyrinchium striatum* with the golden leaves of *Choisya ternata* 'Sundance' behind. Fuchsia 'Tom Thumb' adds colour at the front and the rose 'Kathleen Harrop' covers the arch.

FOR EXTRA COLOUR

Begonias and fuchsias fill a pot to bursting with their dark purple and green leaves and pink, red and white flowers. This mixture is a good choice for a more shaded area of the terrace. Begonia tubers can be lifted in autumn and dried off then replanted in spring. In frost-prone areas many fuchsias will survive if the stem base is planted 5 cm/2 in below the soil surface and a deep layer of mulch is added. Alternatively bring pots indoors.

Special effects

Raised flower beds are used almost everywhere in this garden. These both help to contain the soil and are easier to maintain. The lower beds are edged in a framework of neatly laid bricks. The taller bed, at the end of the garden, has large golden-grey rocks laid in the jig-saw-like manner of a country stone wall. The taller stone-edged bed, at 45 cm/18 in, means that little bending is necessary when gardening, and larger, smoother stones provide a seat when a little quiet contemplation is required.

See also:
- *Raised beds, page 108*
- *Building a low brick wall, page 120*
- *Arches, pergolas and arbours, page 132*

Short, wide garden

The owners of this garden, attached to a 1930's house, wanted it to be modern, minimalist and different. They turned to sculptor and garden designer Paul Cooper to use his combined creative talents to conceive a garden that was both modern and formal.

The original large garden had been sold off as plots, leaving a piece of land that was wide and very short, with a line of tall conifer trees along the end. As these were planted in the adjoining garden they could not be removed, so Paul decided to create a strong feature to detract from them.

▲ Before conversion the garden was laid out with a central lawn and beds around the edges, emphasising its short length and its width.

Trellis panels

Buff chippings, timber edge

THE GARDEN'S PROBLEMS

A line of 6 m/20 ft conifers at the end of the garden, growing in the adjoining garden.

The owners wanted to be able to look out on the garden from the top window of the house and see precise geometric patterns.

The short length of the garden.

Old basic concrete paving slabs were to be retained.

HOW THEY WERE SOLVED

A bold structure that mimicked a gateway was created, alongwith a pergola. Both were painted white to draw the eye away from the conifers.

Using a wide range of hard surface materials, plus grass, Paul has formed an eyecatching minimalist design.

An impression of length was achieved by narrowing lines as they reached the boundary.

Brick edging and the introduction of other materials leads the paving slabs to become part of a wider scheme of defined shapes.

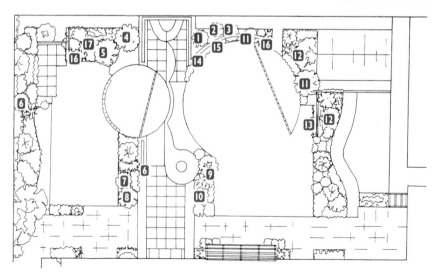

◀ The planting scheme was deliberately tidy and compact with most of the shrubs clipped to form neat globes. Low plants are either ground hugging or form tight hummocks.

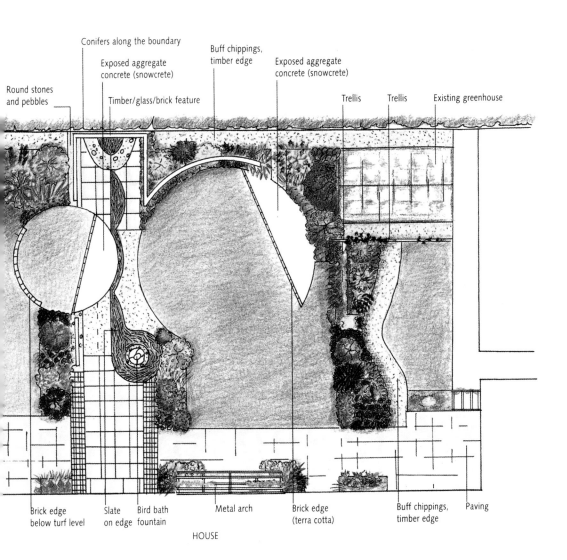

Round stones and pebbles — Conifers along the boundary — Exposed aggregate concrete (snowcrete) — Timber/glass/brick feature — Buff chippings, timber edge — Exposed aggregate concrete (snowcrete) — Trellis — Trellis — Existing greenhouse

Brick edge below turf level — Slate on edge — Bird bath fountain — Metal arch — Brick edge (terra cotta) — Buff chippings, timber edge — Paving

HOUSE

DESIGNER'S PLANTING SCHEME

Key plants
1 Myrtle, *Myrtus communis* 'Variegata'
2 *Mahonia* x *media* 'Charity'
3 Golden Mexican orange blossom, *Choisya ternata* 'Sundance'
4 Privet, *Ligustrum ovalifolium* 'Argenteum'
5 *Rosa xanthina* 'Canary Bird'
6 *Viburnum tinus*
7 *Abelia* x *grandiflora*
8 *Photinia* x *fraseri* 'Red Robin'
9 *Elaeagnus* x *ebbingei*

10 *Viburnum* x *carlcephalum*
11 *Viburnum davidii*
12 *Ceanothus dentatus*

Decorative detail
13 *Agapanthus africanus*
14 Cranesbills, *Geranium macrorrhizum* 'Album' and *G.* 'Johnson's Blue'
15 Foam flower, *Tiarella cordifolia*
16 Iris – tall bearded species and varieties
17 Sage, *Salvia officinalis* 'Icterina'

Plants for added colour
Campanula carpatica – in blue
Coral flower, *Heuchera* 'Palace Purple'
Dianthus 'Doris'
Ceratostigma willmottianum
Red-hot poker, *Kniphofia rooperi*
Eryngium bourgatii

CONSTRUCTION

Designer Paul Cooper has used white for the main structures, arches, pergola and ground surfaces, to highlight the patterns he has formed with the hard landscaping that mixes curves and straight lines. Structures are kept deliberately clear of climbers which would hide the clean lines and eventually blend in colour with the background, so losing the strong outline they are intended to create.

Where trellis is used, some of the spaces have been blocked in with plywood and then painted to enhance the feel of this garden.

The main giant white structure at the end of the garden is in fact a water feature with water tumbling from the centre top down over glass bricks. Two semi-circles of mirror

▲ Looking from the house towards the end of the garden. The main structure and water feature, together with the pergola to the right, take the eye off the line of conifers behind.

PLANTING

This is a garden where man shows his control over nature. Shrubs are kept neatly trimmed in a series of globes, boxes and tidy hummocks. In each space created by the post and rail pergola, a shrub chosen for its colour or leaf shape, forms a simple sculptural silhouette, an unusual alternative to screening the timber with climbing plants.

KEY PLANTS

▲ Long tooth-edged bracts, tinged with pink, create a ruff of silvery spikes that surround the flowers of *Eryngium varifolium*. The strong shape and silvery tints of eryngiums create a perfect foil for the clean lines in this modern garden.

◀ Cranesbill, *Geranium* 'Johnson's Blue', with its bright green leaves and pink-tinged blue flowers, forms good ground cover.

◄ The water feature and central paving seen from the side and looking across a section of lawn. The square arches create strong images against the clipped shrubs and the rest of the planting.

reflect the same-shaped pool below, creating a mirror image of the water that turns it into a full circle. From this pool flow a series of part circles of broken slate used at the edge to mimic water. The line of slate completes its journey near the house as a circle with a bird bath and fountain as a centrepiece.

Ground surfaces are cleverly mixed to create a range of colours and textures that highlight the strong shapes that are such an important part of the design.

▲ Another sculptural plant that highlights the simple architectural shapes in the garden is the silk-tassel bush, *Garrya elliptica*. In winter the grey-green catkins hang like silvery tree decorations and give the bush its common name.

FOR EXTRA COLOUR

An excellent plant to provide flashes of colour in autumn is the bulbous nerine from South Africa. *Nerine bowdenii* has faintly scented and lily-shaped pink flowers with long drooping stamens. It also comes in white, tinted palest pink, as f. *alba*. *Nerine filifolia* has smaller pink and white flowers with frilled edges.

Special effects

Mixing ground surfaces Here Paul Cooper has used a wide range of hard surfaces to highlight the shapes that he wanted to bring into focus. There are square paving stones and smaller pavers, which outline the pathway leading to the water feature.

This incorporated the retained areas of paving with those that are new and brings a range of textures and colours that provide further interest.

Brick and timber edgings create clean-cut shapes for the circular lawns, while white-finished concrete, and light buff-coloured chippings highlight the shapes of the main structures. Slates fixed on edge, together with cobbles, provide a rougher finish that contrasts well with the smoother concrete and paving.

See also:
• Trellis, pages 47 and 123
• Moving water, page 128

Long, narrow garden

This garden was bordered by long, narrow beds and had unattractive views. A new conservatory and terrace of hexagonal paving had to be integrated into the scheme, which was to provide a place for entertaining and a place for two small boys to enjoy and use the garden.

Designer Sally Court divided the length into separate sections. The space nearest to the house became an area for family gatherings with a view of a triangular pool. The second section was reserved for the boys' use, and at the end of the garden, which lies in the path of the morning sun, there would be a place for a relaxed breakfast as well as a screened utility area.

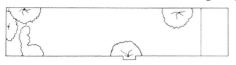

▲**Before conversion** *the garden was lined along both sides with narrow borders which made the space appear even longer and narrower than it actually was.*

THE GARDEN'S PROBLEMS

Ugly views of concrete garages at the end of the garden.

The garden's long and narrow shape.

A new conservatory and a terrace with paving need to be considered in the choice of materials.

HOW THEY WERE SOLVED

Raised beds and tall planting hide the views. Climbers act as a decorative screen along the right-hand side.

Each separate section provided a hint of what lay beyond – a trip down the garden was a journey of discovery.

The geometric paving prevented curves being used and so the designer used straight lines for paths and created a triangular pond, which were more in keeping with the overall design.

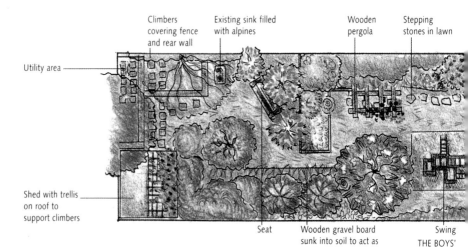

Utility area

Climbers covering fence and rear wall

Existing sink filled with alpines

Wooden pergola

Stepping stones in lawn

Shed with trellis on roof to support climbers

Seat

Wooden gravel board sunk into soil to act as edging to border and lawn

Swing
THE BOYS' GARDEN

THE WILD GARDEN

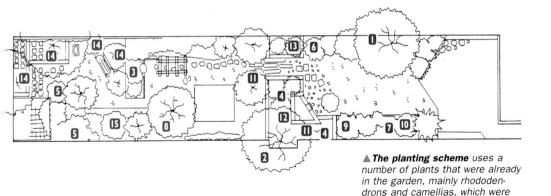

The planting scheme uses a number of plants that were already in the garden, mainly rhododendrons and camellias, which were repositioned nearer to the house.

DESIGNER'S PLANTING SCHEME

Key plants
Already existing
1 Tree of heaven, *Ailanthus altissima*
2 Mountain ash, *Sorbus aucuparia*
3 *Pittosporum tenuifolium*
4 Selection of rhododendrons and camellias – relocated
5 Conifers

New
6 *Malus* 'Golden Hornet'
7 *Prunus virginiana*
8 *Magnolia grandiflora*
9 *Pittosporum tobira*
10 *Ceanothus* 'Puget Blue'
11 New Zealand flax, *Phormium tenax 'Purpureum'*
12 *Photinia* x *fraseri* 'Red Robin'
13 Strawberry tree, *Arbutus unedo*
14 Himalayan birch, *Betula utilis*
15 *Osmanthus delavayi*

Decorative Detail
Clematis macropetala
Japanese maple, *Acer palmatum* var. *dissectum*
Lamium 'White Nancy'
Pulmonaria saccharata
Bergenia silberlicht
Hosta 'Royal Standard'
Romneya hybrid
Ornamental hop, *Humulus lupulus* 'Aurea'
Hydrangea arborescens 'Annabelle'
Paeonia delavayi

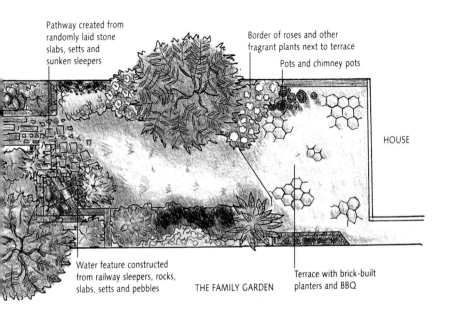

Pathway created from randomly laid stone slabs, setts and sunken sleepers

Border of roses and other fragrant plants next to terrace

Pots and chimney pots

HOUSE

Water feature constructed from railway sleepers, rocks, slabs, setts and pebbles

THE FAMILY GARDEN

Terrace with brick-built planters and BBQ

CONSTRUCTION

Apart from being long and narrow, the garden was also very flat. Sally added height at the end of the first section by constructing slightly raised beds, edged in railway sleepers, together with a raised pool.

The upper pool, constructed of railway sleepers, has a centrally placed funnel that spills water down into a shallow pool below. The water is recirculated back into the top pond. The raised beds and pond divide off the next section, reached by a gravel path, broken up with stepping stones and partly buried sleepers.

The second section is for the boys with swings, space for football and a bed where they can try out their gardening skills. A pergola and evergreen planting screen the

▲ *The conservatory and the paved terrace by the house were the starting point for the garden's design.*

PLANTING

A number of plants in the garden were retained, some being moved to a new position. A tree of heaven, *Ailanthus altissima* was resited close to the terrace as a backdrop, and a mature *Pittosporum tenuifolium* adds privacy to the end of the garden and has been joined by another specimen tree, a *Magnolia grandiflora*.

KEY PLANTS

▲ As a background to the pond a mountain ash, *Sorbus aucuparia*, provides decoration of clusters of white flowers in spring, followed by bright red berries. In autumn the leaves turn yellow and red before they fall.

◀ Next to the raised bed a bear's breeches, *Acanthus spinosus*, banked on either side by roses, shows off its tall spires of purple-pink and white-throated flowers and attractive large, dark green, spiny, divided leaves.

◄ Looking down the garden from the top terrace. On the left are the triangular pond and raised bed that separate this section from the next.

▼ The unusual triangular raised pool with its overspill into a shallow pebble-lined pond below.

end of the garden, where shrubs create a den for the boys. There are areas of rough grass, mature shrubs and trees, and a seat. The mature planting and trellis covered with climbers give privacy and screen the utility part of the garden.

▲The bell-shaped white flowers of a *Pittosporum tobira* along the garden path flourish in late spring to early summer. They are scented and gradually turn creamy yellow with age. The leathery dark green shiny leaves are paler on the underside.

FOR EXTRA COLOUR

For colourful early flowers that brighten a shady position the perennial pulmonaria with its blue, pink or white flowers and white- or silver-spotted leaves is a good choice. *Pulmonaria saccharata*, shown, has unusual lilac to pink flowers whereas the variety *P. saccharata* 'Frühlingshimmel' has bright pastel blue flowers with a darker blue centre.

Pulmonaria likes humus-rich and moist soil, as well as full or partial shade.

Special effects

Mixing path materials By mixing the materials used in creating a path, much more interesting effects can be achieved. This also allows you to curve a path made from rigid materials, such as paving, by introducing gravel or stone chippings and then setting the paving with gaps, like stepping-stones, along the length.

With paving for the main walkway other ornate and less resilient materials can also be used, such as bark chippings, broken slate or even shells.

Here Sally has mixed larger paving slabs, smaller setts and sunken sleepers, all laid in gravel. The slabs continue on as stepping-stones through the lawn that the path leads to.

See also:
- *Paths steps and edgings, page 118*
- *Children's play space, page 138*

Split-level garden

The owners of this garden had differing views of what they required. One wanted a modern, simple and stylish outdoor room, the other preferred a romantic, traditional country-garden look. It was the designer Sally Court's job to bring these two requirements together in a garden that both would like.

The house, on a lower level, was faced from the main downstairs rooms with a blank wall, with the main area of the garden above this. Sally extended the narrow paved areas next to the house outwards so that it became wide enough to use as a sitting and eating area.

The paving and retaining wall were extended in a series of curves, with brick steps echoing this shape up to the top section. The wall was used as a backdrop for a moving water feature to break up the length of the wall and create sound and visual interest on the patio.

Trellis fixed along the boundary fences was stained green (so that it would blend into the background) as was a decoratively designed garden shed at the end of the garden that looks more like a gazebo.

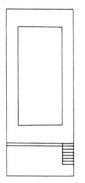

▲ **Before conversion** the lower rooms of this tall town house were below garden level with a narrow paved strip adjoining the house and a blank wall between this and the garden.

THE GARDEN'S PROBLEMS

The large kitchen and family room set below the main garden and facing a blank wall.

Drainage problems in a garden where the house is on a lower level.

Squirrels constantly dug up the garden to store nuts and seeds collected nearby.

HOW THEY WERE SOLVED

Extending the lower terrace with material similarly coloured to that used in the house, linked the inside with the outdoor space.

A gulley was used to take away rainwater from the house and the terrace in wet weather.

Setting up a special squirrel feeder as well as a birds-only feeder. Soon the squirrels were using the feeder and curtailed their digging.

DESIGNER'S PLANTING SCHEME

Key plants

1 Strawberry tree, *Arbutus x andrachnoides*
2 Jelly palm, *Butia capitata*
3 Dwarf fan palm, *Chamaerops humilis*
4 Cabbage palm, *Cordyline australis*
5 Daphne odora 'Aureomarginata'
6 Loquat, *Eriobotrya japonica*
7 *Magnolia grandiflora* 'Samuel Sommer'
8 New Zealand flax, *Phormium tenax*
9 Black bamboo, *Phyllostachys nigra*

◀ **The planting scheme** was planned to use plants that are unusual in this area and very architectural in form.

Decorative detail

10 Japanese mock orange, *Pittosporum tobira*
11 *Cistus x skanbergii*
12 Cardoon, *Cynara cardunculus*
13 Alexandrian laurel, *Danae racemosa*
14 *Dianella tasmanica*
15 Woodrush, *Luzula sylvatica* 'Marginata'
16 Lilyturf, *Ophiopogon planiscapus* 'Nigrescens'
17 Soft shield fern, *Polystichum setiferum*
18 Prostrate rosemary, *Rosmarinus lavandulaceus*
19 *Parthenocissus henryana*
20 Wisteria 'Snow Showers'

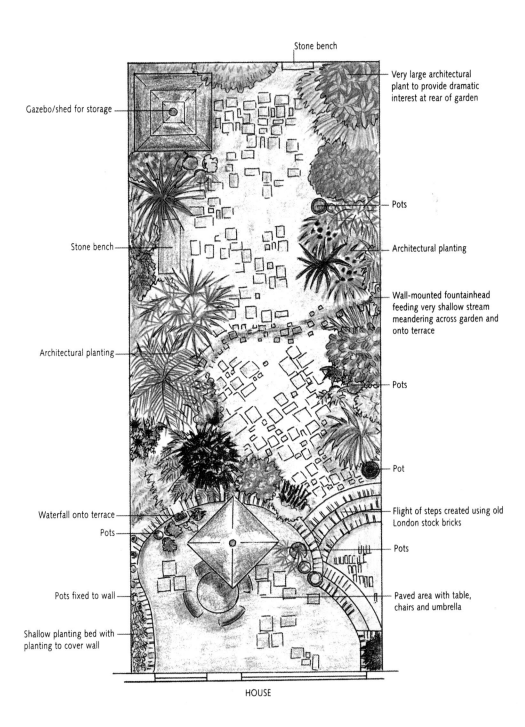

Stone bench

Very large architectural plant to provide dramatic interest at rear of garden

Gazebo/shed for storage

Pots

Stone bench

Architectural planting

Wall-mounted fountainhead feeding very shallow stream meandering across garden and onto terrace

Architectural planting

Pots

Pot

Waterfall onto terrace

Flight of steps created using old London stock bricks

Pots

Pots

Pots fixed to wall

Paved area with table, chairs and umbrella

Shallow planting bed with planting to cover wall

HOUSE

CONSTRUCTION

The major task was to open up the terrace close to the house and to replace the 1 m/39 in retaining wall with a new one that followed a series of decorative curves.

The lower terrace and most of the garden above this were paved in a range of slabs of different sizes with gravel between. Reclaimed honey-coloured bricks were used for the wall and steps.

To create an attractive view from the house, and break up the retaining wall, pots were fixed to the surface around the wall. A fountain was placed on the wall with a stone water-garden trough below it. Three beautiful giant lizards were commissioned, two to act as spouts for the fountain and a third for the top of the wall.

▲The water feature creates a perfect focal point on the wall of the lower terrace. The giant pots holding evergreen shrubs placed on either side break up the expanse of plain wall.

See also:
- *Moving water page 128*
- *Ornamental extras page 136*

PLANTING

A modern theme of structural plants, which provide year-round interest, is used with a range of palms, black-stemmed bamboo, cardoon and New Zealand flax. These blend with verdant climbers to cover the walls, fences and trellis. In frost-prone areas alternative species of these plants may be better suited to winter outside.

KEY PLANTS

▲In a pot on the terrace an evergreen viburnum, *Viburnum davidii*, provides year-roundy interest. It bears small, white, slim, bell-shaped flowers in late spring followed by sprays of metallic, almost black fruit.

◄A mat of brilliant yellow is created by the stonecrop, *Sedum acre* which has star-shaped yellow flowers in the summer. It grows to form a low domed shape 5 cm/2 in high by 60 cm/24 in across.

◀ The view from the upper terrace looking back towards the house. This area is a happy mix of paving and greenery when seen from the house.

▼ The panorama from the tower terrace looking towards the garden shed, masked by trellis and climbers and the stone seat set in the sunshine that looks over the garden.

Other features were introduced to the garden to provide focal points. A second fountain tumbles to a shallow stream that meanders way across to the terrace, and a one bench on the opposite side of e garden provides a good view.

An umbrella plant, *Cyperus* species, ourishes in the damp conditions of the ater feature and makes a natural ome for two of the three basking zards. Water spouting from the lizards' mouths spatters decoratively onto large ebbles before falling into the stone ink below.

FOR EXTRA COLOUR

Container evergreens may not be very colourful but they provide interest around the year. The bay tree, *Laurus nobles* not only has aromatic leaves but can be clipped into interesting topiary shapes. In an exposed spot or in a frost-prone area it is best taken indoors for the colder months. Grown close to the house, its leaves can easily be picked for use.

Special effects

A garden ornament is a very personal thing. Ornaments can be ornate and classical, fun and frivolous or simple and streamline. They may be mass-produced or, as here, specially designed for their location.

Siting is all-important. Here a giant maroon fish stands on its tail to view passers by, its positioning among the planting at the side of the path creating a surprise.

Paved town garden

Garden designer Sally Court inherited a very small town garden on a slight slope that she considered was overplanted. Laurel, privet and Scots pine, as well as some inappropriately large shrubs, made it dark and unappealing.

Sally decided to remove everything that was there and start again, paving the area throughout and allowing space for wider beds. She took advantage of the slope to create the new garden on slightly different levels: shallow steps take you up to the terrace immediately adjacent to the house and then up again from this section to the terrace with the water feature provided by the fountain and pool.

Changing the garden's design also allowed Sally to move the back gate from the centre of the end fence and position it at one side, making room for a shed. Climbers soon covered the fences on all sides of the garden to provide colour and greenery on a second level, and a groups of pots and a sink garden provide extra space for yet more plants.

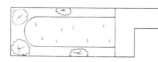

◀ **Before conversion** there were pathways up both sides, and narrow borders, a small lawn and large trees and bushes.

Shed — Gravel boards — Gravel path

Sink planter

Fountain water feature with trellis panels either side of brick pillars

THE GARDEN'S PROBLEMS

Surrounded by houses in almost every direction the garden had no privacy.

Straight paths and beds which ran from the house to the end of the garden, making the garden appear even smaller.

Poor soil condition.

No birds visited the garden.

HOW THEY WERE SOLVED

The birch planted at the end of the garden screens it from the houses at the back. Rampant climbers clothe the side fences, which were topped with trellis to add extra privacy.

The paths, beds and lawn were removed. A water feature placed centrally, part way down the garden, separates the area.

Debris was removed and manure and compost was added to improve the soil.

Planting was chosen to provide birds with berries and seeds.

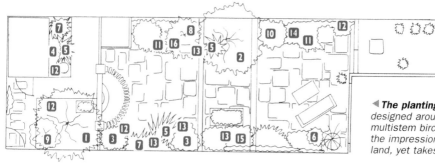

◀ **The planting scheme** was designed around a stunning multistem birch, which gives the impression of a mini woodland, yet takes up little space.

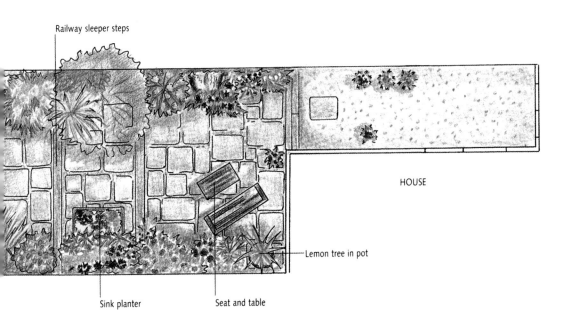

Railway sleeper steps

HOUSE

Lemon tree in pot

Sink planter

Seat and table

DESIGNER'S PLANTING SCHEME

Key plants
1 Birch, *Betula utilis* – multistem
2 *Ceanothus* 'A. T. Johnson'
3 *Pittosporum tobira* – standard
4 *Pittosporum tobira* 'Variegatum' – shrub
5 New Zealand flax, *Phormium tenax*
6 *Pinus mugo* var. *pumilio*
7 *Trachycarpus fortunei*
8 *Elaeagnus ebbingei*
9 *Aucuba japonica* 'Crotonifolia'
10 *Rosa* x *hugonis* – weeping standard

Decorative detail
11 *Astrantia major rubra*, 'Sunningdale'
12 *Hosta fortunei* 'Albopicta', 'Halcyon', *H. sieboldiana*, *H. undulata* and others
13 *Tradescantia* – a mixture of varieties
14 *Trachelospermum jasminoides*
15 *Trachelospermum jasminoides* 'Variegatum'
16 *Rosa* Heritage, Gertrude Jekyll and Tradescant

Plants for added colour
Clematis macropetala, C. cirrhosa, C. armandii, C. 'Vivyan Pennell', *C. texensis, C. viticella*
Cranesbill, *Geranium* – ten species, including *G. renardii* and 'Johnson's Blue'
Paeonia x 'Bowl of Beauty'
Paeonia lutea var. *ludlowsi*

CONSTRUCTION

Sally used reclaimed York stone to pave the major part of the garden, giving it a mature finish. Railway sleepers create wide, shallow steps that take you onto the slightly different levels of the garden.

To increase the garden's privacy and to turn it into a very sheltered spot where she could grow exotics, she added trellis to the top of all the boundary fences.

Two-thirds of the way down the garden she built a centrally positioned low wall from old honey-coloured bricks, with pillars at each end and space at the sides. This is part of the water feature with a lion-head fountain centrally positioned and a deep, semi-circular pool below. This makes an eye-catching centrepiece from the

▲ *The stunning white bark of the multi-stemmed birch,* Betula utilis, *together with the lion fountain set in the wall in front of it, catch the light and draw the eye to the end of the garden.*

PLANTING

Simplicity is the keynote to Sally's planting in a small space. She uses a theme with plants or colour, then repeats it through the garden to create harmony.

Here she chose the birch as the star of the garden and planned the rest of the planting around this to include a range of textures and round-the-year interest.

KEY PLANTS

▲ A large terracotta jar gives height to a group of containers that hold colourful plants. By replacing pots as the seasons change, Sally can provide round-the-year colour in this small space.

◀ A sink garden comes into its own in a small space, bringing the miniature and very decorative plants it holds up to a higher level and enabling good drainage to be provided.

◄ The view from the house, showing the steps that lead onto the terrace. The courtyard is crammed with pots and the boundary fences are smothered in climbers to give a verdant effect.

▼ Looking towards the end of the garden, where the garden shed can only just be seen amongst the greenery.

terrace near to the house and conceales the end of the garden.

The beds are irregular in size, following the staggered edges of the stone paving and together with this groups of pots, create a wide and curving pathway through the entire garden.

▲ A lemon tree, Citrus limon 'Meyer', grown in a container provides an exotic touch with its fragrant flowers in early summer followed by fruit. It has been positioned in a corner where it is out of the wind and gets the sunshine throughout the day.

FOR EXTRA COLOUR

Cranesbills, members of the geranium family, are easy to grow and flourish in sun or partial shade and in almost any soil except very wet. The flowers in pink, blue, purple and white appear in summer.

Compact perennial species grow to about 15 cm/6 in tall, and are ideal for use in a sink garden. Taller clump-forming species look effective grown in a flower border or amongst shrubs.

Special effect

Wall fountains can give visual interest and provide the relaxing sound of moving water to the smallest of outdoor spaces and many are suitable for fixing indoors too. They are ideal for use where there are small children.

Many designs are available, from traditional-looking lion or human heads to figures and animals of stone, concrete or lighter metal resin to simple spouts and modern shapes.

Overlooked garden

Jean Goldberry uses a range of heights and divisions along the garden's length to break up the space in an interesting way, creating the privacy that the owners longed for. She used a mature *Amelanchier canadensis* at the end of the garden to create a miniature woodland area with tree-trunk stepping stones and a seat of timber planks. Paved terraces breaks up the garden's length and groups of larger pebbles add a sculptural effect. There are raised timber-edged beds and two ponds.

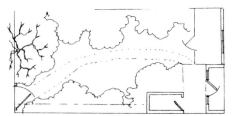

▲ **Before conversion** the garden comprised very overgrown shrubs on either side with grass down the centre, over which a worn-away path led to the back gate.

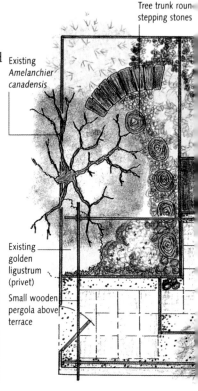

Tree trunk roun stepping stones

Existing Amelanchier canadensis

Existing golden ligustrum (privet)

Small wooden pergola above terrace

THE GARDEN'S PROBLEMS	HOW THEY WERE SOLVED
The original garden seemed very long and narrow.	Garden 'rooms' created by laying paving in squares and rectangles, breaking up the length.
Little privacy, with buildings on the right-hand side looking directly into the garden.	Pergolas hide the garden from the overlooking windows, creating interest and views from the house.
A rectangular space, all on one level, lacking any interest.	The level was dropped in the centre, with steps down. Raised beds of different heights add interest.

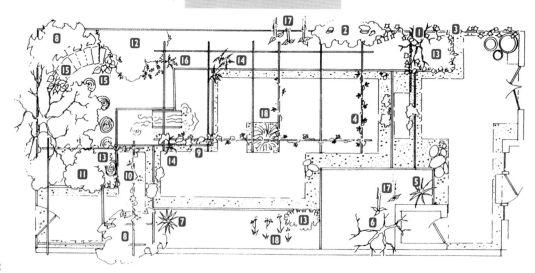

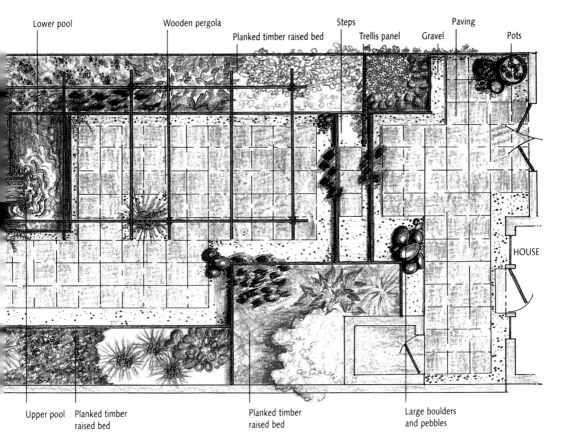

Lower pool · Wooden pergola · Planked timber raised bed · Steps · Trellis panel · Gravel · Paving · Pots

HOUSE

Upper pool · Planked timber raised bed · Planked timber raised bed · Large boulders and pebbles

◀ **The planting scheme** uses cool blues and white in the main, with some rose pink to provide definition and some golden and cream-variegated foliage.

DESIGNER'S PLANTING SCHEME

Key plants
1 *Eucryphia milliganii*
2 *Rhamnus alaternus* 'Argenteovariegata'
3 Vine, *Vitis coignetiae*
4 Golden hop, *Humulus lupulus* 'Aureus'
5 Mountain flax, *Phormium cookianum* ssp. *hookeri* 'Cream Delight'
6 *Cytisus battandieri*
7 *Yucca gloriosa*
8 *Phyllostachys aureosulcata* 'Aureocaulis'

9 *Clematis armandii*
10 *Jasminum officinalis* 'Aureomarginata'
11 *Daphne odora* 'Aureomarginata'
12 *Rhododendron* 'Cilpinense'

Decorative detail
13 *Bergenia cordifolia*
14 Lady fern, *Athyrium filix-femina*
15 *Hosta* 'Sum and Substance'
16 *Euphorbia robbiae*
17 Foxglove, *Digitalis grandiflora*
18 *Iris sibinca* 'Flight of Blue Butterflies'

Plants for added colour
Morning Glory, *Ipomoea tricolor* 'Heavenly Blue'
Busy lizzies and balsams, *Impatiens* – in white where spaces available
Wishbone flower, *Torenia fournieri*
Bells of Ireland, *Molluccella laevis*
Tobacco plant, *Nicotiana* Nicki Series – in white in sunny patches

CONSTRUCTION

Some initial work was needed to transform this garden and produce the privacy required by the owners. Firstly a range of levels was created along the length of the garden. Paving was then laid, with shallow steps edged in timber leading from one level to the next. The change of levels is only slight, dividing the garden into three separate sections but immediately makes it appear much more interesting.

Matching timber was used to make the raised beds. Those in the central sunken area are three planks high and the one nearest to the house, on the left, slightly higher.

The pools are on different levels so that water from the back pool cascades into the lower front pool then recirculates. Positioned directly

▲The view from the central section of the garden, looking up the steps towards the back gate with the pergola posts just in the picture and the water feature out of sight on the right.

See also:
• *Introducing water, page 126*

PLANTING

Summer colour abounds in this garden but winter interest is not ignored. This appears in variegated foliage and in the exotic golden stemmed bamboo, *Phyllostachys aureosculcata* 'Aureocaulis'. Pink is introduced in late winter with the pale pink rhododendron 'Cilpinense' and in spring with the variegated *Daphne odora* 'Aureomarginata'.

KEY PLANTS

▲▲A The lemon yellow and pineapple-scented flowers of pineapple broom, *Cytisus battandieri*, appear in mid- and late summer. Silvery green leaves contrast against the cone-shaped flowers.

◄*Euonymus fortunei* provides winter colour in both its gold- and silver-variegated leaf varieties. *E. fortunei* 'Silver Queen' has bold white margins to the leaves and can be grown as a climber.

▲ Looking from the terrace near to the house down the steps into the sunken garden. A vine (deciduous) and evergreen plants cover the roof of the larger pergola and create a green and private space

▶ Together with the fountain in the front pond the cascading water from the higher pool adds the soothing sound of moving water

opposite the steps that lead down from the terrace, the water feature creates a decorative picture from indoors, all year round. The long pergola also provides interest from the house.

At the end of the garden a soft path of wood chippings is interspersed with stepping-stones made of sliced tree-trunks. These have been covered with wire netting to ensure they remain nonslip, an important consideration.

▲ The water feature has a channel that takes the water down from the higher pool into the larger, lower one.

▲ The large leaves of this vine, *Vitas coignetiae* 'Incana' soon cover the expanse of pergola and provide dappled green shade and privacy during the months of summer.

FOR EXTRA COLOUR

Flowering plants in pots add colour to any area in the garden where it is temporarily lacking. The plants can remain in a secluded spot until they reach their peak, and can then be moved into position when they can take pride of place. Most plants will cope with less than ideal conditions for a short time.

Conservatories can be too hot and dry for many plants in summer, but at this time the plants flourish outdoors to be brought back indoors when the cooler weather returns. In most areas this hydrangea could be wintered outside.

Special effects

Natural sculpture In this garden groups of pebbles form simple but striking natural sculptures very much in keeping with the gravel edging that divides one area of paving from the next. Many other natural materials can be used successfully in this way. Shells and driftwood can be used to add character to a seaside garden. Tree stumps, cones and logs enhance a woodland area.

Concrete garden

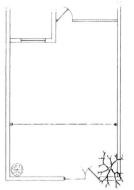

Few outdoor areas are less inspiring to look at, and more daunting to transform, than a concrete backyard. Rather than removing the surface designer Jean Goldberry has built on top of it, using a series of beds stepped up away from the house. A pergola and trellis allow for vertical planting and a raised pond adds a calming influence.

◀ **Before conversion** the yard contained little more than its solid grey base, with a narrow bed down one side and a lilac tree at the end.

▼ **The planting scheme** includes evergreens with leaves tinted in cream, gold and red, as well as other plants in striking shapes for year-round interest.

THE GARDEN'S PROBLEMS

The small size – just 7.7m/25 ft long by 5 m/ 16.5 ft wide.

A concrete surface would be extremely difficult to remove.

Neighbour's upstairs windows overlook the garden.

An uninteresting view from the kitchen window.

The owner has little time to spend on maintenance.

HOW THEY WERE SOLVED

A pergola, trellis, pond and raised beds were introduced to vary levels.

Raised beds were built after drainage holes were made in the concrete.

The pergola will create privacy once the plants grow over the roof and uprights.

The raised beds and the vertical planting create interest all year round.

Maintenance is simple with the raised beds.

DESIGNER'S PLANTING SCHEME

Key plants
1 Choisya 'Aztec Pearl'
2 Fargesia muneliae 'Simba'
3 Climbing rose, Rosa 'Felicite et Perpetue' – along trellis
4 Rosemary-leaved cotton lavender, Santolina rosmarinifolia
5 Daphne odora 'Aureomarginata'
6 Flax, Phormium 'Cream Delight'
7 Helleborus argutifolius
8 Grass, Cortaderia 'Gold Band'
9 Ivy, Hedera canariensis 'Canary Island'
10 June berry, Amelanchier lamarckii
11 Veronica, Hebe 'Red Edge'
12 Romarinus prostratus
13 Lavender, Lavandula 'Hidcote'
14 Trachelospermum asiaticum

Plants for added colour
Smilacina racemosa
Hosta 'Sum and Substance'
Schisandra grandiflora
Alchemilla mollis
Viola, Viola cornuta
Sweet pea, Lathyrus 'Old Spice'
Wallflower, Erysimum linifolium 'Variegatum'
Trailing petunia in shades of purple, petunias, in shades of deep purple
Nasturtiums, apricot and pale yellow
Fuchsia 'Tom Thumb'
Lady fern, Athyrium felix-felina
Lenten rose, Helleborus orientalis
Herbs, sage, chives, thyme.
Pink, Dianthus 'Mrs Sinkins'
Madonna lily, Lilium candidum

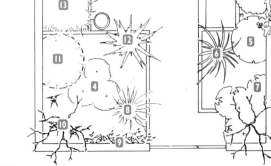

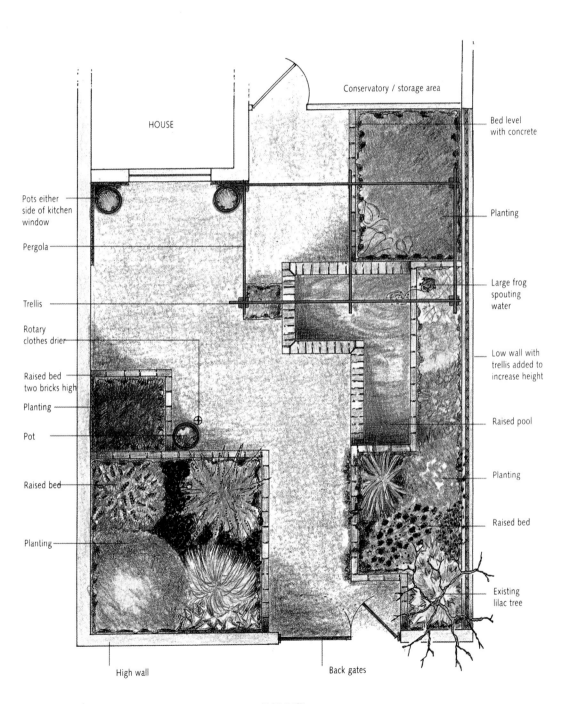

HOUSE

Conservatory / storage area

Pots either
side of kitchen
window

Bed level
with concrete

Pergola

Planting

Trellis

Large frog
spouting
water

Rotary
clothes drier

Raised bed
two bricks high

Low wall with
trellis added to
increase height

Planting

Pot

Raised pool

Raised bed

Planting

Planting

Raised bed

Planting

Existing
lilac tree

High wall

Back gates

BACK ALLEY

CONSTRUCTION

The design involved the building of raised beds over the concrete, the erection of a pergola and trellis, and the addition of a pool. Areas of path between the beds are covered with softly shaded slabs.

The raised beds start near the house, gradually increasing in height near the end of the garden. The original bed makes it possible to plant large deep-rooting shrubs like the Mexican orange blossom, Choisya, on the right-hand side.

The pergola and the trellis, on the low wall on the right hand side of the garden, bring support for colourful climbers as well as giving privacy to this small space. More rampant, leafy plants are ideal for areas where shade is required, while those plants with

▲ *Looking towards the house through the arch-way of the pergola. Later, the burgeoning plants will turn this into a comfortable and shady sitting-out area.*

See also:
- *Raised beds, page 108, 120*
- *Introducing water, page 126*
- *Arches, pergolas and arbours, page 132*

PLANTING

Jean chose the plants for this garden with special care so that they would create a verdant look and maintain privacy around the year. The secret of success was to pick key plants for their stunning shape (ensuring that this is well displayed) and to choose as neighbours those plants that best show off each other's colours and leaf shapes.

KEY PLANTS

▲ For ground cover *Alchemilla mollis*, lady's mantle, was chosen. The leaves spread out to show off the hairy surface that holds the water in place after rain has fallen.

◀ By the house, the scented white flowers of *Choisya* 'Aztec Pearl' can be seen in late spring, followed in late summer to autumn by a second lot of blooms.

slimmer, neater growth allow filtered sunlight where this is preferred.

The L-shaped pool creates a soothing, reflective spot and the supporting wall is designed to form a comfortable seat for those enjoying its calming influence.

▲ The view from the house looking towards the original lilac tree, included in the new design.

▶ The L-shaped bed at the end of the garden echoes the shape of the pond and its plants are on view from the kitchen window.

▲ A dense, low evergreen shrub with bright green aromatic leaves, *Santolina rosmarinifolia* is positioned partway down the garden in full sun. In mid-summer it produces round heads of bright yellow flowers.

FOR EXTRA COLOUR

For a natural effect, in comparison to the bolder pansy cultivars, Jean introduced the smaller, but scented, pale lilac, pink and white flowers of violas, *Viola cornuta*, which appear early, in spring, and flower through to summer.

Grow these, like pansies, in moist, but well-drained soil in sun or partial shade and divide clumps in spring or early autumn to increase plant numbers.

Special effect

Shaped pergolas A pergola can be designed to fit into almost any shape or space in the garden. Once they are covered in climbers, they soon provide a shady spot for relaxing out of the direct sunlight.

For alternative pergola materials and designs to the one shown here, see those on pages 16–27, 40–43, 58–61, 70–73, 76–79, 90, 94–95.

Steeply sloping land

This garden, on the side of a hill, with a high bank at the end of the garden and concrete retaining wall near to the house, was difficult and dangerous to manage. Jean Goldberry terraced it, forming three flat areas, one above the other, linked by wide, shallow steps.

First Jean placed the sitting area at the top of the garden where there were stunning views and positioned a pergola to obscure the view of the town behind it. She next placed a water feature in the centre of the garden, to include a waterfall, where water splashed down from one garden level to the next spreading out into a shallow natural-looking pool. She also added a series of beds of cascading plants to provide colour that could be enjoyed from the house below.

▲ **Before conversion** the garden contained a lawn that sloped steeply towards the house, making mowing difficult. There was a narrow slip of concrete near the house from which steps went up to the garden.

▼ **The planting scheme** Part of the brief was to produce a garden which placed special emphasis on autumn colour. Jean also used the steep slope to create a water-fall of blues, reds and oranges.

THE GARDEN'S PROBLEMS

The very steep, sloping land.

The slope made working in the garden difficult. No flat areas were wide enough to work in safety.

Old bank on the top boundary.

The steep slope made it difficult to use the mower.

HOW THEY WERE SOLVED

The sitting area was positioned at the top end of the garden where there were good views over local countryside.

Railway sleepers form an edging for steps and to terrace the space into a series of flat beds and paved areas.

This area was designed to mimic the effect of roadside banks covered in wild flowers.

Grass was deliberately avoided in the design as even after the area was terraced, it would have been difficult to get a mower into position to mow it.

DESIGNER'S PLANTING SCHEME

Key plants
1 Juniper, *Juniperus communis* 'Sentinel' – vertical trees to balance the slope
2 *Rosa* 'Rushing Stream'
3 *Sorbus aucupana* 'Sheerwater'
4 *Fothergilla major*
5 Cedar of Lebanon, *Cedrus libani* 'Sargentii'
6 *Buddleia davidii* 'Nanho Blue'
7 *Prunus* 'Okumiyako'
8 *Ceratostigma plumbagnoides*
9 *Rosa* 'Danse de Feu' up pergola posts
10 Vine, *Vitis coignetiae*
11 *Euonymus alatus*
12 *Berberis* 'Rubrostilla'

Decorative detail
13 *Juncus inflexus* 'Afro'
14 Sweet woodruff, *Galium odoratum*
15 *Nepeta* 'Six Hills Giant'
16 *Farfuglum japonicum* 'Argenteum'
17 *Dryopteris filix-mas*

Plants for added colour
Pelargonium 'Lila Mini Cascade'
Lobelia in dark and sky blue to fill spaces
Nasturtium, *Tropaeolum majus*
Zinnia haageana 'Persian Carpet'
Pansy, *Viola* hybrids
Salvia farinacea 'Victoria'

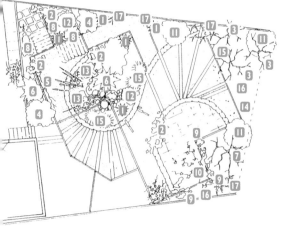

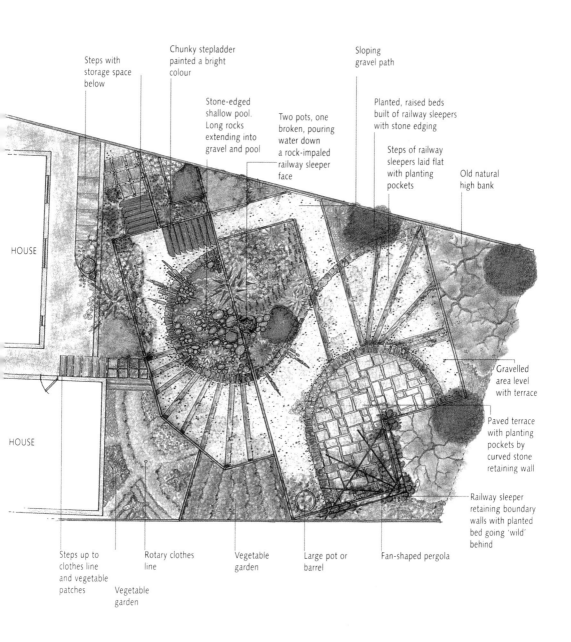

Steps with storage space below

Chunky stepladder painted a bright colour

Stone-edged shallow pool. Long rocks extending into gravel and pool

Two pots, one broken, pouring water down a rock-impaled railway sleeper face

Sloping gravel path

Planted, raised beds built of railway sleepers with stone edging

Steps of railway sleepers laid flat with planting pockets

Old natural high bank

HOUSE

HOUSE

Gravelled area level with terrace

Paved terrace with planting pockets by curved stone retaining wall

Railway sleeper retaining boundary walls with planted bed going 'wild' behind

Steps up to clothes line and vegetable patches

Vegetable garden

Rotary clothes line

Vegetable garden

Large pot or barrel

Fan-shaped pergola

CONSTRUCTION

Terracing involves a lot of initial construction work but it is almost always the best method of dealing with a steep, sloping garden. Being thick, wide and tough, railway sleepers make ideal edging supports for this sort of terraced construction but any treated timber of similar strength would be just as suitable. Stone, a readily available local material, was used to form a low retaining wall alongside the steps and around the top terrace.

The centrally placed water feature uses the same materials. The water tumbles down the height of the retaining wall to end up in a shallow pebble and rock-lined pool on the terrace below.

The sun terrace, at the top of the garden, is made with a surface

▲ *The view of the house looking down from the end of the garden and showing the series of wide and shallow timber-edged steps that are lined with gravel.*

See also:
- *Windy location, page 58*
- *Arches, pergolas and arbours, page 132*
- *Plants for dry soil, page 186*

PLANTING

This garden has glowing autumn colour with *Fothergilla major*, *Ceratostigma plumbaginoides*, the vine *Vitis coignetiae* and *Euonymus alatus* all showing brilliant orange and scarlet leaves in autumn, highlighted by the coral red fruit of the berberis 'Rubrostilla' and splashes of red, orange and yellow in the flowers of the nasturtiums.

KEY PLANTS

▲ The deep purple flowers of lavender, *Lavandula angustifolia* 'Twickel Purple' edge a raised bed alongside the path joining the terraces to provide scent for passers by on sunny summer days.

◀ Thyme 'Pink Chintz' forms tight mats between the paving slabs and is also used in the free-draining gravel. Mat-forming thymes need cutting back hard if they are to remain compact.

◀ A view, not long after construction, shows the steep path that leads up to the paved seating area at the top of the garden.

of paving and retained by a stone wall. Spaces at the edge of the paving provide planting areas for cascading plants and the pergola forms a framework for climbers such as a vine and the scarlet and orange rose 'Danse du Feu'.

▲ A natural effect is achieved by the timber and stone used to form the waterfall and the shallow pond lined with pebbles and rocks below.

FOR EXTRA COLOUR

Nasturtiums, *Tropaeolum* hybrids, are easy to grow from seed in moderately fertile, well-drained soil and in full sun. They provide a colourful mass of red, orange and yellow flowers. *T.* 'Alaska' series (shown) have specially decorative leaves speckled and blotched in creamy white. These form good ground cover colour. *T.* majus is a climber, and *T.* 'Peach Melba' has pale creamy yellow flowers with streaked orange-red centres.

Special effect

Waterfalls provide visual interest and the sound of falling water helps to bring a sense of harmony with nature.

The water appears from between boulders. Vertical sleepers provide the backing to the fall and slivers of stone act as natural breaks to the tumbling water before it enters the pool below. The water is pumped back up to the top of the fall, to follow the same procedure again and again.

This circulating water can be powered by a submersible pump if the height is not more than 1.2 m/4 ft. Otherwise a surface pump would be needed and this requires a separate electricity supply.

▲ By using a range of climbing plants growing up a post of the pergola, Jean has rung the changes and provided blooms through much of the year. A large early flowering clematis intermingles with the rose 'Danse du Feu' which has scarlet flowers later in the year.

DESIGNS WITH SPECIAL FEATURES IN MIND

A garden that is planned with a central theme, a particular use, or has a distinct advantage or specific requirements, needs special thought in its design and choice of planting.

In this chapter we show how our garden designers have dealt with six gardens, each planned around a specific requirement.

Low-maintenance garden

With a garage and a lane at one end of this very long garden (and the house itself the other side of the lane), it was important to draw people into and through the garden to the opposite end. Jean Goldberry created the main areas of interest at the far end and these include a pond, decked terrace for eating and a pergola above the extended original patio. Along the side of the garage she created a zig-zag pergola to follow the lines of the ground surface of gravel, grass and planting.

▲ *Before conversion* the garden was surrounded with a conifer hedge on one side, with a high wall and a timber fence on the other and was mainly weed-covered soil.

THE GARDEN'S PROBLEMS

The owners both work full-time and prefer to enjoy the garden rather than spend time working in it.

The space is very long and thin with a garage and the lane at one end.

A flexible space for eating, which could accommodate a range of numbers of people, was required.

HOW THEY WERE SOLVED

Decking, gravel and paving provide hard, easy to care for surfaces. Terracota pots hold geraniums, which need little watering, and the planting is mainly of evergreens with a bark chipping mulch.

Heavy timber railway sleepers set in a diagonal design help to break up the length. Features were added to draw visitors through to the end of the garden.

The eating area is formed of decking. Raised beds and paving around this area create a well. The surrounding surfaces can then be used as seats.

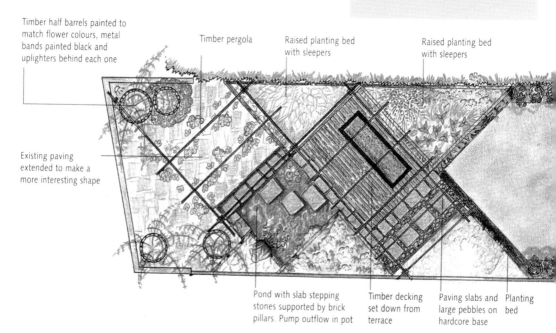

Timber half barrels painted to match flower colours, metal bands painted black and uplighters behind each one

Timber pergola

Raised planting bed with sleepers

Raised planting bed with sleepers

Existing paving extended to make a more interesting shape

Pond with slab stepping stones supported by brick pillars. Pump outflow in pot

Timber decking set down from terrace

Paving slabs and large pebbles on hardcore base

Planting bed

DESIGNER'S PLANTING SCHEME

Key plants

1 Japanese angelica tree, *Aralia elata*
2 Common myrtle, *Myrtus communis*
3 *Sophora tetraptera*
4 *Leptospermum scoparium* 'Red Damask'
5 Spotted laurel, *Aucuba japonica* 'Crotonifolia'
6 Spurge, *Euphorbia characias* ssp. *wulfenii*
7 *Cytisus* 'Killiney Red'
8 *Holboellia latifolia* – climbing
9 *Lonicera x tellmanniana* – climbing
10 *Rosa* 'Etoile de Hollande'– climbing
11 *Vitis vinifera* 'Purpurea'
12 Black bamboo, *Phyllostachys nigra*

Decorative Detail

13 Aquatic grass, *Glyceria maxima* 'Variegata'
14 *Rudbeckia fulgida* var. *sullivantii* 'Goldsturm'
15 *Nymphaea tetragona* 'Helvola'
16 *Doronicum carpetanum*
17 Daylily, *Hemerocallis* 'Frans Hals'

Plants for added colour

Pelargonium 'Mme Fournier'
Nasturtium Jewel Series
Pot marigold, *Calendula* 'Geisha Girl'
Antirrhinum majus Coronette Series
California poppy, *Eschscholtzia californica*
Bells of Ireland, *Moluccella laevis*

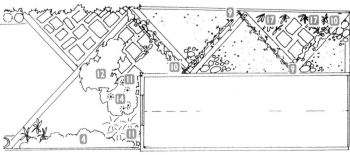

▲ **The planting scheme** uses low-maintenance evergreens that need little pruning and bright yellow, orange and red which stand out against the dark blue-green pergola and decking.

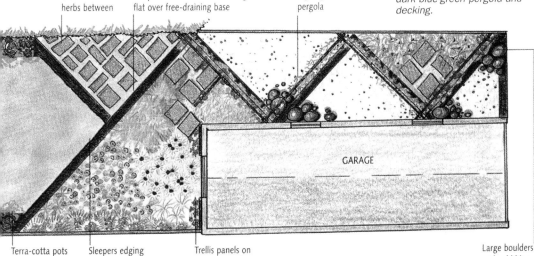

Slabs with herbs between

Sleepers covered in wire netting laid flat over free-draining base

Zig-zag pergola

GARAGE

Terra-cotta pots with bright red geraniums

Sleepers edging lawn

Trellis panels on either side of garage window

Large boulders and pebbbles

CONSTRUCTION

Strong diagonal lines and a range of heights divide this narrow garden into a number of interesting areas. The paved terrace at the far end was extended to form a diamond-edged pattern which allows more space and a pergola was added to create interest at a higher level.

The square pond, set at an angle, is edged with paving. It is set below the level of the terrace but at the same height as the decking. The yellow pine decking is pressure-treated to make the pine rot-proof and non-slip when wet. The higher sides provide seating and a low table completes the eating area.

The lawn that follows is edged with sleepers to retain the neat shape. These are set just below lawn level for easy mowing. Beyond

▲ The strong shape of the paved patio at the far end of the garden is repeated in the decking and pond, and the materials used contrast and complement each other, highlighting the clean design.

PLANTING

Raised beds and potted plants are used highlight the planting and this helps to keep trees and shrubs small. Three triangular raised beds border the sitting areas. The climbers – *Holboellia latifolia, Lonicera* x *tellmanniana* – and the crimson rose 'Etoile de Hollande' are grown against the garage and over the pergola.

KEY PLANTS

◄ Runner beans and sweet peas grow up a wigwam of canes in a half barrel container. These provide both height and colour, and the fresh young beans are easy to pick for use in the kitchen.

▶ The aquatic grass, *Glyceria maxima* 'Variegata' grows in a corner of the pond where the striking leaves contrast well with the shorter foliage that surrounds it. This grass can grow to 80 cm/32 in.

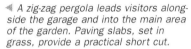

A zig-zag pergola leads visitors along-side the garage and into the main area of the garden. Paving slabs, set in grass, provide a practical short cut.

The square pond, set at an angle, has a raised bed behind it with planting that softens the straight lines. Brick edging contrasts with the other materials used.

See also:
- Raised beds, pages 108, 120
- Introducing water, page 126
- Containers, page 134

this, just before the garage, are slabs set on compacted soil with herbs growing in the spaces.

As running cables for electricity would have been costly, illumination comes from floating candles on the pond and jam jars of night lights hung from the pergola.

▲ Meadow rue, *Thalictrum* species, are lovers of damp and shady places and are at home in a semi-wild area by a water feature. They thrive in climates where summers are fairly cool.

FOR EXTRA COLOUR

Pelargoniums prefer a situation in full sun but require less regular watering than most container plants, which makes them easier to look after. Flowers continue through most of the summer if they are regularly deadheaded.

Move container-grown pelargoniums indoors in winter, in areas prone to frost, and cut back by about one-third. Repot in spring when the plants begin to grow.

Special effect

Easy-care plants in pots
Evergreens and pelargoniums are a good choice if you are looking for pot plants that need minimum care. Adding water retaining crystals in the potting mix, ensures that soil will retain moisture for longer. Plants grown in containers need regular feeding if they are to flourish but slow-release fertilizers can help.

Pot-grown plants also need repotting, or at least some of the compost replaced, every year or two.

Terracotta dries out quickly in hot weather and so is not always the best material to use in a low-maintenance garden. In areas that are subject to frost check that the terracotta is frostproof as it can flake or crack when the water in the compost expands on freezing.

Lining a wooden container with plastic will help it to retain water and also lengthen the life of the timber.

Children's garden

The children of the house wanted the garden to have a sand-pit, a football pitch with goal posts, a climbing frame, a home for the family tortoise, and some magic and mystery.

Jean designed a whale-shaped lawn which doubles as a football pitch, space was found for the frame and sandpit near the house and the tortoise was given its own house by the bicycle shed. A secret area was created within a ring of Amelanchiers, and adults were not forgotten with seats and a hammock to relax on and a paved area for outdoor meals.

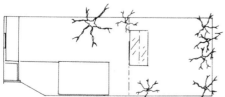

◀ *Before conversion* *the area was divided into two by a wire net-ting fence. There was a bare, weed-infested lawn, a flower border and a beautiful copper beech and lime trees on the boundary.*

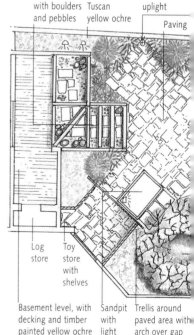

Timber steps with boulders and pebbles   Wall painted Tuscan yellow ochre   Trellis with uplight

Paving

Log store   Toy store with shelves

Basement level, with decking and timber painted yellow ochre   Sandpit with light   Trellis around paved area with arch over gap

THE GARDEN'S PROBLEMS

The boys wish for a football pitch was very important.

The tortoise needed a home and this had to be included in the plan.

Space was needed for the climbing frame already in existence.

A strip of paving outside the basement kitchen and main living area which was too narrow to use.

HOW THEY WERE SOLVED

A long whale-shaped lawn provides the pitch at an angle to prevent balls being aimed at the house.

An area beside the bike shed forms night and winter quarters.

Sited behind the circle of trees, the equipment was painted a deep blue. A blue slide and a climbing rope were introduced.

This area was widened, floored with decking and painted yellow to link indoors with outdoors.

▼ *The planting scheme* *uses very bright colours and includes plants that are easy to grow such as sunflowers and nasturtiums, as well as trees picked for autumn colour.*

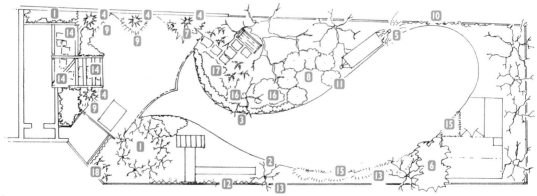

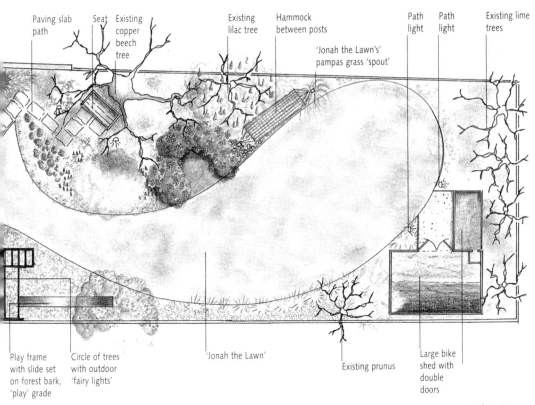

Paving slab path · Seat · Existing copper beech tree · Existing lilac tree · Hammock between posts · 'Jonah the Lawn's' pampas grass 'spout' · Path light · Path light · Existing lime trees

Play frame with slide set on forest bark, 'play' grade · Circle of trees with outdoor 'fairy lights' · 'Jonah the Lawn' · Existing prunus · Large bike shed with double doors

Area for pet hutches

DESIGNER'S PLANTING SCHEME

Key plants

1 *Amelanchier lamarkii* – to create a circle of trees
2 Crab apple, *Malus* 'John Downie'
3 *Sorbus* 'Joseph Rock'
4 Juniper, *Juniperus communis* 'Hibernica'
5 Pampas grass, *Cortaderia selloana* 'Albolineata'
6 Yellow-groove bamboo, *Phyllostachys aureosulcata* var. *aureocaulis*
7 Rosemary, *Rosmarinus* 'Prostratus'
8 Redcurrant, *Ribes rubrum*
9 Lavender, *Lavandula angustifolia* 'Hidcote'

10 Vine, *Vitis coignetiae*
11 *Tropaeolum speciosum* – growing over currant bushes
12 Thornless blackberry, *Rubus lacinatus*

Decorative detail

13 Black-eyed Susan, *Rudbeckia fulgida* var. *sullivantii* 'Goldsturm'
14 Daisy, *Bellis perennis* Roggli Series
15 Sedge, *Carex* 'Frosted Curls'
16 Catmint, *Nepeta* 'Souvenir d'André Chaudron'
17 Male fern, *Dryopteris filix-mas*

Plants for added colour

Sunflower, *Helianthus annus* 'Russian Giant'
Nasturtium, *Tropaeolum majus*
Love-in-the-mist, *Nigella damascena* Persian Jewel Series
Lettuce, green and red 'Salad Bowl', *Lactuca sativa*
Livingstone daisy, *Dorotheanthus bellidiformis*
China aster, *Callistephus* 'Kyoto Pompon'

CONSTRUCTION

Once the area outside the basement had been laid with decking, and painted yellow to match the colour scheme in the house, the timber-edged steps were built up to the terrace. This was laid with an integrated sandpit. The patio paving also extends to a seat beneath the copper beech which looks towards the house and the children's play area.

The giant whale-shaped lawn, created from tough perennial rye grass, extends almost to the end of the garden and the shape allows the goal posts to be positioned at an angle to the house, to avoid accidents with balls.

At the far end of the garden a shed takes the bikes and in front, to one side, is the tortoise pen with

▲ The play space has a 'carpet' of a thick layer of bark chippings for a soft landing.

▶ The brilliant yellow, dark-centred flowers of the black-eyed Susan, *Rudbeckia fulgida* var. *sullivantii* 'Goldstrum' grow alongside the 'whale' and provide patches of bright colour behind the lettuce border.

PLANTING

Plants were chosen for a range of different reasons. The whale lawn was decoratively edged with cut-and-come-again red and green salad bowl lettuces to provide the tortoise, as well as the family, with a constant supply of food, and a pampas grass provides the whale's water spout.

The circle of amelanchiers makes a magic fairy-ring when hung with lights, and these together with the sorbus 'Joseph Rock' and the vine, *Vitis coignetia*, provide rich highlights of red and gold as winter approaches.

KEY PLANTS

◀ The seat that overlooks the play area and the house is backed by euphorbia. The scented *Choisya ternata* is deliberately allowed to grow over it on one side.

◄ Looking down the curving 'whale' lawn towards the bicycle shed and tortoise house. The patio provides ample space for eating outdoors.

▼ The sandpit, which is set into the patio, can be watched over from the seat under the beech tree opposite and the sand is kept clean by the use of a cover, (below).

sleeping quarters in the shed itself. The climbing frame and slide are tucked away behind the circle of Amelanchiers and the hammock provides a viewing point for games and football.

▲The timber-sided paved steps that lead from the basement are lined with pebbles and overhung with evergreen shrubs, including a bushy hebe, the silver-grey lavender, *Lavandula* 'Hidcote' and an artemisia, all benefiting from the good drainage and sunny position.

FOR EXTRA COLOUR

Brilliant orange French marigolds, *Tagetes* 'Safari Tangerine' can be easily grown from seed by young-sters. The large seeds are easy to handle and can be sown *in situ*. They provide a patch of long-lasting bright colour.

Another great favourite with children is the sunflower, *Helianthus annuus* 'Russian Giant' which grows to a towering height.

Special effect

A sandpit soon falls out of use as the family grow up and take up new interests. However, it is not difficult to turn the dug-out area to new use as an ornamental pond when children stop playing with the sand. Alternatively, with the sand removed and the space filled with good topsoil, a bed can be created for ground-hugging plants.

Garden with a view

The owners of this new house wanted an informal effect to tie in with the countryside behind the garden. The garden was sited on steep land emphasizing the view beyond.

The garden was divided into two, with each area having a different feel. The section nearest the house became a traditional country garden while the lower area was more wild, to blend into the landscape. Small waterfalls, rocky streams, and plants create a jungle-like luxuriance.

Utility area   Gazebo   Railway sleepers act as steps and paving

◀ **Before conversion** *As the house was newly built there was no garden, just a lot of builder's rubble.*

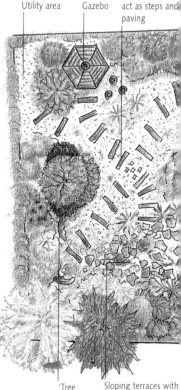

'Tree benches'   Sloping terraces with a series of small pools spilling into the bottom pool. Dramatic planting scheme creates a 'jungle' effect

THE GARDEN'S PROBLEMS

A steep slope facing away from the house.

Making the most of wonderful views.

A new house with a garden full of builder's rubble and no topsoil.

A cold garden with very little sun.

HOW THEY WERE SOLVED

The area near the house was flattened and a terrace built to catch the morning sun.

The view was accentuated by planting tall specimens on the sides, leaving the central area low.

Rubble was removed, the land was contoured and topsoil added.

A wet woodland feature with paths and streams running through it was created in the lowest part of the garden.

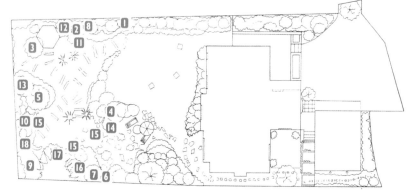

◀ **The planting scheme** *The section of the garden nearest the house had a traditional country garden scheme while there was more exotic planting on the lower level.*

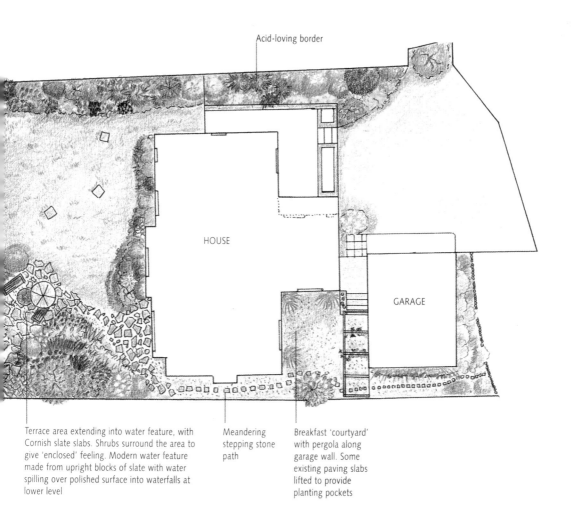

Acid-loving border

HOUSE

GARAGE

Terrace area extending into water feature, with Cornish slate slabs. Shrubs surround the area to give 'enclosed' feeling. Modern water feature made from upright blocks of slate with water spilling over polished surface into waterfalls at lower level

Meandering stepping stone path

Breakfast 'courtyard' with pergola along garage wall. Some existing paving slabs lifted to provide planting pockets

DESIGNER'S PLANTING SCHEME

Key plants
1 *Phillyrea latifolia*
2 Hawthorn, *Crataegus laevigata* 'Crimson Cloud'
3 Ornamental cherry, *Prunus avium* 'Plena'
4 *Elaeagnus* x *ebbingei* 'Limelight'
5 Maple, *Acer griseum*
6 Chusan palm, *Trachycarpus fortunei*
7 Strawberry tree, *Arbutus* x *andrachnoides*

8 *Osmanthus decorus*
9 *Robinia pseudoacacia* 'Frisia'
10 *Eucryphia* x *nymansensis*

Decorative detail
11 Lenten rose, *Helleborus orientalis*
12 Spindle tree, *Euonymus europaeus* 'Red Cascade'
13 Spindle, *Euonymus f. albus* var. *intermedius*
14 Maple, *Acer griseum*

15 Hostas, ferns and *Iris sibirica*
16 *Gunnera manicata*
17 Spurge, *Euphorbia characias* ssp. *wulfenii*
18 Foxglove tree, *Paulownia tomentosa*

CONSTRUCTION

Once the builder's rubble had been removed the garden was landscaped, with a level section created near to the house which dropped to sloping land below. Seen from the house, the lower section of the garden is not in view until the edge of the top terrace is reached and so forms a secret garden waiting to be discovered.

Small flat terraces were dug out at points on the slope of the lower area as places to sit. Here water forms in small pools before running down the slope again ending up in a larger pool at the bottom end of the garden, where a utility area is kept well out of sight. The terraces are linked by timber steps and gravel pathways that pass close to waterfalls and fast streams

▲ *Steps of railway sleepers in the gravel in the lower section of the garden lead down the slope and link one small flat terrace with another.*

PLANTING

The garden nearest to the house contains a long, wide herbaceous border along one side, and shrubs and trees opposite this provide shelter for the terrace. In the lower section of the garden a jungle-like effect was created with plants such as the foxglove tree, *Paulownia tomentosa* with its fragrant lilac-pink flowers.

KEY PLANTS

▲ *Elaeagnus* x *ebbingei* 'Limelight' planted in the border between the top and lower sections of the garden forms a link between the traditional upper section of the garden and the more exotically planted lower section.

◄ The seat on the lower terrace looks down the timber-edged steps. Cranesbill geraniums provide foreground colour and a newly planted *Robinia pseudoacacia* 'Frisia' adds colour beside the seat.

▲ The top terrace of gravel and sunken railway sleepers, and the timber bench, are enclosed by planting to create a sheltered area and a place from which to enjoy the view of the countryside.

▶ Water tumbles down from the top garden in small waterfalls, along streams lined and edged by large craggy rocks.

of tumbling water, ending up at a gazebo hidden from sight.

The water feature starts from close to the top terrace in a pool, this position is highlighted by giant standing stones (right). The water then runs between rough-edged slabs of slate, some of which act as stepping stones, to spill over from the top terrace. It continues its run through the sloping section of the garden to the end of the garden below.

FOR EXTRA COLOUR

Eucryphia x *nymansensis* bears its cup-shaped white flowers from late summer through to autumn and provides colour at a time of the year when flowers are often in short supply. It is a tall evergreen shrub that can grow to as much as 15 m/50 ft, so is only suitable for a garden like this that backs onto open countryside. Here it acts as a frame to the view behind.

Special effect

Running water Beautiful effects can be created by moving water. In this garden slabs of slate are used for areas of paving and spaces are left between the slate at intervals to form crevices for running water while other slates form stepping-stones for crossing the water.

A similar effect for a more formal area can be created with granite setts, with spaces left between them for the water to flow around.

▲ Pictured here in summer, the decorative peeling bark of the paper-bark maple, *Acer griseum* creates a focus even in winter.

With the elderly in mind

This garden, devised by Barbara Hunt in conjunction with the charity Age Concern, was created for a garden exhibition at Hampton Court, London. It seeks to help to compensate for some of the problems that arrive as we get older, from lack of energy and mobility, to failing eyesight. With wide, paved areas, the garden uses a range of materials, and has a pergola, raised beds and a raised pool. The pond and many of the beds are edged with seating so that they can be enjoyed from close at hand. A bird bath, bird table and the inclusion of plants to attract bees and butterflies bring nature to the garden.

POINTS TO CONSIDER

Mobility – a problem for some of those for whom the garden was designed.

Eye-sight may be poor for some garden users.

Scent is particularly important for older people.

SOLUTIONS

Wide paths provide access for wheel chairs and for people to walk side-by-side. Gentle slopes rather than steps. Lots of seating in both sun and shade.

Using strong and contrasting colours helps to overcome the problem older eyes have in adjusting to a move from an area of light to one in the shade.

When eye-sight or hearing are reduced, flowers which give off scent provide a lot of pleasure.

▶ **The planting scheme** uses bright colours and positions plants of contrasting colours side by side. It also includes a number of plants with either aromatic foliage or fragrant flowers and others to attract bees and butterflies.

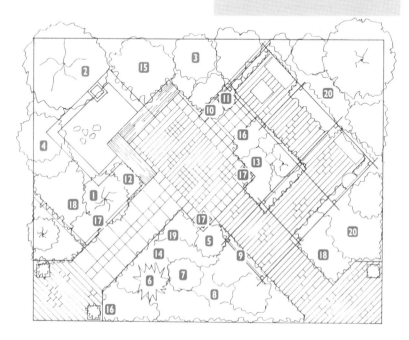

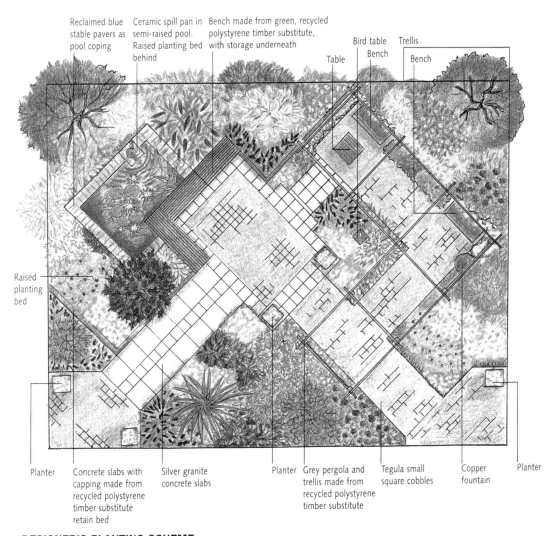

Reclaimed blue stable pavers as pool coping

Ceramic spill pan in semi-raised pool. Raised planting bed behind

Bench made from green, recycled polystyrene timber substitute, with storage underneath

Table

Bird table
Bench

Trellis

Bench

Raised planting bed

Planter

Concrete slabs with capping made from recycled polystyrene timber substitute retain bed

Silver granite concrete slabs

Planter

Grey pergola and trellis made from recycled polystyrene timber substitute

Tegula small square cobbles

Copper fountain

Planter

DESIGNER'S PLANTING SCHEME

Key plants

1 Japanese maple, *Acer palmatum f. atropurpureum*
2 Rock maple, *Acer saccharinum* 'Wieri'
3 Indian bean tree, *Catalpa bignonioides* 'Aurea'
4 Golden bamboo, *Phyllostachys aurea*
5 Dwarf mountain pine, *Pinus mugo*
6 New Zealand flax, *Phormium tenax*

Plants with aromatic foliage

7 *Artemisia* 'Powis Castle'

8 *Eucalyptus gunnii*
9 Mint, *Mentha rotundifolia* 'Variegata'
10 Jerusalem sage, *Phlomis fruticosa*
11 Rosemary, *Rosmarinus officinalis*
12 *Salvia officinalis* 'Icterina'
13 *Santolina virens*

Decorative detail

14 *Achillea* 'Moonshine'
15 *Buddleia fallowiana*
16 Lavender, *Lavandula vera*
17 *Argyranthemum* 'Jamaica Primrose'
18 *Rudbeckia* 'Marmalade'

19 *Salvia officinalis* 'Purpurascens'
20 *Lilium* 'Connecticut King'

Plants with fragrant flowers

Jasmine, *Jasminum officinale*
Lavender, *Lavandula angustifolia* 'Hidcote'
Japanese honeysuckle, *Lonicera japonica* 'Halliana'
Philadelphus 'Virginal'
Rose, *Rosa* 'Dreaming Spires'
Viburnum x *bodnantense* 'Charles Lamont'

CONSTRUCTION

The paving was picked for its non-slip and non-reflective properties. Changes in colour and materials are used to herald clearly, for the less well-sighted, that they are entering a new area. Seating surfaces in dark green are made from a recycled polystyrene waste material which is warm to the touch and relatively maintenance free. It does not absorb water so can be quickly dried after rain.

The pergola provides a frame for climbers, and shade for the seating area below, from which the scent of the climbers can be enjoyed.

Raised beds and the raised pond bring the pleasures of plants and water up to a more accessible level to those walking, sitting or in wheel-chairs.

▲ The pond has a wide raised edge that provides comfortable seating and a chance to view plants and water close to.

PLANTING

Apart from providing a number of specimen plants with decorative leaf-shapes and autumn colour, Barbara picked plants for their aromatic leaves or fragrant flowers. She chose bright colours that could be seen clearly by those with poorer sight. Orange and yellow have been used extensively, often side-by-side for vivid contrast.

KEY PLANTS

▲ A mix of leaf and flower shapes and colours allows each plant to be defined against the other. The silver leaves of a *Eucalyptus gunnii* overhang the pale yellow flowers of Achillea 'Moonshine'.

◀ The bright sunny colours of black-eyed Susan, *Rudbeckia fulgida*, the yellow flowers of the lily 'Connecticut King' and bright orange marigolds show up strongly against a green background.

▲ A bird table is ideally placed if it is close to buildings so that it is possible to view the feeding birds whatever the weather.

▶ The water feature tumbles water into the pond below and acts up as a bird bath. The water is recycled from the pond back up to the top saucer again.

▲ In these raised beds Barbara has used the two colours most easily seen by older eyes. The bright orange flowers of *Rudbeckia* 'Marmalade' are elevated to eye-level creating a strong contrast against the paler yellow daisy-like heads of the *Argyranthemum* 'Jamaica Primrose'.

FOR EXTRA COLOUR

Flowers in tones of a single colour work well in a container. Here the small, soft pink flowers of *Nemesia* Carnival Series rise above the rim while the pendent deep pink flowers of the climbing *Rhodochiton* appear around the edges and trail down to the ground.

Special effect

Attracting the birds Bird baths and bird tables not only bring wildlife close to home but they create attractive garden sculptures. Provided the situation is suitable and safe for birds, hidden from circling birds of prey and protected from marauding cats, bird baths and tables can be used as a focal point on a small terrace, at the crossroads of paths or the end of a pathway, and in many other situations.

Here potter and designer, Denis Fairweather has created a bird bath from which water pours into the pond, adding sound to the enjoyment of the other senses.

The table and water spill are made from recycled polystyrene waste material which can be sawn, drilled, nailed, glued and jointed in the same way as timber. He has formed a pair of pecking birds on the rim of each to attract real birds to enjoy the facilities also.

Integrating a swimming pool

The owners of this garden decided to include a swimming pool, but wanted it to be out of sight of the house so that it would be a surprise feature, and when the children invited friends for a swim the noise of their enjoyment would not be too close to the house. The spot had to be free of trees, must not interfere with the line of the house drains, and should be in the sun for most of the day and in a sheltered situation. They chose a spot at the end of the garden with access through the flower garden and a pergola arch. As the garden is on a slope this meant digging out to create a flat terrace for the pool.

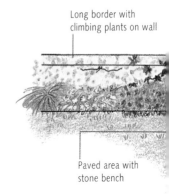

Long border with climbing plants on wall

Paved area with stone bench

LAWN AREA

▼ *Before conversion* *the area used for the pool had been a lawn adjacent to the fruit garden.*

THE GARDEN'S PROBLEMS

The line of the house drains was an important consideration.

The pool had to receive sun for the longest possible time every day.

A position sheltered from wind was needed but away from trees.

The large expanse of water and the size of the pool had to be considered.

HOW THEY WERE SOLVED

Experts checked the route of the drains before the final position was decided.

The final position was chosen as it would receive sun from first thing in the morning until evening.

A lawned area was chosen with a wall running down one side to provide wind shelter. A pool terrace was created by digging out the sloping land.

Siting the pool out of sight of the house with a sunken terrace surrounding it.

▼ *The planting scheme* *Little extra planting was necessary. A retaining wall on one side backed onto a mature bed and these plants could then be enjoyed from both sides. A second narrow bed, with a low fence behind it, was newly planted and pots were arranged by the pool for additional colour.*

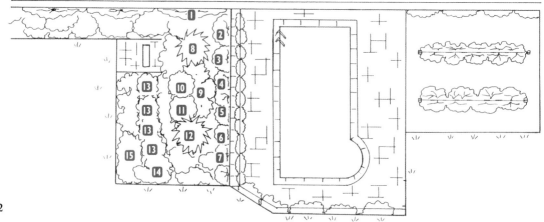

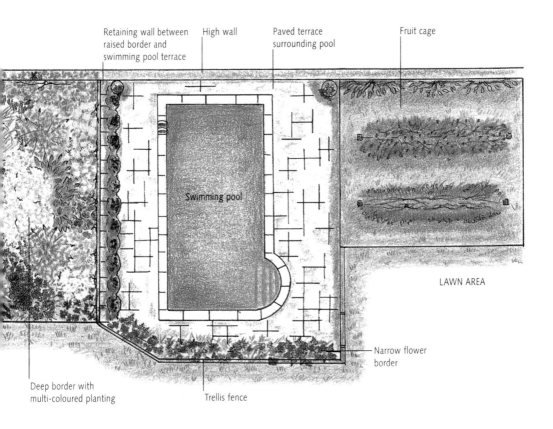

Retaining wall between raised border and swimming pool terrace

High wall

Paved terrace surrounding pool

Fruit cage

Swimming pool

LAWN AREA

Narrow flower border

Deep border with multi-coloured planting

Trellis fence

DESIGNER'S PLANTING SCHEME

Key plants
1 Climbing rose, *Rosa* 'Compassion'
2 Shrub rose, *Rosa* Graham Thomas
3 Shrub rose, *Rosa* Troilus
4 Shrub rose, *Rosa* Fair Bianca – a group of three
5 Shrub rosa *Rosa* The Prince – group of three
6 Shrub rose, *Rosa* Chaucer
7 *Rosa* x *xanthia* 'Canary Bird'
8 *Mahonia* x *media* 'Charity'
9 *Viburnum davidii* – a group of three
10 Mock orange, *Philadelphus* 'Belle Etoile'

11 Mock orange, *Philadelphus* 'Manteau d'Hermine'
12 *Mahonia* x *media* 'Lionel Fortescue'

Decorative detail
13 Peonies, *Paeonia* – mixed species and varieties
14 Lavenders, *Lavandula* species
15 Cranesbill, *Geranium sanguineum* var. *striatum*

Plants for added colour
Cosmos bipinnatus
Lavatera assurgentiflora
Phlox species

313

CONSTRUCTION

The owners set out to design the surrounding area themselves with some help from the pool construction company. A digger was used to dig out the pool and landscape the surrounding area to form a flat, partially sunken terrace, with the excavated soil being used elsewhere in the garden. Removing the soil is expensive, so it is worth finding an alternative use for it, for example, as a rockery, or in raised beds.

The water is heated by electricity with all the equipment concealed. It is possible to use solar energy in many areas if the panels are sited well. The pool is kept covered when it is not in use to maintain the water temperature, allowing it to be used for long periods throughout the year.

▲ The sunken terrace in which the pool has been sited is sheltered from the wind in all directions and has the added advantage of mature planting along one side, with climbing roses that tumble over trellis to add colour to the pool area as well as the flower garden.

PLANTING

Climbing roses cover trellis that divides off the main flower garden from the sheltered pool terrace. These provide summer colour on one side of the pool. Along an adjoining side a low trellis fence, built to keep out a young puppy, has been made almost instantly colourful with the addition of cosmos and lavatera species.

KEY PLANTS

▲ A vigorous, magenta pink cranesbill, *Geranium* x *oxonianum* forms clumps and flowers right through from spring to early autumn.

◀ The brick-built pergola is surrounded by deep beds with mixed planting giving colour and interest throughout the year. The scarlet flowers of *Crocosmia* 'Lucifer' stand out against the pink of the lavatera in the background and the campanula.

▲ A view-point from the flower garden close to the house pinpoints the pool's position on a lower terrace. It also shows the advantage of adding a pool where plants are well established.

▶ A stone seat on the route from the house to the pool shows how well hidden the pool is. It also highlights the garden's mature and colourful summer planting.

▲ Surrounding the ground around the trunk of a tree the cranesbill *Geranium nodosum* 'Whiteleaf' adds colour in what is usually a difficult spot to get plants to flower. This is an ideal plant for use in just such a situation as it flourishes in shade and dry conditions.

FOR EXTRA COLOUR

The exotic-looking flowers of clematis species and hybrids come in a range of colours. If carefully selected, it should be possible to have one in flower from spring to autumn.

Clematis armandii, an evergreen with small, scented white flowers, is one of the earliest. *C.* 'Nelly Moser' with its pale pink flowers decorated with a deep pink stripe, appears later, in spring to early summer. In mid-summer the brilliant magenta to scarlet flowers of *C.* 'Ville de Lyon' arrive, followed by the pinky purple flowers *C.* 'Comtesse de Bouchaud' (below) which continue until late summer.

Special effect

Brick structures are expensive to erect but bricks are one of the most durable materials for use in the garden. Here bricks have been used to build a series of pillars to hold up the timber beams for a pergola. The pergola itself extends from one side of the garden to the other and also divides up the garden into a series of 'rooms'. In addition it also helps to screen the pool area from the house itself.

GROUNDWORK

Recognizing the type of soil you have, and knowing how to improve it and what plants will thrive in it, ensures that the plants you grow will flourish. This chapter describes how to identify your soil type, how to enrich what you have and how to keep it in good condition. It also tells you when and how to water your newly planted plants to give them a good start and a strong and self-reliant root system. How to set about installing power in the garden is also covered, as this allows you to highlight decorative plantings and create wonderful effects with water. Lighting also extends the period you can sit outdoors and enjoy the garden, as well as making it safer to walk around in at night, and more secure from unwanted intruders.

Identifying your soil

Clearing the site

A new garden may appear to be little more than a heap of rubble with little or no topsoil. However, it can be radically improved if you take the following steps:

- Dig out and heap up bricks and larger stones if you think you can use them in the design. Otherwise dispose of them.

- Fork over, or dig the soil to let in air and water. In the autumn cover with a thick layer of organic matter, then leave until the following spring.

- In the spring dig, then rake the surface smooth. Allow weeds to germinate and remove.

- After planting mulch well to suppress further weed growth.

Soil is rock which over thousands of years has been crushed and mixed with decayed organic matter, known as humus. The three main types of soil are light, sandy soil, which is made up of large particles that do not adhere to each other and through which water and plant food pass easily; medium silt, which is made up of medium-sized, smoother particles; and heavy clay, which is made up of minute particles which pack together, retain moisture and form sticky lumps that dry solid. Most garden soil is a mixture, with one of the above predominating.

Topsoil is the name given to the relatively thin, darker top layer of soil which has built up over the years as it has been enriched with humus through the natural decay of organic matter such as dead leaves, animals and plants, and through cultivation. The subsoil lying below this gives the soil its general character and to a large extent determines whether it is rich or poor in nutrients, and whether it is warm or cold and has good or poor drainage, as well as whether it is acid or alkaline. In a new house and garden there may be no topsoil at all, but subsoil can be converted into topsoil by good cultivation.

Fertile soil, loam, is an approximately equal mix of sand, silt, clay and humus. Humus is a vital, organic, ingredient which introduces a wide range of chemicals and bacteria into the soil. It improves soil texture in its own right, and encourages the activity of earthworms, whose work not only breaks it down and releases its vital ingredients as food for plants, but also aerates the soil.

SOIL TEST

To check what type of soil you have do the following test:

Pick up a handful of damp soil. Rub it between fingers and thumb.

It is sandy if it feels gritty, the grains do not stick together and it is difficult to roll your sample into a ball.

It is a sandy loam if it is gritty but can be rolled into a ball.

It is silt if it feels silky and can be rolled into a ball.

It is a sandy clay loam or a clay loam if it is gritty or sticky and can be rolled into a cylinder.

It is clay if it feels sticky and will form a cylinder which can be curved to form a ring.

See also:
- Mulching, pages 104, 111
- Digging, page 107
- Checking acid or alkaline levels, page 108

SOIL TYPE	ADVANTAGES	DISADVANTAGES
Sandy soil	Light, so easy to work Warms up quickly in spring	Free draining, so quick to dry out Nutrients easily lost
Silty soil	Retains moisture well Often very fertile; improves well	Dries into hard clods
Clay soil	Retains nutrients well Improves well Good for growing a wide range of plants	Hard to work Retains water, so sticky when wet and compacted when dry Slow to warm up in spring

OTHER SOIL TYPES

Chalk soil, which is pale in colour, has many of the disadvantages of clay. It may form only a shallow layer and often contains a lot of stones. It is also usually very alkaline, see page 108.

Peaty soil is dark in colour and spongy in texture. It may be waterlogged and need draining but is often very fertile, being rich in organic matter.

Creating a sump

When installing drainage, you need to provide somewhere for the drained water to collect and disperse from. You may be lucky enough to have a natural drain or ditch that you can use, but you will generally need to dig out a pit into which your water pipes can drain. This is known as a sump or soakaway. The sump should be situated at the lowest part of the garden, and needs to be at least 60 cm/2 ft deep and square. When you have chosen the site and dug the hole, fill it with building rubble or gravel (or a rubble topped with a gravel layer). Then place inverted turf over the drainage material and cover with more turf or soil.

LAYING LAND DRAINS

Poorly drained soils are cold and inhospitable, and their compacted structure deprives the plants' roots of the air they need. Very wet soils cause roots to rot and plants to die. If rain does not drain away but continues to lie in your garden, if only moisture-loving plants thrive, and if the lawn is full of moss, it may be that you need to install drainage.

Dig trenches in the garden for the drains leading into a soakaway (see above, right). Make these at least 30 cm/1 ft deep, with a slight fall towards the soakaway (following any natural slope). Place a layer of coarse grit or fine gravel along the bottom.

Lay the drains (which may be made of clay or perforated plastic) on the bed of gravel. Use a T-shaped connector if you are adding side drains.

To finish off pack more grit or gravel around and over the drains to improve drainage and to help to prevent the holes in the pipes from becoming clogged. Cover with inverted turfs or perforated polythene sheet, then replace the soil or re-lay grass turf.

Improving soil condition

Testing for nutrient deficiency

To check if your soil is deficient in nutrients use a soil-testing kit. However, if you think you have a serious nutrient deficiency it is wise to send off soil samples for a professional laboratory test.

To take soil samples use a trowel and take soil from about 6 cm/2 1/2 in below the surface. Take several samples from around the garden and test individually.

Measure into a jar 1 part soil to 5 parts water. The lid makes a good measure. Shake well then leave to settle and become reasonably clear. This can take from half an hour to a whole day.

(continued opposite)

To improve the structure of the soil dig in lots of bulky organic matter each year (see page 107). In a good loam the soil is made up of crumb-sized pieces that can be seen by the naked eye. The spaces between the crumbs provide channels for aeration and drainage. This structure helps to maintain water and nutrients within the soil. On sandy and silty soil the addition of humus coats the soil particles to form crumbs. On clay soil it works conversely and helps to break down the solid clods into a crumb-like structure.

The benefit of worms to the soil

A good worm population is a sign of a good soil. Worms consume fresh organic matter, breaking it down and release nutrients which are immediately available to plants. At the same time their burrows through the soil create aeration and drainage channels.

▲ *Organic mulches improve the soil.*

In planted areas

To keep the soil in good condition once you have put in your plants, add compost, manure and other organic matter as a thick layer of surface mulch. It will gradually be worked down to continue to improve the structure. Mulch also helps to prevent the soil from drying out, and suppresses weeds. Mulch when the soil is damp, or the material will draw water out of the soil.

▲ *Add coarse grit to improve clay soil.*

On heavy, clay soil

Apply lime to improve the structure (not suitable for alkaline clay, or for acid-loving plants, see page 109). Also dig in a good supply of coarse sand or grit as well as plenty of compost and manure. Do not be sparing with quantities, rather deal with one smaller area at a time.

SOURCES OF ORGANIC MATTER

- Horse, cow or pig manure
- Garden compost
- Compost from municipal waste
- Treated sewage sludge
- Spent mushroom compost
- Fresh, dried or composted seaweed
- Composted straw
- Spent hops

Quantities to use annually
- Manure: 5.5 kg per sq m /10 lb per sq yd
- Good compost: 2.5 kg per sq m/ 5 lb per sq yd or 1 barrow load per sq m/sq yd

Checking for nutrients

For healthy growth plants need a wide range of nutrients in the soil. By annually digging in bulky organic matter, the soil should remain fertile. Mulching the soil throughout the growing season helps to improve the soil's fertility. At the start of a soil-improvement plan the soil may be deficient in some nutrients and quantities take some time to build up using this method. In a small garden, planting has to be concentrated, and extra nutrients may be necessary.

The most important nutrients are nitrogen, which aids growth and gives leaves their green colour, phosphorus, for strong root growth, and potassium (potash), which affects the size and quality of flowers and fruit. Nitrogen is likely to be in short supply as it is washed out of the soil and not replenished in cold, wet weather. By digging in bulky organic matter phosphorus and potassium levels should remain high. Potassium deficiency is more likely to occur in light, sandy soil or chalk, and phosphorus deficiency in heavy clay soil or peat.

Trace elements such as iron, zinc, copper manganese and boron are also vital to plant growth. Very alkaline or limy soils can reduce take up of these important elements.

Applying fertilizers

Fertilizers can be powders or granules, or a concentrated liquid to be diluted. Once diluted, the liquid is watered onto the ground around plants. If the soil is dry, water it first. Liquid fertilizer can also be used as a foliar feed, applied in the evening or in dull weather, by spraying the plant's leaves thoroughly.

On bare soil apply dry fertilizer by first dividing the ground into 90 cm/3 ft squares. Spread the fertilizer as evenly as possible.

On established plants scatter the fertilizer around each plant to feed the roots, keeping it away from the stem.

Lightly hoe in the fertilizer and water the area, unless rain is forecast. This makes it available more quickly.

(continued from opposite)

Draw off clear liquid from the top with a pipette and transfer this to the test and reference chambers of the kit container.

Pour the powder from the capsule provided into the test chamber. Shake well until the powder is dispersed.

Allow a short time for the colour to develop then check this against the comparison chart.

See also:
- *Digging page 107*
- *Checking acid or alkaline levels, page 108*

FERTILIZERS TO USE

General fertilizers that contain the three main nutrients
Organic Blood, fish and bone, sea-weed meal, liquid animal manure
Inorganic Growmore formula and slow-release fertilizers that are released over a period of time, plus controlled-fertilizers that are regulated by the soil's temperature

For nitrogen deficiency
Organic Rock potash, dried blood, liquid seaweed, hoof and horn, fish meal
Inorganic Nitro-chalk, Ammonium sulphate (but makes soil more acid)

For potassium deficiency
Organic Liquid seaweed, wood ash
Inorganic Potassium sulphate

For phosphorus deficiency
Organic Bone meal, fish meal
Inorganic Superphosphate of lime

Trace elements
Organic Seaweed meal
Inorganic Chelated iron compound, proprietary tonics, and trace element granules

Garden Compost

Compost bins

You can make compost by simply piling the materials up in a corner but using a bin is a neater and more efficient alternative.

Compost bins are readily available. Buy the largest you can fit in. It should be at least 1 m/3–4 ft square to produce more heat and help the contents to rot down quickly. Ideally you need two, one to take fresh material and one for partially broken-down compost, which can be forked over and left covered to go through the final stages of decomposition.

Plastic compost bin with lid, that comes in three slot-in sections.

A timber bin that is simple to construct as it comes as a kit The timber is pre-cut and the bin is sold ready to assemble. Simply slot or nail the sections together, following the instructions.

Homemade compost provides organic matter to improve your soil. Compost is decomposed kitchen and garden waste, including grass clippings. Using a container is neater and speeds up decomposition. The bacteria which break down the vegetable matter need air, warmth, moisture and nitrogen to decompose successfully.

Making compost

It is best to stand the bin on bare soil. Fork over the soil in the base area to aid drainage. Place a layer of twiggy material or straw in the bottom to provide good aeration, 8–10 cm/3–4 in deep. Bulky material soon shrinks down. Continue to fill the bin until you reach the top. Contents should be forked over to even out decomposition. Cover the heap to keep in the warmth. In summer your compost should be ready for use in three to four months. Winter cold slows down decomposition and it may take until the spring for it to be ready.

Pile on kitchen and garden refuse that rots easily. Stems and twigs will need shredding first. It is best to add compost materials in larger, mixed quantities if possible. A good way of doing this is to keep two plastic bags beside the bin, one for kitchen waste and the other for garden waste, then mix together before adding.

Include a layer of manure when a thickness of about 15 cm/6 in has been reached. If this is not available use garden soil and add an activator such as seaweed meal, blood, fish and bonemeal or a proprietary compost activator to introduce more bacteria into the heap. Keep the material in the heap moist you may need to water it in dry weather. Continue to add in layers as above.

Once the bin is full, lift it away and place it by the side of the rotting heap. Cover the heap and start a new one.

◀ With two heaps side by side, one pile can rot down and be used in the garden while the other is being built up.

WHAT TO COMPOST

- Kitchen vegetable waste
- Teabags, tea leaves, coffee grains
- Eggshells
- Vacuum cleaner waste
- Old potting soil
- Lawn mowings
- Thin prunings
- Bonfire ash
- Straw
- Animal manure
- Seaweed
- Autumn leaves. It is best to rot down autumn leaves on their own in a wire basket. These take longer to decompose – up to two years – but the resulting leafmould is ideal for use as potting or seed compost.

WHAT NOT TO COMPOST

- Animal waste such as meat scraps, which could attract rats
- Diseased plant material
- Perennial weeds
- Evergreen leaves like holly or ivy (you can include conifer needles)
- Woody material
- Any man-made waste (plastic etc.)

EXTRA COMPOSTING MATERIALS

You can never have too much compost. For extra supplies visit market stalls and greengrocers' shops at the end of the working day. Use seaweed, straw or green bracken (check first with local regulations that gathering them is legal), or manure from riding stables.

Quick compost tips

- When you use eggshells on your compost heap, crush them before adding them to the waste. This will speed up the rate at which they break down.
- If your garden produces a lot of thick, tough plant material such as woody stems and shrub and tree prunings, consider investing in a shredder.
- The bigger the pile, the more heat builds up inside it and the faster it will break down.
- Forking the heap as it rots, to turn the drier outside material to the middle, helps it to rot evenly.

DIGGING

Digging not only allows you to introduce soil-improving conditioners but also aerates the soil and exposes pests to be gobbled up by enthusiastic predators. To incorporate manure or compost put a layer in the bottom of the trench, then half-fill it with soil. Add more manure and finally fill the trench with soil.

First mark out size and position of the trenches using tough garden string. Dig out a square of soil the width and depth of the spade, starting at the end of the first trench. Pile up the soil at the end of the bed.

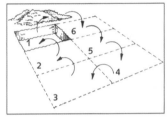

Drive the spade into the soil at right angles to the surface, and a spade's width away from the first opening, then pull back on the handle to lever and loosen the bite of soil.

Lift the spadeful of soil and twist it over, with a flick of your wrist, to invert the clod of soil into the first space. Keep your back straight while doing this, and lift with your knees.

At the end of the row remove the first bite in the next row by driving the spade in at right angles to the first row, then insert the spade between these cuts and parallel to the first trench.

Checking acid or alkaline levels

Growing plants unsuited to your soil

If you long to include plants unsuited to your soil, build a raised bed and import soil to suit the plants you have chosen.

Raised beds

The construction tips on page 120–121 can be used for building a raised bed, but omit mortar from some joints in the first line of bricks. These gaps provide spaces for excess water to escape. When building a raised bed, lay the complete rectangle of bricks that form the bed sides at each level, so that the sides are tied in with the front and back. To fill the bed, first put in rubble to one-third of its depth, then complete by adding soil to the top.

A raised bed or a planting area can be made with wooden boards. Pressure-treated timber should be used.

See also:
• *Digging, page 107*

Soil fertility and what you can grow, is affected by the pH level, or the amount of lime in the soil. The pH is measured on a scale of 1 to 14. The low numbers denote an acid soil, a neutral soil has a pH of 7 and the higher numbers show that the soil is alkaline or limey. Most soil is slightly acid: a pH of 6.5 is ideal for a wide range of plants, including vegetables. A drop of only one point on the scale shows a soil ten times more acid and a rise of one point shows it to be ten times more alkaline.

When a garden has been cultivated for a long time, the soil tends to become slightly more acid, whereas an alkaline soil is less likely to be affected long-term by the treatment it gets. A soil can be made more alkaline by the application of garden lime, used for improving the soil condition for vegetables.

If the pH falls below 5.0 nutrients are affected. Below this phosphate can become unavailable to plants, the soil becomes more acid and calcium, potassium and magnesium can be washed away. A very alkaline soil is equally hostile to many plants, and can cause nutrients to be 'locked' into the soil. Some plants only survive in acid conditions while others thrive if the soil is alkaline. It helps to know the pH level of your soil and which plants suit it and will thrive – see page 109 for examples.

If your soil is acid you can raise the pH level fairly simply by adding lime. It is important to do this at a different time from using manure, compost or fertilizer. If these are mixed there is a harmful reaction. If you apply manure in the autumn then leave liming until the early spring, about six weeks before planting. Add only a little lime at a time, then test again later and add more if necessary as it can quickly build up.

Measuring the pH level Use a pH kit (right) or a probe meter to check this. Take samples from around the garden. Follow the instructions for whichever method you use.

▲ *Adding lime improves acid soil.*

Raising the pH on sandy and other acid soils Divide the area to be limed into 1 m/1 yd squares, using pegs and string and weigh out enough lime for each square. Use gloves or a spade to apply the lime one square at a time, sprinkling it as evenly as possible over the surface.

▲ *Adding garden compost and manure will help to make the soil more acid.*

Raising the pH on clay soil Follow the instructions for sandy soil; but thoroughly dig the lime into the soil, (see digging page 107).

Lowering the pH It is hard to make an alkaline soil more acid, although digging in compost and manure helps. Use liquid seaweed foliar spray to provide a quicker method of correcting deficiencies. To create a successful garden choose plants that prefer the natural conditions you have.

LIME

Ground limestone and calcified seaweed are expensive but last longer in the soil. Alternatively use slaked or garden lime. Hydrated or builders' lime can also be used, but in smaller quantities – approximately three-quarters of the quantities given below. It needs to be replaced annually as it is quickly lost.

Use the following quantities of ground limestone to raise pH by 1pH.
- On sandy soil 225 g per sq m/ 8 oz per sq yd
- On loamy soil 450 g per sq m/ 16 oz per sq yd
- On clay soil 680 g per sq m/ 1 lb 8 oz per sq yd

Some plants for acid soil

If you have an acid soil you are lucky, as most garden plants thrive in a fairly acid soil, and over-acidity can be easily corrected by the use of lime. A few plants, including most heathers and lilies, must have acid soil and refuse to grow without it. Camellias (right), azaleas (below, right) and rhododendrons (below) are among the species that will not tolerate lime.

Some plants for alkaline soil

Alkaline soils can demand a more selective approach to choosing your plants. Many species fail to thrive when too much lime in the soil prevents them taking up all the nutrients they require. However, there are also many chalk and lime lovers, including lilacs (right), all the clematis (below, right), and buddleia (below).

Watering

Installing an automatic watering system

These systems include a huge range of sprinkler, spray and dripfeed heads as well as pop-up nozzles for watering the lawn that sink below the surface when they are not in use.

Connect the master unit to a hose from the garden tap. This reduces the water pressure and contains a filter that can be removed for cleaning. An electronic timer can also be screwed to the tap to turn the system on/off automatically.

Lay out the main supply tube. Position this where it will not be too visible: beneath a hedge, alongside a path or just beneath the soil surface.

Connect smaller diameter branch tubes. Position these, using the special connectors, where you need to take water to another part of the garden.

In tubs and baskets or for individual plants fit drip-feed heads to the pipe. These are held in place with special pegs.

For general localized watering use a spray head (see below).

We need to water wisely as this is important for the production of strong, healthy plants. Plants that are watered sparingly but often produce a root system close to the soil surface and these roots soon suffer in dry periods. The healthiest plants are those that develop a strong, deep root system which is able to tap into more reliable reserves well below ground level.

Watering systems

Automatic systems work from a garden tap. A main pipe is laid around the garden then smaller branch tubes are added which lead away to areas where water is needed. Spike fittings are positioned alongside plants to be watered,

▲ Micro-adjustable dripper.

then tiny spray or sprinkler units are screwed into these. The system can be used to water containers and hanging baskets as well as beds and lawns. It is estimated that the system needs to be turned on for ten minutes twice a day, in dry weather to provide sufficient water. A timer is also available which, fitted to the tap, automatically controls the water on and off.

Seep hoses can be part of the above system or laid separately along the ground. Tiny perforations allow the water to seep out slowly and sink well into the soil. Seepage hoses are similar but can also be buried just below the soil's surface. This minimizes water loss through evaporation.

Sprinklers can be difficult to train accurately and are easy to forget, so they can be very water wasteful. Oscillating sprinklers can be adjusted to cover areas of different sizes, static and rotating sprinklers water in a circle, and pulse-jet sprinklers rotate to eject the water in a series of pulses.

Hand watering, using a watering can or a garden hose with a spray attachment, is accurate but time consuming. It does allow you to check the health of your plants as you water each in turn, and is ideal for watering containers and baskets. Allow at least a full can for each large container.

▼ A soaker hose in use.

What and when to water

▲ *Adjustable lawn sprinkler in use.*

Lawns A lawn of newly sown grass-seed or newly laid turf needs regular watering in dry weather. However an established lawn can survive a period of drought and soon turns greens again when rain arrives. If consistently green grass is particularly important to you give the lawn a good soaking once a week. In dry periods mow frequently but adjust the height of the blades to a longer 4 cm/1½ in. This encourages dense growth and helps to trap any dew.

Large shrubs and trees need regular watering when first planted to

▼ *A hose extension can be useful.*

create a healthy root system. Once deep roots are established they can find water for themselves and rarely need watering, even in dry conditions.

Small shrubs and hardy perennials start to droop as a sign that they require water. Give the plants a good soaking in the evening when the sun is off the area.

Bedding plants and vegetables need regular watering in dry weather if they are to thrive. Water these plants either first thing in the morning or during the evening (never when they are in strong sun). The closer together plants are the more water they need.

▼ *Compost in pots can dry out quickly.*

Tubs, window boxes and hanging baskets should be treated as for bedding plants and vegetables. They can dry out very quickly in hot weather, and may need to be watered every morning and evening. Revive hanging baskets by soaking them in a bucket of water.

Saving water

Fix water butts to downpipes to store as much waste rain-water as you can. It is also possible to divert bath and shower water into storage tanks where it can cool prior to being used on the garden.

Watering tips

- Never water plants when the sun is on them. This not only causes leaf burn but wastes water in evaporation. Instead, water in the evening.

- A good layer of mulch, about 8 cm/3 in, spread over the soil surface will prevent evaporation and so help to keep the soil below moist. Mulch when the soil is wet. Never add mulch to dry soil or the mulch will draw water away from the soil instead of holding it in.

- Use ground-cover plants to fill any spaces of bare soil. Once established they look decorative and help to shade the soil and prevent it from drying out.

See also:
- *Ground cover, page 174*

Electricity in the garden

Safety pointers

The often damp conditions outdoors, and direct contact with the earth, make safety considerations vital. A fault could easily lead to a fatal accident.

- Ensure that installation work is carried out by a fully qualified professional electrician.

- Never service or work on equipment without first switching off and disconnecting from the power.

- Use only fittings and cables designed specifically for outdoor use.

- Check on the condition of cables and equipment and service them regularly.

- Use a residual-current circuit breaker on all sockets used for garden tools so that power is cut off if any thing goes wrong.

If garden lighting or a pump to power a fountain or waterfall is required, it is best to organize this early on, to avoid digging up the garden at a later date. Security lighting, if fixed to the house walls, can be run off the house supply. Some low-voltage garden lighting does not need installing, but uses cables that can be run above the ground. From a safety point of view, consider installing an outdoor socket or fitting one under cover in a garage or porch. This helps to obviate the need for lengths of cable running from within the house.

Hidden power The best way to provide permanent power in the garden is to run it underground. Either special cable must be used

▼ Electricity in the garden enables you to install water pumps and garden lighting.

or the cable must run through a galvanized steel or rigid plastic conduit. Both run in a channel well below ground level. This type of installation needs to be fitted by a professional electrician as there are strict regulations which must be met and cables and connectors must be weatherproof.

Above-ground cables Low-voltage lighting, which uses a low-voltage transformer sited under cover in an outbuilding, can often be installed with the cables running along the ground. Lay the cable where it is easily seen when you are working in the garden to avoid accidentally cutting through it. Avoid taking the cable over sharp edges like steps or paving which could damage it. If you need to join pieces of cable, use special outdoor cable connectors and for extra protection wrap these in plastic.

Outdoor socket A weather-proof socket outlet is useful, and safer, for use with power tools (such as those shown below). It must be protected by a residual-current circuit breaker (RCCB). This reacts to break the current circuit when a fault occurs or a cable is accidentally cut.

Where to use power

Garden lighting This falls into two main categories. Lighting which is installed for safety, to help find your way around the garden in the dark, or for security, to highlight and deter interlopers, may be run off the mains supply if the lights are fixed to the house walls. Cable that runs along the wall outdoors must be protected by a length of metal or plastic conduit and all fittings must be weatherproof.

If you wish to highlight the garden's decorative features, such as a shapely or colourful tree or shrub, you have the option of using underground cable or a kit that connects to a low-voltage transformer. Follow the manufacturer's instructions for connecting the light fittings to the flex.

Fountains and waterfalls An electric pump can be sited in a garden pool to provide the power for a waterfall or fountain, both of which continually recycle the same water. Pumps can run from

▲ *Free-standing lantern lights both the path and patio area. Night-time lighting can be activated just when the area is in use and as a security measure.*

the mains supply or use a low-voltage transformer. Hire a qualified electrician to install a mains-supply pump.

▲ *An elaborate and unusual water feature, powered by a simple pump, in which little frogs spurt jets of water into the lowest fountain tier.*

FORM AND SHAPE

With a strong 'skeleton' the garden will look interesting at all times of the year, even if there is the odd planting disaster. This chapter covers the materials that, together with the way they are used, make up the nuts and bolts of a garden's design.

The colour, texture and size of the paving or other materials you choose for paths and sitting areas, the way you define the boundary – whether you outline it with walls, fences or hedges, or a mixture of these – all these choices create quite different final effects. The way the space within the garden is broken up by special water features or given height with arches and pergolas contributes to its form, as does the arrangement of highlights such as containers and ornaments. Children as well as adults need to be able to enjoy the garden. And, finally, once the garden design is in place you will want to be able to sit back on comfortable and complementary furniture, with the addition of a barbecue and garden lighting, to enjoy it in all its moods, both during the day and in the evening.

Ground surfaces

Working out quantities

Paving, bricks and timber
Multiply width by length to work out the number of square metres/square yards of material that will be needed.

Gravel or shingle Multiply width by length, then by depth. One cu m/35 cu ft will cover an area of 20 sq m/215 sq ft to a depth of 5 cm/2 in.

Hard surface choices
- Concrete paving slabs
- Setts and pavers
- Stone and reconstituted stone
- Timber
- Bricks
- Cobbles
- Shingle and gravel

Soft surface choices
- Grass seed
- Turf
- Wildflower meadow
- Chamomile
- Creeping thyme
- Clover

Brick is traditional looking and hard-wearing

Timber decking gives a warmer, softer look

The materials used for paved or hard-surfaced areas and lawns, together with the shape of these key areas, are extremely important in forming both the style and the bold background outline of a garden. Paving or other hard materials provide hard surfaces, in the same way as vinyl, tiles or timber do this in a house, while the lawn creates the softer, gentler effect of a carpet.

▲ *Paving is both durable and pleasing to the eye.*

Planning paved areas

When planning the positions of areas to sit in, balance the practical use of the garden with aesthetic effect. Consider the position of the sun, the need for shade, shelter from wind, views, and privacy.

Once you have decided on the position, size and shape of a paved area use hosepipe or rope to out-line it on the ground. Allow plenty of space for chairs and tables and plant containers. Arrange furniture within the outlined area to check that it will all fit in the space com-fortably. You may need to adjust the area size to take into account the paving material you choose so that you avoid having to cut slabs.

Planting in containers, which can be moved around, is a flexible solution in paved areas.

Choosing the materials

Consider both the garden style and the materials used in the construction of the house. A paved area next to the house should have a slight fall away from the house so that rain drains away from the building rather than towards it.

Pre-cast concrete paving slabs are reasonably priced and easy to lay. They also come in a wide range of colours, shapes and finishes. Avoid a highly textured finish where you intend to use furniture. Check the change of colour when slabs are wet and how slip-resistant they are.

Bricks blend well with a traditional brick-built house and provide a natural, country effect. They can also be laid in a range of patterns. House bricks are too soft to be suitable and flake if exposed to winter weather. Choose frostproof, hardwearing bricks such as engineering bricks or brick pavers.

Setts are another small-sized and decorative alternative. Granite setts

▼ *Pebbles or other materials can be mixed with paving slabs.*

are hard-wearing, and look at home in areas where granite is the local building material. Concrete setts give a similar effect, and are cheaper. **Timber decking** is a popular surface, sympathetic to the surroundings in most gardens. Paint or stain can be used to add colour. Old railway sleepers are a very strong, and cheaper, alternative. If timber becomes dangerously slippery when wet, or in frost, staple fine chicken wire over the surface. **Stone** Sandstone, limestone, ironstone, York stone, and slate all blend well with most garden styles but these materials are expensive and difficult to lay. Reconstituted stone is cheaper. Both come as straight-sided slabs or with uneven edges to be laid as crazy paving. Alternatively you can use broken stone or concrete slabs for this. **Cobbles** are uncomfortable to walk on but ideal for forming smaller patterned areas in plain paving. **Gravel and shingle** are both cheap, easy to use and give a softer finish. But they provide some problems too. They are best retained by edging as they tend to 'walk' with you into the house and

▼ *Gravel is more suitable for pots than furniture.*

▲ *Natural stone is perfect next to an old house.*

onto the lawn, where they can create a danger when mowing. Some plants can look very effective growing through the surface, but regular weeding will be necessary or the area to be overtaken by seedlings. Laying plastic sheeting underneath the gravel helps to avoid this but holes will need to be made in the plastic for drainage.

Gravel and shingle both provide a measure of security in a front garden as any visitor's arrival is very audible.

SOFT SURFACES

A lawn from turf gives you an instant result, once the ground is prepared, and turf can be laid at most times of the year, but it is cheaper to sow a lawn. The best time to create a lawn, whichever method you use, is spring or early autumn. There are two widely available alternative grass mixes you can use. Those that include rye grass are hard-wearing and easy to care for. Garden owners who want a good-looking finish and are prepared to spend time on looking after a lawn should go for a fine, dense grass.

Alternatives to grasses are clover, camomile and creeping thyme but these are suitable only for small areas. You can also sew an area as a wildflower meadow using a mixture of recommended grass and wildflower seeds. In the first year this should be cut at two-monthly intervals so that the grass does not smother the wild flowers. After this cut only early in spring and then in the autumn once the seeds have been shed.

Mixing materials

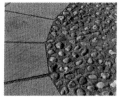

By combining materials you can create decorative effects. For instance use larger quantities of cheaper paving and provide character, pattern and design detail with small-sized, more expensive alternatives such as granite setts or cobbles to create an uneven surface. This makes a paved area or a path more interesting. Below, pebbles are introduced between areas of paving slabs on a pathway.

Lay the pebbles in spaces left between paving slabs. Fit them as closely together as you can on a bed of mortar.

Lay a stout piece of wood across the pebbles from one slab to the next to check that the pebbles are flush with the paving. If necessary tap the wood with a hammer to bed them in and ensure the surface is completely even.

Paths, steps and edgings

Laying stepping-stones

Stepping-stones that meander across a lawn are less intrusive than a path. They also provide a way of moving across gravelled areas without taking the tiny chippings with you.

Work out the positions of the stones by walking along the route the path will take. Take normal strides and mark the position of each step as you go.

Place the stones in the positions marked and check the effect visually. Walk over the stones to double-check the spacing.

Cut around each stone with a spade, to a depth slightly more than that of the stepping-stone.

Cut beneath the slice to be removed and lift the turf out.

Level the base of the cut-out space with sand Position the stone, check that it is level and just below surrounding grass to avoid damage to the mower.

Path and step choices
- Concrete paving slabs
- Setts and pavers
- Stone and reconstituted stone
- Timber and bark chippings
- Bricks
- Cobbles
- Shingle and gravel
- Grass

Edging choices
- Bricks
- Tiles
- Terracotta strips
- Timber, logs, railway sleepers
- Rocks or giant pebbles
- Low-growing plants
- Low hedges or fences
- Shells

Paths, and paved areas, highlight the design of the garden, providing definition, while the materials you use to create them enhance (or detract from) the character. Steps which lead from one level in a garden to another work in the same way, and can follow the form and materials used for the linking path or add new and interesting textures by introducing different materials. Most of the options covered in Ground surfaces – not forgetting grass, if the area will not get much wear – are also suitable for paths and steps. Edgings add definition and act as a practical divide to keep soil off paths and lawns and to contain softer path materials.

▲ *The contrast of bricks with stone can be effective for steps and raised beds.*

Providing links
Paths supply a link with each section of the garden from the house, allowing you to wander and admire as well as to work without damaging soil structure. They can be straight or meandering, but need to lead to a specific point of interest, which may be the garage or garden shed, a place to sit and relax, or a closer view of a point of special interest such as a statue, pond or group of pots. Where

paths meet there is an opportunity to create a central pattern using the same or a different material. Pebbles or bricks are ideal for this. This area can then be used to show off a sculpture, or a container holding a topiary bush or a shrub or tree.

The narrowest width advisable for a path is 30 cm/12 in. This will be wide enough for just one person to use the path. If you need to use the path for a wheelbarrow just over twice this width will be more suitable.

If a path will create too hard a line, consider using paving slabs as stepping-stones instead. These can also define a route along a path made of softer materials such as grass or gravel.

Moving from one level to another
Garden steps, both for safety and for aesthetic reasons, are best constructed as wide and shallow as possible. A flight of steps does not have to be straight.

▼ *Steps should be broad and shallow.*

▲ *Terracotta edging on a brick path.*

▲ *Plants soften the edge of a path.*

Laying timber edging

Timber edging comes as wood strips wired together. You can cut the wire to shorten the strip, or wire two lengths together.

Unwind the roll and use wire-cutters to cut it to length.

Dig out a trench for the edging, having first worked out the height you want the edging top above the ground.

Lay the edging in the trench, checking the height and that it is level along the length. Backfill with soil and firm well.

For a straight top place a length of timber over the edging strip. Use a club hammer to knock it firmly in place.

Curving steps look good and provide a range of aspects as you pass up or down them. Angle the steps slightly forward to avoid the danger of standing water.

Consider using a different material for the riser and step surfaces – for example bricks topped with stone slabs.

Edging paths, patios and beds

Edging not only defines the shape of a path, patio, flower bed or steps but it is a practical method of containing soft materials such as soil, chippings or gravel. Apart from materials made specially for the role – for example, timber

▼ *An informal combination of materials.*

edging, corrugated plastic strip and coiled terracotta – you can use hard materials such as bricks (either flat or set diagonally on edge), paving, tiles or logs, and even railway sleepers. For a purely decorative effect consider the use of large pebbles, shells or other suitable natural material.

Beds can take a softer edging with low hedges or a line of ground-hugging plants, which are ideal for showing off the shape, but to keep the soil and grass in place first fit a lawn edging strip. Make sure that the top of the strip sits just below lawn level to avoid damage to the mower.

▼ *An inventive but formal design.*

See also:
- *Ground surfaces, page 116*

Walls and screens

Building a low brick wall

Even a low wall needs to be built on a firm foundation, or footing, of hardcore and concrete.

Form the footing by excavating a 30 cm/12 in deep trench. Fill it to a 13 cm/5 in depth with consolidated hardcore. Drive in pegs as a guide for the top of the concrete and check that peg tops are level.

Complete the footings by pouring in concrete. Level it off with the peg tops. Use a piece of wood to tamp the concrete level and to remove large pockets of air. Leave to harden for a few days.

Lay the first course of bricks. Form a pier at each end by placing two bricks sideways. On a long wall you will also need to repeat piers at regular intervals.

(continued opposite)

A brick wall is the traditional way of outlining a boundary to a garden and providing it with privacy, and is long lasting and attractive to look at. It can help to keep out intruders and animals, provide shelter, or screen an ugly view. A boundary wall highlights its size and shape. To give the shape less emphasis, to make the space appear larger, or to create more interest, vary the materials used around the perimeter, or vary the wall's height. When mixing walls and fences, construct areas of fence on a low brick or stone wall to create a more integrated look. Where complete privacy is not required pierced concrete or open terracotta blocks provide another visual effect.

Walls are also used as retainers, to hold the soil in a series of stepped terraces in a sloping garden or to create a sunken area. High or retaining walls are not easy to construct and are best erected by a specialist. Materials used may be bricks, stone, reconstituted stone, flint, or concrete blocks, which can be faced

▼ *A low brick wall can make a screen or divider.*

▲ *A dry-stone wall is a haven for plants.*

with stone if preferred. A wall needs capping to protect the construction. Some choices for capping are bricks, set side-by-side across the width, concrete slabs, or some other weatherproof material.

Walls as internal dividers

Within the garden, strategically placed openwork screens can divide the garden into a series of 'rooms' with an enticing view of something interesting beyond. Alternatively, with a covering of plants, they can hide necessary eyesores, like the garden shed or dustbin, or provide privacy for a paved sitting or eating area. Apart

▼ *Raised beds can team with boundary walls.*

(continued from opposite)

▲ Trellis-work breaks up an otherwise dull surface and filters the wind.

▲ Combining painted trellis panels with picket fencing creates an original look.

Lay subsequent courses after running a ribbon of mortar along the top of the previous row. As shown, 'butter' one end of each brick before you position it.

Frequently use a spirit level to ensure bricks are level. As you work strike off any surplus mortar from the wall sides.

Firm and adjust the level of each brick as you lay it, using the handle of the bricklaying trowel.

Finally fix coping and pier caps to complete the wall and protect the brickwork from excessive moisture.

from openwork masonry walls, timber trellis, slatted wood, and even openwork wire mesh can be used to form slim dividers. Screens of this type also filter wind and sun very effectively. As they allow some air-flow they do not act as a total barrier creating eddies of wind in the way that a solid wall can do.

Low walls can edge a pond or patio, or act as a decorative divide between different areas and levels in the garden without supplying a feeling of enclosed spaces. To soften the hard lines of a wall use dry-stone walls with cracks for plants, or create a double-shell wall with a space in the centre to take soil for planting. A higher, flat-faced brick or stone wall can be used as a sheltering background for climbers and a wall that faces the sun makes a home for tender plants. Brick wall piers can act as plinths for containers of flowering plants, and wall baskets and similar containers can add the softness and colour of plants to an otherwise bleak wall.

Wall materials
- Reconstituted or natural stone
- Bricks
- Flint
- Concrete blocks
- Pierced concrete
- Pierced terracotta

Screen materials
- Timber trellis, stained or painted
- Openwork terracotta or concrete walling
- Slatted wood

GATES

An opening in the garden boundary wall, fence or hedge usually needs a gate to complete it and to keep children or pets inside the garden. Several factors help you decide what type of gate is best suited to your specific situation. The general surroundings, the purpose of the gate, and the materials used for the boundary are all involved in deciding on the best design and materials. High, closeboarded gates provide privacy and security, while low, openwork designs allow a sight of the house or a view from it. Timber or ironwork gates are popular and look best if they match the boundary in height.

See also:
- Fences, page 122
- Hedges, page 124

337

Fences

Erecting a panel fence

The simplest way to erect a fence is to set the posts in metal spikes.

Position the spike with the protective head inside the top and drive it in with a sledge-hammer. Make sure that the spike remains vertical. Check often with a spirit level.

With the post in position in the spike top, check that this is absolutely vertical.

Lay the first panel in position, next to the post, and mark the spot for the next post spike. Drive the spike in as before.

continued opposite)

Fences are a quick and cheap alternative to walls. They act as windbreaks, hide an ugly view and outline a boundary. Height provides privacy but high walls or fences throw long shadows, keeping off sun and rain, which can be a major problem in a small space. While hedges and trellis filter the wind and reduce its strength, wind is only diverted by a solid barrier. A lower fence, topped with trellis and covered in climbing plants, provides a better alternative and still gives privacy.

▲ *A closeboard panelled fence.*

Fences make an instant boundary, take little space and provide instant privacy. They are erected on posts which may be of wood, concrete or metal. These can be fixed into the ground directly, set into concrete, attached to a concrete spur or pushed into the top of a metal spike driven into the ground. In the two latter methods a timber post is not in contact with the soil and so is likely to last longer. Concrete posts are the longest-lasting but are visually less compatible with timber fencing.

Style options
Fences come in a wide range of materials and designs to suit every situation and type of garden.

Panel fencing is the simplest high fence to construct and is cheap to buy. There are two designs, overlapped and interwoven. The overlapped panels provide more privacy. Panels of either design are fixed to posts but are not very strong and are difficult to repair.

Closeboard fencing is tougher and can be made to any height. It is made from overlapped boards held into position on horizontal, triangular-shaped rails. The best method of construction for both types includes a gravel board. This runs along the bottom to protect the board ends from damp, and is easy to replace. The top edge of a closeboard fence can be straight or shaped between posts.

Woven hurdles are used in the classic cottage-garden fence. Hurdles come in a range of heights and are usually made from pliable stems of willow or hazel (which is coarser), which are woven in and out of stouter upright stems. Hurdles are not long-lasting but are easily portable and provide a good temporary barrier while shrubs or a hedge grow.

▼ *Woven hazel hurdles as fencing.*

▲ *Diagonally set timber gives a contemporary look.*

▲ *Picket fencing is a country classic.*

(continued from opposite)

Nail panel brackets to the first post. Nail matching brackets to the second post, then remove the second post temporarily.

Picket fencing, either stained or painted white, provides a good, low boundary for a front garden. It is constructed in a similar way to closeboard fencing but with spaces between the uprights. The top edge of each upright may be rounded, pointed or cut in any design.

Post and rail baffle, or ranch fencing, is simpler in design, constructed from posts linked with two or three horizontal rails. Wire is often fixed between the rails in country areas to keep animals out.

Wire with concrete posts forms the simplest of designs. To hide the basic structure plant fast-growing evergreen climbers along its length. Plastic-coated chain link or chicken wire provides additional plant supports.

Plastic fencing is an easy-maintenance option but is not as strong as most other materials. Available in ranch style or as post and plastic-coated chain.

Trellis fencing comes in a wide range of widths, heights and thicknesses, in both timber and plastic and in square or diamond shapes. Expanding trellis is also available but is not very strong. Trellis makes an excellent internal divider. It can also form attractive open areas in a tall boundary fence and can be fixed to the top of a wall or fence to give extra height for climbing plants.

Position the panel and get someone to hold it while you position the second post. Check the panel is horizontal, then nail into it through the brackets.

Nail a post cap to the top of each post to complete the fence.

Materials choice
• Timber, metal or plastic

Style choices
• Woven panels
• Closeboard
• Wattle hurdles
• Picket fencing
• Post and rail fencing
• Trellis

See also:
• Walls and screens, page 120
• Hedges, page 124

▼ *Post and rail fencing is available in rural or more cultivated style (as shown).*

▼ *Diamond-shaped trellis panels finish off this opening in a plain fence.*

Hedges

Planting a hedge

Before you plant a hedge it is important to prepare the ground well. Dig a trench and, to improve the soil's structure, dig in lots of garden compost or well-rotted manure. The prepared strip needs to be at least 60 cm/2 ft wide. Before planting break down large clumps of earth and sprinkle on a balanced garden fertilizer. If planting in autumn or winter use a slow-acting fertilizer.

Caring for bought plants
Hedging plants are often sold in bundles of bare-rooted plants. Keep the roots moist, for example by placing them in a temporary planting hole. Separate them as you plant.

To ensure a straight hedge use a garden line and insert markers spaced as recommended for each plant. Do not place too close together when there is a risk that individual plants may die. In a windy situation or on a boundary stagger the planting of the trees as shown here.

(continued opposite)

Hedges can mark a boundary, divide the garden into smaller, spaces or form a low, neat outline to formal beds. They can protect plants from adverse weather, deter burglars, help to lower noise levels and attract wildlife. Hedges rarely collapse in a storm in the way that fences, or even walls, can do.

Formal hedges

Clipped, compact evergreen hedges look much the same throughout the year and are ideal for creating a formal outline in or around the garden. They provide a good backdrop for flowers and plants. These hedges need regular clipping to maintain their shape.

The traditionally grown plants for evergreen hedges are privet, yew, laurel, and box. Conifers are also commonly used. Avoid fast-growing Leyland cypress and go for slower-growing alternatives such as *Chamaecyparis lawsoniana* 'Ellwoodii', which will produce a more satisfactory hedge. For neat, low hedges there is the dwarf box, *Buxus sempervirens* 'Suffruticosa'.

Less formal effects

There is a wide range of flowering and fruiting shrubs that can be

▼ *A clipped yew hedge is always attractive.*

trained to form decorative but looser-growing hedges. For spring colour go for forsythia with its sunny yellow flowers that appear before the leaves. For a low hedge *Berberis thunbergii* 'Atropurpurea' has purple-bronze foliage turning a rich red in autumn. Hornbeam, *Carpinos betrays*, has yellow or green catkins in spring and turns a yellow-orange in autumn before the leaves fall. Beech, *Fagus sylvatica*, can provide a formal or informal outline depending on how you trim it. Although it is deciduous, the autumn leaves often remain on the hedge all winter; the copper beech, *F. s. purpurea*, has purple leaves that turn a deep, rich copper colour in autumn.

Plant a mixed hedge for a traditional country look and to attract a wide range of birds who will enjoy the food, protection and

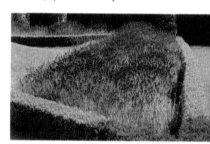

▲ *A box hedge encloses a lavender bed.*

nesting potential. Country hedges may include some of the following: hawthorn and black-thorn, hazel, beech, holly, spindle, privet, dog-wood, dog roses, honeysuckle and guelder rose.

Hedges for security

Thick, prickly hedges form ideal

▲ *A country hedge is laid to become thick and impenetrable.*

▲ Rosa rugosa *is usually still in flower when the first hips ripen.*

(continued from opposite)

Dig a large hole for each plant and position it, spreading out the roots. Fill the hole with soil and firm it well.

Finally rake the soil level and water plants thoroughly. Keep well watered for the first season.

deterrents to unwanted visitors if you plant them along road-sides or bordering a front garden. The common holly, *Ilex aquifolium*, is excellent for this. For a variegated form choose 'Ferox Argentea' with cream-edged leaves or 'Golden Queen' with golden margins. *Berberis* x *stenophylla*, also dense and thorny, is a colourful alternative, with its gold flowers in spring and purple-red leaves.

A rose hedge can be both decorative and extremely prickly. Choose *Rosa rugosa* varieties for their closely prickled stems. Many also have flowers with a beautiful scent and large red hips in autumn. The flowers come in white, yellow, and tones of pink through to deep crimson. *Berberis thunbergii* is also

thorny but grows to only about 1 m/3 ft high. Its fresh green leaves below, turn orange in autumn and it has red-tinged, pale yellow flowers and red fruit. Hawthorn, *Crataegus monogyna*, is also suitable and has white or pink-tinged flowers in spring followed by red fruit.

▲ *A fuchsia hedge, is an attractive alternative to a formal clipped hedge.*

Some hedge plant choices
Evergreen hedges
- Box, *Buxus sempervirens*
  Holly, *Ilex aquifolium*
- Viburnum, *V. tinus*
- Cedar, *Thuja occidentalis*
- Laurel, *Prunus lusitanica*
- Yew, *Taxus baccata*
- Privet, *Ligustrum ovalifolium*

Colourful hedges
- Rose, *Rosa rugosa*
- Hawthorn, *Crataegus monogyna*
- Cotoneaster species
- Hornbeam, *Carpinus betulus*
- Escallonia varieties
- Mexican orange blossom, *Choisya ternata*

Low herbal hedges
- Lavender, *Lavandula* species
- Sage, *Salvia* species
- Cotton lavender, *Santolina chamaecyparissus*
- Rosemary, such as *Rosmarinus officinalis* 'Severn Sea'
- Hyssop, *Hyssopus officinalis*

FORMING A FEDGE

A fedge is a combination of fence and hedge and is a good way of creating the effect of a hedge in a narrow space. Plant ivies about 2.5–3 m/8–10 ft apart against a fence until they intermingle to form a dense cover over the framework, then clip to control growth. The traditional hedge is made by pushing in and weaving willow stems, which soon root and grow to form a narrow, green barrier.

BEWARE FAST-GROWING HEDGES

The fast-growing Leyland cypress, *Cupressocyparis leylandii*, is not really suitable for a small garden, particularly if you wish to remain on good terms with your neighbours. The advantage of its speedy growth is outweighed by the fact that it does not simply stop when it reaches the required height but continues on apace and so needs topping as well as trimming every year.

See also:
- Fertilizers, page 105
- Digging, page 107

Introducing water

Creating a pond

A pre-formed shape enables you to install a pond very quickly, and little skill is required.

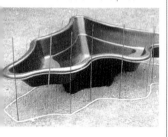

Place the pre-formed pond on the ground and mark out its outline with canes. Lay rope around the canes to mark the shape.

Dig out the the pond area, taking into account shelves and changes in depth. Make your hole slightly bigger than the shape.

To check depth measure down from a plank across the hole. Use a spirit level placed on the plank to check that the pond is also level.

(continued opposite)

There is room for a pond or pool in the smallest garden. Although a larger pond creates a light-reflecting focal point, a waterproof tub can hold a miniature pond where space is at a premium.

The pond should be situated in an open, sunny spot. Overhanging trees cast shadows which prevent water plants from flourishing and their falling leaves create problems.

The next decision is whether to go for a formal or informal effect. An informal pond is best sited where a natural pond would occur: that is in a low-lying area of the garden. If you wish to place it elsewhere, build up the background, using the excavated soil, to create a bank or rockery behind. On the other hand, a formal pond sits well in the centre of a paved area, or a lawn. A series of interlocking ponds creates a stunning water garden. Fountains and waterfalls, using a pumped recycling system, will keep the water in good condition, whereas care needs to be taken to balance a still pond if the water is to remain crystal clear.

▼ *To get a natural effect, place the pond in the lowest part of the garden.*

▲ *A tub can be made into a pond.*

Formal effect

In a symmetrically planned formal garden simple rectangular, square or round ponds look most in keeping, although a semi-circular pond placed against a wall or fence on the patio can also fit into the design. Formal pools can be raised, with a surrounding wall providing a seat. This is ideal for a pond on a patio. Alternatively the pond can be sunk into the ground.

Use a pond to alter the apparent shape of a garden. A long, narrow pond placed across the width in a long, narrow garden will help to make the space appear wider. Or, equally effective, take the pond almost from one side of the garden to the other at an angle. A walkway across the water can lead you from one area to the next.

The natural look

An informal pond needs to look as natural as possible, in both

MINIATURE PONDS

Wooden tubs, old sinks, plastic plant containers, fish tanks are all suitable. The pond can either be sunk into the ground or placed on top of it. If you add a 15 cm/6 in layer of compost to the base you can plant a small water lily and one – possibly two – aquatics. Cover the soil with a layer of gravel and add a few large pebbles, then fill with water.

▲ *For a natural look use a liner.*

shape and surroundings. Liners should be black or brown. Natural ponds looks smaller once planted, so allow for this in your choice of size. If you want the water to attract wildlife take grass right up to the edge and provide a shallow beach at one end to make it easy for animals to enter and leave the water. Birds will use this area for drinking and bathing.

Pond-making materials

The simplest way to construct a sunken pond is to use either a pre-formed shape or a flexible liner. Buy the best quality material you can afford as once the pond is installed it becomes a major problem to fix leaks. A flexible liner gives more freedom as you can make the pond any shape you like. If you want to

▼ *A stone surround finishes off the pond and keeps the lining anchored.*

add fish or larger waterlilies you will need a depth, in part of the pond, of 45–60 cm/18–24 in. Shelves around the edge allow you to include marginal plants which thrive in shallow water.

A sunken formal pond can also be created using these materials. A raised pond is usually constructed using concrete for the base and tough external bricks or reinforced concrete blocks for the sides.

Pond edgings

With lined ponds it is important to cover the pond edge to create a natural finish. If you use paving, tuck the liner underneath the slabs and allow the paving to overlap above the water. If you run grass right up to the pond edge the flap of the liner should be turned down and buried so that the grass has soil to grow in. Allow the grass edge to meet the water and hide the liner. Pebbles also create a natural-looking outline.

POND SAFETY

Avoid ponds while you have small children. It is possible to drown in very shallow water. Instead, consider installing a wall-fixed recycling fountain. A mill-stone or a low basin of pebbles, where water jets out then trickles over the surface, are also suitable.

(continued from opposite)

Place the pool in the hole and check that the edges are completely level from all angles, using the plank and spirit level

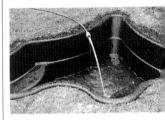

When the pond is snugly in place run water into it, packing fine soil around the edges as the water level rises. Finally push soil firmly under the shelves, ramming it down with a piece of wood.

Material choices
- Pliable plastic or rubber liner
- Pre-formed rigid liner
- Concrete raised pool

Miniature pond containers
- Half-barrel
- Trough
- Saucer-shaped stone or concrete container
- Plastic or other waterproof container

See also:
- *Moving water, page 128*
- *Water plants, page 178*

343

Moving water

Choosing a pump

A pump is needed to provide the power to circulate the water for a waterfall or fountain. Pumps can either be submersible, sited in the water or surface-fixed nearby, in which case they need a housing to protect them.

Submersible pumps are less powerful but deal adequately with most fountains up to about 1.2 m/4 ft high or a small waterfall. They work silently, and low voltage models can be connected to the house electricity supply.

Surface pumps are more powerful, and with a surface pump a range of fountains and waterfalls can be run from one system. The pump and its housing should be positioned as close to the pond as possible so that only short lengths of tube are necessary.

When buying materials for a water feature, discuss with the suppliers exactly what effect you want to create. They will then be in the best position to advise you on the pump most suited to the effect you wish to achieve.

Moving water features
- Fountain
- Waterfall
- Cascade
- Millstone
- Bridges, stepping stones, and walkways

Moving water provides exciting effects and creates a tranquil atmosphere. A fountain, tumbling stream, or waterfall all provide the tinkling sound of moving water. Water-garden centres, television gardening programmes and

▲ *A multi-bowl fountain.*

specialist water-garden books, provide inspirational ideas on ways to use moving water. Some novel ideas include vertical falls of water which stream down light-reflecting backdrops, and slow-drip bamboo pipes, as well as the more traditional tumbling streams and gullies. You will need to install a pump for moving water features.

There are innovative fountain heads using almost any shape or material through which a pipe can be threaded, as well as specially produced animals, heads, figures, shells and flowers.

Fountains These are the simplest moving-water structures to fit and usually suit a formal area or formal pond best. A fountain can be an independent feature of single or multi-storey bowls where water falls from a head at the top to ever-larger dishes set one below the other. In this case no extra work is needed except to site the fountain and set up the electricity required to power it and recirculate the water. A fountain added to a garden pond can be positioned centrally in the pond or placed at the edge. Bear in mind that it will look most effective if it is in scale with the pond. A large ornament and wide-spreading jet of water will look incongruous in a small pond and vice versa.

According to the head you choose, water from a fountain can appear in a wide number of shapes from a single spout to multi-tiered sprays, whirls, bells, fishtails and geysers. Fountain kits are available which include a fountain jet, a flow adjuster to alter the speed of the water, and a submersible pump. The pump should be positioned on

▼ *Water spilling into a trough over wood in tiers stimulates thinking.*

▲ Water cascading over stone ledges needs a natural-looking setting.

a brick or other block to keep it raised above the bottom of the pond. The electricity to power the system can either be taken direct from the mains or make use of a low-voltage connector.

Waterfalls and cascades Waterfalls look best in a natural setting. The soil excavated from the pond can be used to form the base for a rocky outcrop from which the water tumbles in tiers. A waterfall can be built from the same materials used in making a pond. Additional rocks and stones embedded in the

surface give a more natural finish. Pre-formed stream sections are available. The distance from the pond surface to the top step of the waterfall should be no greater than 90 cm/36 in. Get advice on the most suitable pump for the job when planning the design.

Millstone and pebble fountains Water spouting out of the centre of a millstone or falling to over a layer of pebbles creates an effective small-sized feature. These usually come as a kit and are simple to install. Wall-fixed fountains for use indoors or outside can enliven the end of a small terrace or pathway. For a stronger impression use a wall-fixed fountain that sprays the water into a larger semi-circular pond below.

Bridges, walkways and stepping stones A series of interlocking ponds creates a stunning water feature. Ponds can go from one side of the garden to the other, provided a safe method of crossing the water is included in the design.

Ornamental timber bridges are the traditional method used but flatter concrete or timber walkways on a level with the pond edges, or stepping stones of slabs, provide a less obvious route.

▲ A millstone fountain takes very little space. The gurgling sound of the water bubbling up from the centre is soothing and water brings a shine to the surrounding stones.

▲ An arched timber bridge is the traditional way to cross a pond or garden stream although there are plenty of equally attractive alternatives.

POND LIFE AND MOVING WATER

Fish benefit from the introduction of a fountain or waterfall. The splashing increases the oxygen in the water and the rate at which carbon dioxide is released, and helps to stop ponds from freezing over. Waterlilies and surface plants, plus some deep-water aquatics, are best kept away from splashes and turbulent water. Waterlilies need warm, static water, and are damaged by constant splashing which submerges the flowers and rots pads.

Plant frameworks

(continued opposite)

Some simple plant supports

Lines of crossed canes set in pairs in a row give support to runner beans or sweet peas. Tie pairs together near the top, then slide a long horizontal cane into the 'V' and secure.

Wigwams of tall canes arranged in a circle are pulled together at the top and tied in place with string. You can also use a specially produced holder (above) through which the canes are pushed which holds them evenly spaced.

In small gardens utilize vertical surfaces as frameworks to grow plants. Walls and fences are obvious choices but free-standing structures covered in plants can enhance the garden's design, providing colour at a higher level and supporting plant stems at the same time. Climbing plants may be trained up timber trellis, wire, plastic or twine to clothe walls or fences, and the use of cane wigwams, ornamental obelisks or metal corkscrews allows you to add extra height wherever you feel it is required, without the need of a wall. Herbaceous plants form the best shapes and remain *in situ* in windy weather if supported by wire frames or twig cages.

Unobtrusive or deliberately decorative

Frameworks may be unobtrusive, simply holding a plant in place, and can be home-made from bamboo canes, plant sticks or stems and twigs cut down in the garden. They can also be very decorative in their own right if they are woven in arched or wigwam shapes. Metal corkscrews, timber obelisks, metal or timber arches and pergolas create strong features as part of a garden's design. Tall and decorative supports such as obelisks, wigwams and corkscrews add height attractively to an area of low growing plants. Arches and pergolas can divide up a garden, forming a number of separate areas, each with a different theme or colour scheme. A strategically placed support densely planted with climbers can also hide an eyesore.

Home-made frames

Supports made from natural plant stems, saplings or twigs are less obtrusive than manufactured alternatives. Willow, hazel, birch or any other supple wood, can be bent and used to create a support as an alternative to more rigid vertical bamboo canes and pea sticks. A circle of canes is easily arranged

▲ *A wooden framework for climbers is a shady sitting area.*

▲ *A climber grows around the front door giving height to this garden.*

346

▲ An obelisk makes a pretty focal point.

to form a wigwam with the cane tops tied together. If a string is wound around the poles in a spiral effect, plants are more easily trained and the result can be very decorative. Place the canes in a circle of at least 75 cm/30 in diameter. If extra strength is required for robust climbers add a central stick and use canes of larger diameter. A double line of angled canes, the pairs crossed at the top with a horizontal pole placed in the V forms a straight barrier and support for a row of climbers such as sweet peas or runner beans.

Shorter twiggy stems, pushed well into the soil in a circle or square and intertwined, make a cage shape which is a good support for herbaceous plants. Provided

QUICK-GROWING COLOURFUL CLIMBERS

Clematis hybrids • Runner beans
• Canary creeper • Sweet peas
• Nasturtiums • Morning glory
• Honeysuckle • Golden hop • Ivy

▲ The framework for climbing plants can be an ornamental feature in itself.

the cage is positioned early on in the growing season the plants will happily grow through the support to hide it as it keeps them in shape.

Supports to buy
A wide range of metal supports is available to suit many plant shapes, heights and arrangements. Most last longer than home-made alternatives. Some are designed to blend into the background as the plants grow. In others, such as obelisks and metal spirals, the frame itself forms an important part of the final effect and looks best if it is not completely obliterated by plant life.

▼ Climbing roses on the verandah posts enhance this timber structure.

Twiggy sticks can be pushed well into the ground to support plants. Insert them early on to allow the plants to grow up through them.

Metal supports come in a wide range of sizes and can be linked together to suit individual plants.

A sturdy stake, hammered well into the ground, is needed to support most trees. Use a special tree tie that holds the stem away from the stake, thus avoiding any damage to the stem.

Choice of plant supports
• Walls and fences
• Arches and pergolas
• Wigwams
• Crossed canes
• Herbaceous plant frames
• Metal corkscrews
• Obelisks
• Trellises or wires fixed to fences or walls

Arches, pergolas and arbours

Building a rustic arch

These tips on building an arch could also be followed to construct an arbour.

Sketch a design on paper. To suit your situation and the height and width you require.

When fixing a horizontal section to an upright use this basic joint.

Where two pieces cross, mark the position and cut halving joints in each one, using a saw and chisel.

Use wood glue and a rust-proof nail to hold each joint.

(continued opposite)

Arches, pergolas and arbours add a new dimension to a garden. They also provide a perfect opportunity to grow a wide range of climbing plants.

▲ *Tubular metal arches such as this can be bought as ready-made units.*

Arches come in a range of shapes which may be round-topped, pointed or square. An arch may be to frame a view or lead the way from the house to the patio, or can highlight the entrance to a pathway or the route beyond a fence or hedge. A row of arches may be lined up along a path.

A pergola is a larger structure made up of a series of joined arches. This may form a single divide between one area of the garden and another but it is commonly made of a double row of uprights held together by roof struts and placed to span a path or form a covering for a patio. A pergola can also be attached along one side to a wall or fence.

Depending on where it is sited, an arbour is a partially enclosed space that may be a garden hideaway, a place in which to sit in private, or a ring-side seat from which the whole garden can be viewed. An arbour or a pergola can be made more rainproof by adding a translucent roofing material to the top.

Construction materials

Arches, pergolas and arbours all form a striking part of a garden's design and look most in keeping if they suit the house and the garden's style. Stained or painted squared-off timber is popular for modern situations, while rustic poles are often used to recreate a country-garden style. These can have the bark removed to help prevent rot and insect infestation or left on to attract small insect-eating birds. Iron or tubular steel with a galvanised, painted or plastic coated finish can also be used. For a longlasting, but more expensive, alternative brick or stone

▼ *This timber pergola crowned with roses adds a vertical element.*

SCENTED CLIMBERS

Include some of these scented plants amongst those you choose to clothe arches, pergolas and arbours.

Honeysuckle Common honeysuckle, *Lonicera periclymenum*, has white to yellow flowers in mid- to late summer, followed by bright red berries. *L. hildebrandiana* is evergreen or semi-evergreen with fragrant cream-white flowers in summer, also followed by red berries (which are poisonous).

Jasmine Common summer jasmine, *Jasminum officinale* has white flowers in mid- to late summer. *J. beesianum* is evergreen with fragrant pink-red flowers in early and midsummer.

Rambler and climbing roses 'Etoile de Hollande' is a climbing rose with dark crimson, fragrant flowers, 'Sutter's Gold' blooms early with yellow, pink-veined flowers, and 'Compassion' has salmon pink to apricot flowers in summer. 'Felicite et Perpétue' has small, double, pale pink to white flowers.

Bird's mouth joints are useful for connecting horizontal or diagonal pieces to uprights. First mark the position carefully then cut out a V-shape about 2.5 cm/1 in deep in one piece and saw the second piece to fit. Drive a nail diagonally through the joint.

uprights may be built and married up with timber roof struts. Garden seats with a built in arch can be placed against a solid background, forming a simple arbour.

Arches, pergolas and arbours can be made on site or bought in a range of sizes already to be easily erected on site. In most cases you will need to allow for poles which are at least 60 cm/24 in longer than the height required, to provide a fixing into the ground. A span of about 1 m/3–4 ft is about the widest suitable for an arch.

Siting an arbour

An arbour is usually sited in a sunny spot, with the frame and plants providing shade. In a windy situation it is best to site an arbour with its back to a wall, fence or hedge to provide protection. The structure can be positioned parallel with a side or end boundary, run diagonally across a corner, or sited centrally within an open space.

As a seat is the central ingredient of an arbour decide on its size and shape first, then construct around it. The frame material and thickness need to be strong enough to take the span required and also to support vigorous climbers. Draw up a rough sketch of the design you

▲ *A white arbour with a built-in seat.*

prefer. Include the measurements and take this with you when buying the materials so that you can obtain advice on the thicknesses required. The frame will soon be transformed by clambering plants to make an enclosed space. Scented climbers will make sitting in the arbour a special pleasure.

QUICK COVER-UPS

Your chosen climbers may take some time to get established. While they are growing, sow seeds of annuals such as morning glory, *Ipomoea indica*, which has rich blue flowers; sweet peas, *Lathyrus odoratus*; or the cup-and-saucer plant, *Cobaea scandens*, which has bell-shaped flowers that open creamy green and age to a deep purple, followed by large, decorative seed heads.

(continued from opposite)

Assemble each arch side and the top separately on the ground first. Insert the uprights in already prepared holes, fix temporarily with wooden struts, then drill and screw the top in position. Secure the uprights firmly.

Materials choice
- Sawn timber
- Rustic poles
- Wrought iron
- Tubular steel – galvanized, painted or plastic-coated
- Posts of brick or stone

Containers

Container plant care

Plants grown in containers need a little extra care if they are to flourish and reward you with a constant show of colour. In hot, dry weather water at least once, and if possible twice, a day.

Watering Water retaining granules in the compost can save on watering. A hosepipe makes watering a number of containers relatively quick and easy. For out-of-reach hanging baskets use a lance attachment, compression sprayer or special basket pump. Alternatively, attach a cane to the hose end to lengthen it and keep it rigidly upright.

Feeding To avoid having to feed regularly use a slow-release or controlled-release fertilizer and add it to the compost when you plant the container.

For shrubs and trees sprinkle either of the above fertilizers on the surface in spring, then fork lightly into the compost surface.

(continued opposite)

Plant-filled containers are a must for roof gardens and balconies. They are very versatile, allowing you to clothe a wall in colour or transform an area of the garden.

Containers can lead the eye down a pathway, highlight a paved sitting area, to create a welcoming doorway or line a row of steps. Hanging baskets and window boxes add colour and greenery at a higher level. By grouping different sizes of containers you can create a 'bed' of colour in any area or, conversely, you can use a beautifully shaped container-grown shrub or tree to form a focal point. By under-planting a container-grown tree or shrub you can add a splash of temporary colour when needed.

Plants in smaller pots can be moved about. Tender plants grown in pots can be transferred to a more sheltered spot in colder weather. Pot-grown annuals can be partially immersed in a flower bed when added colour is required, then easily removed and transferred elsewhere.

▲ *A rough-hewn stone trough.*

Choosing containers

Plastic and fibreglass containers are cheap and come in a wide range of shapes and sizes. They are lighter than most of the alternatives and therefore ideal for roof gardens and balconies. Fibreglass, often made to imitate lead, is the stronger and more durable of the two. With careful planting a plastic container can almost disappear behind the contents, or you can use paint to antique or decorate the outside. Check before buying that a plastic container is suitable for use outdoors.

▲ *Terracotta pots come in a range of shapes and sizes.*

▲ *Potted plants can be moved in the winter for frost protection.*

▲ Regular watering and feeding aids growth, which soon hides the container.

▲ Window boxes make a mini garden but must be securely fixed.

(continued from opposite)

Terracotta pots come in a range of shapes and sizes, from plain clay pots to those with ornate raised patterns, as well as urns with handles and those with side pockets for planting. Earth or compost in terracotta dries out quickly in hot weather so check plants regularly. Ensure the terracotta is frost-proof as it can flake or crack in freezing weather. In winter do not use water-retaining saucers as the water may freeze and crack the pot.

Wooden tubs, half-barrels, and troughs can look rustic or classic depending on the shape and finish. Timber will rot but if treated with paint or a plant-friendly preservative its life can be extended. Lining a wooden container with plastic will also lengthen its life.

Large baskets have become popular because they make unusual and reasonably priced containers. Prolong a basket's short life by oiling it well before planting. Cover the bottom of the basket with cut-down plastic plant-pot bases to keep the soil off the basketware and line it with plastic in which drainage holes have been made.

Glazed pots in bright colours are easily available. Not all are frost-

proof, so check when buying. Choose a colour to complement the intended contents.

Concrete is a cheaper alternative to reconstituted stone. To age a new exterior spread it with yoghurt to encourage algae to grow.

Window boxes come in all the materials mentioned above and look most effective when plants cascade over the sides and conceal the container. Boxes filled with compost are very heavy and need to be securely fixed in position.

Recycled containers Many holders can be transformed into plant containers. They need to be deep enough and should have a base that can take drainage holes. Suitable plant containers are chimney pots, clay land drains, buckets, paint pots with all paint removed, and wheelbarrows.

Hanging baskets and wall troughs may be made of plastic-coated or plain wire, of iron, basketwork or solid plastic. Liners are available in many types of materials. Baskets look best when young plants are inserted in the sides as well as the top so that the plants grow to form a flowering ball.

Routine care Once a week check containers, dead-head flowers, remove yellowing leaves and those that show signs of pests or disease. Control pests and disease as soon as you find them.

Container choices
- Plastic
- Fibreglass
- Timber
- Concrete
- Reconstituted stone
- Terracotta
- Glazed pots
- Baskets
- Buckets
- Chimney pots and clay drains

See also:
- *Ornamental extras, pages 136–7*

▼ A wooden half-barrel can make an ideal container for a small conifer and colourful pansies.

Ornamental extras

Tips on disguising an eyesore

- A carefully positioned upright tree can obscure a power pole. Have someone help you position the tree until the best planting position is found.

- Climbers grown up trellis will soon hide a fixture such as a garden shed, dustbin area or coal bunker.

- Grow climbing roses up a chicken-wire framework to hide drain pipes. The thorns deter burglars and other intruders.

- Stand a low pot containing trailing annuals on a man hole cover to hide it, or buy a specially designed bowl-shaped cover which can be planted but still removed if necessary.

- Use a pergola to hide an ugly overhead view, with a fastgrowing climber forming a roof.

Ornamental choices

- Classic figures
- Birdbaths
- Wildlife and pet sculpture
- Water features
- Beach bounty
- Rocks and pebbles
- Logs and tree stumps

▲ Stone mushrooms– a fun feature on the lawn.

A well-positioned ornament or decorative feature will add the final touch to your garden. This kind of feature gives a small garden its final flourish, and can provide extra interest, an element of surprise or even amusement. It may be a

▲ A classical urn for timeless elegance.

traditional stone figure, a decorative urn or a modern sculpture or something entirely natural, such as a group of giant stones, a heap of logs or sea-washed driftwood and shells. It may add a touch of humour – plastic decoy ducks on a pond, a concrete cat sitting amongst the catmint or life-sized metal birds pecking at the lawn.

Choosing the right site

Positioning is all-important. Drawing the eye, a focal feature can be placed where it is instantly seen centre stage in the garden or can be placed where it is instantly seen centre stage in the garden. Hidden around a corner, a light-coloured ornament set on a plinth amongst shrubs provides a surprise and brings life to a dull spot. At the end of a path, forming the view that draws you on, a figure can be set beneath an arch.

An ornament also needs to work with its surroundings. Bear in mind both plants and surface materials used in the spot where you want to place it. Be flexible about the position, moving the object around until you are sure that you have found the best place for it. Groups of pots, natural materials, figures or gnomes will create an interesting focus. Take time to arrange the positions until you are happy with the overall result.

Range of choices

Make sure that the container is suitable for all weather conditions.

Pots and urns Glazed pots are available in rich tones, ideal for providing colour and texture to an overshadowed part of the garden. Classic terracotta urns with handles, or narrow-necked tall, slim jars also make perfect focal points on their own or grouped, perhaps with one lying on its side.

Classic figures in traditional designs are produced in reconstituted stone or concrete, or in fibreglass with a finish that looks like lead.

Animals and birds specially made for outdoor displays come in concrete, metal and plastic. Arrange water birds around or in a pond, animals under a tree or amongst low plants in a bed.

▲ A metal resin lizard wall fountain.

Birdbaths, birdtables and sundials combine usefulness and decoration.

Water features A small moving-water feature immediately forms a focal point. Many preformed designs are available or you can construct your own. The only requirements are a drainage hole in the base and matching hole in the top section so that the water can be circulated, and a position for the pump. Use an urn on its side to drip or pour water into a shallow saucer as part of a small water feature.

▲ An armillary sphere that is also a sun-dial.

Garden gnomes Colourful, cheerful and eye-catching, gnomes make a strong and humorous focus wherever they are positioned, alone or in a group.

Natural materials Some of the most effective garden ornaments are designed by nature and available free to be picked up on the beach or in the woods. Smooth, colourful pebbles, big pieces of stone, a group of scallop or spiral shells and driftwood can be used to enhance a water feature. Tree stumps, cones and logs add interest to a woodland area.

▲ A garden elf water feature adds winsome humour in a green pond-side corner. Water features like this and the one shown top left are relatively simple to install.

▲ These 'stone' birds are made of fibreglass.

▲ This inventive yet realistic bird is made from recycled pieces of metal welded together.

▲ This wooden bird house provides a striking feature whilst taking up little space.

Children's play space

Safety points

In a garden where there are small children their safety is paramount and the following points should always be considered.

- Position play features so that they are clearly visible from the house, so that you can keep a watchful eye on what goes on from indoors.

- Keep chemicals and garden tools locked away. Ensure that the garden shed is always kept locked, or erect a special locked cupboard in the garage.

- When in use make sure that electric cables on garden tools are easily seen, and use a residual-current circuit breaker on all sockets used for garden tools. Ensure that power tools are never left unattended.

- Check gates and fences regularly to make sure that they remain child-proof.

- Never leave small children playing unattended near a pond or water.

- Ensure that the garden contains no poisonous plants. Foxglove, deadly nightshade, laburnum, ivy, caster-oil plant, lily of the valley, rhododendron, oleander are just a few to be avoided. Most fungi are best eradicated.

- For a safe landing under swings and climbing frames use a thick layer (10–15 cm/ 4–6 in) of pulverized bark.

Play structures
- Sandpit
- Swing
- Climbing frame
- Playhouse
- Personal garden

Fine weather draws children, like a magnet, outdoors to enjoy the freedom of space. If you provide a range of exciting play choices to stimulate the imagination they will be happily occupied for hours. In a small garden there is rarely room for a completely separate area for children's play projects. If you don't

▲ This all-in-one play structure would keep any child happy for hours.

want play structures to overpower a small garden consider position and materials at the design stage, along with the needs of all of the family, so that sandpits, swings, climbing frames or playhouses can be built to blend in, using materials that appear elsewhere in the garden.

Lawns need to be tough if they are to endure energetic play so use a high percentage of perennial rye-grass, which can survive the rigours of pounding feet.

The garden provides a wonderful first insight for small children into the world of nature. Take time to explain how wildlife and plants of the garden live and grow. Involve children in the siting and fixing of

bird tables and nesting boxes, as well as feeding the birds. This provides a useful introduction to looking after pets responsibly. Involve the child when choosing an area of the garden specially put aside for him where he can grow his own plants from seed. Quick-result plants such as sunflowers and sweet peas are a good choice, as are beans, carrots, lettuces and spinach which can be picked, cooked and eaten.

Structures that adapt
Flexibility is important as children's requirements change quickly and play structures soon fall out of use. With some forethought equipment can be erected with the future in mind, so that a play space can take up a new role when the children lose interest in using it.

Swing A well-constructed archway can form a sturdy frame for a swing. Provide a surface of grass or bark chippings for safety. When the swing is no longer in use the arch can form a frame for climbers and soon become a decorative feature.

Sandpit Dig out an area large enough to take sand construction projects of buildings, boats, or whatever catches the imagination. A sturdy surround will help to keep the sand in place, but avoid sharp-edged materials and use sawn logs with the bark removed. If you form the sandpit in an interesting shape the framework can be used to edge a flower bed or pond when the sand is removed.

Climbing frame If you need to fell a tree at any time this could easily become part of an exciting natural frame. Add platform, steps and swings to create extra stimulus. A mature tree in the garden begs to become a climbing frame and will undoubtedly be used, so it pays to add rope ladders and platforms that make it a safer spot to play.

Alternatively construct a climbing frame as part of a pergola or build it with a future use as a pergola in mind. A thick layer of bark chippings, extending well beyond the frame, provides the safest ground surface.

Playhouses Playhouses provide hours of fun and form the inspiration for all sorts of fantasy situations. Adapt a small garden shed by painting it and adding special decorative features inside. Use only unbreakable glass, plastic or PVC for the windows. The house can go on to become a teenagers' retreat or revert to storage space. If you lack the space for a permanent playhouse make an instant one by using a wigwam frame as a base. When required simply cover the frame with blankets or a specially decorated old sheet. Later grow runner beans or peas up it or introduce scent with honeysuckle or roses.

◀ *A little raised play house, with its own ladder access, makes a perfect secret hideaway.*

▲ *When making a play area for your children, line the ground with a thick layer of bark chippings to soften their inevitable falls. This material also makes the area look more in keeping with a gardener's garden and will help to improve the soil.*

Including water

As a small child can quickly drown in water as shallow as 4 cm/1.5 in, it is not wise to include a pond at an early stage in a youngster's life. If you move to a house with a pond, drain it and use it for a sandpit instead. Water does not have to be completely excluded from the garden – instead add a wall fountain or a small running-water feature such as water flowing from an upturned pot into a shallow pebble-filled saucer.

See also:
- Ground surfaces, page 116
- Plant frameworks, page 130
- Arches, pergolas and arbours, page 134

Garden Furniture

▲ The ultimate in pool-side luxury: loungers with drinks tables attached that can be wheeled back into store.

Caring for garden furniture

Timber needs checking out once a year. Sand down and stain or paint when signs of weathering appear. Some timber needs oiling.

Metal needs regular attention if it is not protected by a plastic coating. As soon as any rust appears, sand to remove, and repaint to seal the surface.

Plastic only needs wiping down with a damp, soapy cloth.

Stone and concrete need a periodic wash down with soapy water and a soft brush. Rinse well to remove all soap traces.

Materials choices
- Timber
- Reconstituted stone or concrete
- Cane and wicker
- Metal
- Plastic
- Canvas
- Metal or plastic frame with padded cover

Well-chosen and well-sited garden furniture extends living into the garden in the most comfortable and relaxing way possible. Garden furniture either needs to be tough enough to stay outdoors all year or be fold-up or stackable so that it is easily stored away when not in use. There are two main types of garden furniture – that used for eating outdoors or that which is for periods when you simply want to lounge in the sun or the shade.

Furniture used for eating outside will usually double up as a temporary resting spot, but garden benches spaced around the garden allow the opportunity of moving from sun to shade at any time. Place a single bench to create a visually attractive element as part of the garden design and where it provides a new and different view of the garden from that of the main sitting area. This type of furniture needs to be robust enough to remain permanently in place.

The most popular chairs for sunbathing, or relaxing in the shade,

▼ Teak furniture suits most areas.

usually have a light, fold-up plastic or plastic-coated metal frame that can be placed at several angles on a ratchet system, and a long, padded, slip over cushion. These chairs can be moved about with ease so that anyone can follow the sun or shade as required.

▲ This well-designed and sturdily built garden furniture comes ready-painted.

Material choices
Furniture can either be chosen to blend with its surroundings or to make a colourful statement. In most cases permanent furniture looks best if it blends with other materials used in the garden, for example natural timber for a brick patio, or a wooden bench to stand below a tree at the end of the garden. For painted furniture, choose colours to blend with those used in nearby rooms of the house or mimic the colours of nearby garden flowers. White furniture works well where white or bright colours are used and green blends attractively into a leafy background.

Timber furniture may be natural in colour, and in tough hardwood such as oak, teak or less robust stained softwood, or it may be painted. Unless wooden furniture

Moulded plastic may not have a long life but it is cheap and light.

is fold-up, it is designed to stay in place around the year. However, wood takes a beating from the wet winters and hot, dry weather in summer, so needs to be regularly maintained with oiling or painting if it is to last when kept outside.

Stone or concrete seats are tough and easy to maintain, requiring no more than a periodic scrub. Curved designs are available, that can be placed around the trunk of a tree.

Cane and wicker, like timber, blend beautifully with the natural surroundings of a garden but they cannot be left outdoors as sun and rain will damage them. Their light weight makes them easy to transport but storage can be a problem. If the patio leads off a conservatory then the furniture can double up for indoor and outdoor use.

Metal furniture may be traditional wrought iron, which is heavy and needs constant maintenance if it is not to rust, or a lighter aluminium copy. Plastic-coated metal is easier to maintain, only needing to be wiped, although a cheaper surface coating can deteriorate.

Moulded plastic furniture, usually in white or green, is now very popular as it is easy to look after, light weight, and weather resistant. Most table tops and legs come apart for storage and chairs stack

to take up a minimum of space over winter. Plastic furniture can be left outdoors throughout the summer. Buy good quality furniture if you want it to last. Cheaper alternatives can crack and discolour on exposure to sunlight.

Canvas-covered director chairs or deck chairs are light to move and fold flat for storage. Director chairs are smart enough to use indoors when required. Canvas rots in time but is easy to replace.

Padded fabric loungers with metal or plastic frames can be used in a lounging or upright position, are light weight and fold up for storage.

Home-made seating adds an individual look to your garden. Concrete paving slabs can be built onto the top of a low wall, a plank screwed to a couple of tree stumps could make a temporary stopover spot in a wild garden or, for something very different, use a special metal chair frame shape and plant it with box to make a topiary seat.

▲ *A marble-topped metal bistro table and co-ordinating folding chair. This type of furniture is decorative and useful for summer drinks, and the table can be left out all year.*

▼ *This wooden lounger seat comes with a well-padded mattress, and with built-in wheels is easy to move around.*

Barbecues

Barbecue choices

- Built-in barbecues
- Kettle barbecues
- Portable table-top designs
- Trolley barbecues
- Gas wheel-around barbecues

Safety points

- Always site barbecues well away from overhanging trees, and from shrubs and timber fences or buildings. A gust of wind can easily send sparks flying which could start a fire.

- Never light a barbecue with petrol or paraffin always use special barbecue lighters and begin about 45 minutes before you want to start cooking.

- Don't leave a barbecue unsupervised at any time while it is alight.

- Remember that charcoal takes a long time to cool down. Spray with water to speed up the process. This also saves the loss of any coals still burning, which can be stored for future use.

- Have a bucket of water or sand available to damp down flames in an emergency.

- Think of the neighbours and make sure you site the barbecue where the wind won't blow your smoke, and cooking smells, into their garden. This also applies if they have hung out their washing to dry on a line.

In good weather the garden provides a relaxed place to eat, daytime or evening, and whether it is a family mealtime or you are entertaining friends. If you regularly eat in the garden it is well worth building in a barbecue area as an integral part of the patio design. The best place to site a barbecue is a sheltered spot, well away from trees and large shrubs, and close to the kitchen so that it is easy to transport any food and equipment to and fro.

Choosing a barbecue

Choice of barbecue depends on how often you will use it, how easily and quickly you want results, how many you will cook for, and whether you have easily accessible storage for the barbecue when it is not in use. For those who prefer heat at the turn of a switch there are wheel-around gas barbecues, or if you are only one or two, and like to take the barbecue with you on day trips a small portable barbecue may be more appropriate.

Built-in designs A barbecue that is incorporated in the patio design and uses the same materials is much the least obtrusive, can stay in position around the year and can be made to measure your needs exactly. Barbecue boxes that come in a range of sizes are widely available and these can be slotted into a brick- or stone-built frame allowing you to build the barbecue to your own specification. If you include weatherproof storage space for fuel to one side and a good-sized work-top area for utensils, plates and food, the barbecue will be ready for use whenever you want it.

Wheel-around gas barbecues If you have the space close by to store a barbecue run on bottled gas this is by far the quickest and simplest to use. Heat arrives almost instantly at the turn of a switch and the lava rocks used give food a similar taste to that of a charcoal barbecue. Another feature is that the heat is easy to control, with several types of adjustable flame.

◀ Brick-built patio barbecues are available commercially (as shown here), but if you are good at DIY you can design and build your own custom-made version.

Gas barbecues come in a range of sizes, with a lid that keeps heat in and will also keep the food warm. Many of the designs provide work-tops at either side and storage space below. Weatherproof covers allow you to keep the barbecue outdoors during the summer months, so that it only needs to be stored away during the winter. Gas-powered barbecue woks and griddles are also available, and wheel-around charcoal-burning barbecues are another option.

▲ Gas barbecues, with wheels, and lids that close down over the cooking area, are available in a range of sizes and styles.

▲ A simple portable barbecue is ideal for campers and picnic lovers, and can still be used in the garden.

◄ Portable gas-fired woks and griddles are an alternative to barbecues for outdoor eating.

Portable barbecues These are easy to store and transport if you like taking the barbecue with you on day trips. There is a huge range of sizes and designs available from small, briefcase slim styles to bigger and more robust shapes. If you want to use the barbecue regularly at home it is a good idea to build a platform to bring smaller and flatter portable barbecues up to a working height to avoid bending.

Lighting

Points to bear in mind

- Consider the neighbours when siting garden lighting. Avoid positioning lights that shine directly towards them. Position lights to point downwards.

- Use only lighting fitments designed specifically for outdoor use and use a professional electrician to fit stronger permanent lighting.

- Lights that play on moving water are very effective. Follow any installation instructions very carefully and conceal ground-level fitments among tall water side plants.

- Show off stylishly shaped plants or striking garden features with hidden spotlights.

- Use diffused, softer lights to highlight a specific area of the garden.

- Give a party feel to a special evening event with strings of hired coloured lights, garden flares and protected candles.

Materials choice
- Fixed buried lighting
- Low-voltage lights from a transformer
- Solar-powered lights
- Gas lights
- Lanterns
- Pond lights
- Garden flares
- Garden party lights

See also:
- *Electricity in the garden, page 112*

Garden lighting greatly increases the enjoyment of the garden. In winter you can view the plants or decorative features in the frost or snow. On a summer night you can eat outdoors or just sit and admire the surroundings. Lights can show off plants, a pond or statue or simply create a romantic ambience. Most important are those lights which allow safe passage through the garden or provide working light for barbecue chefs, and security lights to illuminate unwelcome visitors.

Highlighting plants or special features In a small garden it is usually most effective to pick out only two, or three, features to spotlight. Whether you choose a tree, shrub or special architectural feature, highlighting shape rather than colour usually provides the most effective result. This lighting needs to be professionally installed as there are strict rules governing outdoor cables, which need to be buried, plus the waterproof connectors and fittings that are needed.

Angle the lights to shine away from the viewing position and avoid allowing the source itself to show. The fitting can be concealed

▼ *Garden flares are attractive.*

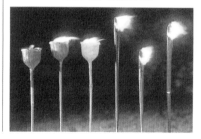

behind a low shrub, wall or other fixture or use stones or logs. Before deciding on the final position for a light source move the fitting around, trying different heights for the best effect.

▲ *Outdoor dining area by candle-light.*

For a softer light use low-wattage lights which run off a transformer that brings down the power to a safe level. A lighting set of this type usually includes the transformer and cable (which can be run above the ground), connectors that clip into the cable at any point you choose, and the light fittings, which push into the ground on spikes. This makes it comparatively easy to move the lights about, allowing you to highlight different areas when plants look their best.

Solar-powered lights that draw off energy from the sun in the daytime to give off a soft, diffused light at night conserve energy, cost nothing to run and need no wiring. Gas lighting also provides an attractive, gentle glow.

Walking around with safety

Eating and cooking areas need good lighting for safety reasons as well as decorative effect. If the patio is close to the house, undrawn curtains may provide enough light. Alternatively fix lights to the exterior house walls. These are easy to fit as they can be connected to the internal mains power supply. Illuminating house names and numbers is an aid to newcomers to your home, and lighting beside the front door allows identification of callers before you open the door. Paths and routes around the garden also need to be well-lit. Arrange fittings to point out any hazards such as steps or water features.

An aid to security Lights that sense body heat, switching on when they are approached, are an excellent security measure but can double up as safety lighting. The alternative is to use timed lighting which comes on and goes off at a prearranged time every evening.

Temporary party lights Coloured garden party lights can be bought or hired to string around the patio.

If you use oil-filled lamps or candles position them where they cannot be knocked over. Special garden candles and flares add atmosphere, and insect-repellent candles keep the bugs away. Candles need to be placed in open-topped containers, such as jam jars, to keep any breeze from fanning the flame and blowing them out. Safety is important: remember to keep a bucket of water close at hand. In dry weather plants can soon catch fire.

KEY PLANTS

The background plants form the basis for the garden's living framework and create round-the-year interest and form. These are the plants to consider first when designing a garden, as they will look decorative whatever time of the year it is.

Shrubs and trees are the backbone of any garden planting and even the smallest garden can accommodate some of each. Their bold outlines, textures or leaf-shapes bring architectural plants to the fore wherever they are grown. Those plants with variegated leaves of green and silver, white or gold are a wonderful source of colour all year round, especially when flowers are in short supply; while distinctively shaped climbers bring the eye up to a new level, as well as providing privacy, breaking up wind flow and hiding an eyesore.

This chapter provides a taster of the huge and exciting range of these key plants.

SHRUBS

Shrubs provide the vital backcloth to the garden's planting. Foliage comes in many tints and there is a huge range of leaf shapes. Some shrubs have variegated leaves, others provide stunning colour, while some keep their leaves throughout the year. Their flowers some wonderfully scented, come in every shape and colour, and many produce decorative fruit. And the huge range of shrubs available means that there will always be some in flower whatever the time of year.

Moving an established shrub

If you decide a shrub has been planted in the wrong position it should be possible to move it to another part of the garden. However, before you start removing the shrub make sure that you have dug a hole large enough to take it and have prepared the soil by digging in well-rotted manure or compost.

Dig out a trench all around the shrub, having first tied up the branches to make it easier. Use a fork and gently loosen the soil around the deeper roots.

To reduce the size of the ball of soil, if it is too large to remove, use the fork carefully so as not to damage the roots – and remove more soil.

(continued opposite)

Arbutus unedo, Strawberry tree
Height and spread up to 8 m/ 26 ft • A. unedo 'Elfin King', is smaller, with height up to 2 m/ 6 ft, spread 1.5 m/5 ft • Full sun • Fertile, well-drained soil; suitable for alkaline soils
    Really a tree, but shrubby in growth, the strawberry tree provides lots of winter interest with white flowers in winter to early spring, strawberry-like autumn fruit and a rough, shredding red-brown bark.

Camellia, Camellias
Height and spread up to 4.5 m/ 15 ft, depending on the variety • Good specimen plants • Suitable for containers Partial shade; plant away from early morning sun • Moist, well-drained, acid soil
    Camellias, with deep green, glossy, round-the-year leaves, thrive in acid soil, although many will tolerate neutral soil. They provide wonderful winter or early spring colour.

Cornus stolonifera, Dogwood
Height up to 2m/6ft, spread 4m/12ft • Full sun – partial shade • Fertile, well-drained, neutral to acid soil; also tolerates wet soil
    A deciduous shrub grown for its decorative, dark red young winter stems. Some dogwoods have bright yellow, orange or green stems. The small, white, late spring flowers are followed by white, often blue-tinged fruit. Variegated forms are available.

▲ *Camellia japonica.*

Cotinus coggygria, Smoke bush
Height and spread up to 5 m/ 16 ft • Full sun – partial shade • Moderately fertile, moist soil
    The fluffy festoons of purple flowers in mid-summer and autumn almost hide the small green leaves to give this decorative shrub its common name. Leaves turn yellow, orange and red in autumn.

Height and spread 60 cm/24 in to 3 m/10 ft, depending on variety • Full sun • Moderately fertile, moist soil
    In mid-summer, the pretty pink or white, small, star-shaped flowers, cover this deciduous bush.

Escallonia, Escallonia
Height and spread 2.5 m/8 ft • Full sun, with shelter from wind • Fertile, well-drained soil
    A frost-hardy, evergreen shrub, especially good in coastal areas. E. 'Apple Blossom' has early and mid-summer flowers in mixed tints.

Euonymus alatus, Winged spindle
Height 2 m/6 ft, spread 3 m/ 10 ft E. alatus 'Compactus' is smaller, with height and spread 1 m/3 ft • Full sun – partial shade • Well-drained soil
    This is a dense, bushy, deciduous shrub with dark green leaves that turn a brilliant scarlet in autumn.

▼ The Dogwood, *Cornus alba 'Red Stems'*.

▲ Catkins of *Garrya elliptica*.

Garrya elliptica,
Silk tassel bush
Height up to 4 m/12 ft, spread 24 m/6–12 ft • Full sun to partial shade, with shelter from wind and frost • Moderately fertile, well-drained soil

An upright, evergreen shrub grown for its long, slim, silvery green catkins that, in the male form, can be up to 20 cm/8 in in length and cover the plant in late winter to look like silver rain. Prune in spring to keep down in size.

Hamamelis x *intermedia,*
Witch hazel
Height and spread up to 4 m/12 ft • Sun–partial shade • Moist, well-drained, acid to neutral soil

Witch hazel is grown for the fragrant yellow or dark red winter flowers. *Hamamelis* x *intermedia* 'Pallida' has clusters of large yellow flowers. (See also *H.* x *intermedia* 'Diane', page 169.)

Mahonia x *media,*
Mahonia
Height up to 5 m/15 ft, spread 4 m/12 ft • Shade • Moderately fertile, well-drained soil

An ornate shrub throughout the year, with sharply toothed, long, dark, evergreen leaves, and long streamers of bright to lemon-yellow, highly fragrant flowers from late autumn to late winter. This makes a good specimen plant.

Philadelphus,
Mock orange
Height and spread 1.5 m/5 ft • Full sun – partial shade • Moderately fertile, well-drained soil

The white flowers that appear in mid-summer have a scent similar to orange blossom. *Philadelphus* x *lemoinei* has arching branches and fragrant, pure white flowers. Makes a good specimen plant.

Potentilla fruticosa,
Potentilla
Height up to 1.5 m/5 ft, spread 1 m/3 ft • Full sun – partial shade, depending on type • Poor, well-drained soil

This compact, bushy, deciduous shrub likes bright sun and produces flowers over a long period from late spring to mid-autumn. Colours vary from white, yellow and pale pink to deep red.

Pyracantha, Firethorn/
Pyracantha
Height up to 3 m/10 ft, spread up to 2.5 m/8 ft • Full sun – partial shade • Fertile soil

A spiny, evergreen shrub pyracantha is usually chosen for its colourful yellow, orange or red autumn berries.

Rhododendron,
Rhododendrons
Height up to 3 m/10 ft, spread 4 m/12 ft or more • Mostly shade, where colour is highlighted • Most require moist, well-drained, acid soil

▲ *Rhododendron* 'Cynthia'.

A huge range of species and cultivars provides us with the showy flowers of rhododendron from autumn through winter and, most commonly, in spring, in an enormous range of sizes and shapes. Flower colours can be: white, pink, apricot, red, yellow, purple, lilac; and sizes range from dwarf alpines and small shrubs to large trees. Some shrubs have attractively coloured young growth.

Viburnum plicatum
' Mariesii' Japanese
snowball tree
Height up to 3 m/10 ft, spread 4 m/12 ft • Full sun – partial shade • Moderately fertile soil

This deciduous shrub has a spreading, layered shape with white flowers held in swathes above the green leaves in late spring. Leaves turn red In the autumn. Good specimen shrub.

▼ *Viburnum plicatum* 'Mariesii'.

(continued from opposite)

Use a sharp spade to cut beneath the plant, once the root ball is of a manageable size. Work around the plant from each side.

Have ready a piece of hessian or tough plastic for carrying the shrub. Roll this up, tilt the plant and slip it underneath, then rock the root ball back over it and unroll the hessian around it.

Lift the shrub with assistance, move it to the new planting hole and gently lower it into position. Check that the soil height on shrub and surrounding earth is the same, and remove the wrapping. Fill in the hole, firm the soil, and water thoroughly. In dry weather water well for several months.

DECIDUOUS TREES

Planting a tree

To provide a new tree with the best start in life plant it with care, and in the right position.

First remove the soil to a depth of 30 cm/12 in. Fork over the rest well, working in plenty of garden compost or well-rotted manure.

Insert a stake, placing it on the side of the prevailing wind, leaving plenty of space for the root ball. Hammer it in well.

(continued opposite)

There is room for one or two carefully chosen trees in the smallest garden. Some can be kept small by growing them in a pot. They provide a focus, can hide unattractive structures and create interest at a higher level. A tree may be chosen for its decorative leaf shape or colour, for its flowers or the fruit that follows, or for the colour or texture of its bark – and sometimes you can find all these features in one tree. Dimensions are for maximum growth, often reached only after many years.

Acer griseum, Paper-bark maple

Height and spread up to 9 m/ 30 ft • Full sun – partial shade • Fertile, well-drained soil
This slow-growing tree has a spreading canopy of dark green, hand-shaped leaves that turn a wonderful orange then crimson in the autumn. Yellow flowers hang from the branch ends in summer. In winter it has beautiful orange-brown peeling bark.

Amelanchier lamarckii, Shadbush

Height up to 9 m/30 ft, spread up to 12 m/40 ft • Full sun – partial shade • Acid, fertile, moist, well-drained soil
Small tree or shrub which has white hair-covered young shoots and leaves. The new bronze leaves turn green, then orange and red in autumn. Small white flowers, up to 12 cm /5 in long, appear in spring, followed by black fruit.

Betula pendula, Silver birch

Height up to 25 m/80 ft, spread up to 10 m/33 ft • Full sun – partial shade • Moderately fertile, moist, well-drained soil
Graceful garden tree, well known for its eye-catching silvery bark. Male catkins up to 6 cm/ 2.5 in long appear in spring and leaves turn from green to yellow in autumn.

Cercis canadensis, Eastern redbud

Height and spread up to 10 m/ 33 ft • Full sun – partial shade • Deep, fertile, moist, well-drained soil

Often multi-stemmed, *Cercis canadensis* 'Forest Pansy' has crimson to pink flowers which appear in clusters before the leaves. The heart-shaped leaves are a deep red-purple when new, turning to orange in autumn before falling. In frost-prone areas they will require protection in winter when young.

Cornus mas, Cornelian cherry

Height and spread 5 m/15 ft • Full sun – partial shade • Fertile, well-drained, neutral to acid soil
The dark green leaves of this small, spreading tree turn a wonderful red-purple in autumn. Balls of yellow flowers appear in late winter, followed by the leaves, and bright red fruit are usually produced in late summer.

Betula pendula, Silver birch.

Acer palmatum 'Autumn colours'.

Crataegus monogyna, Common hawthorn

Height up to 9 m/30 ft, spread up to 8 m/26 ft • Full sun – partial shade • Any soil, except very wet
Thorny tree with small, dark green, glossy leaves and fragrant white flowers with pink central anthers in late spring. Glossy red fruit (haws) appear in autumn. Suitable for a hedge (kept trimmed) or specimen tree, and suitable for towns and coastal areas.

Crataegus monogyna, with haws.

Crataegus laevigata 'Paul's Scarlet', May
Height and spread 8 m/26 ft
• Full sun – partial shade
• Any soil, except very wet

Similar to Crataegus monogyna, above, C. laevigata 'Paul's Scarlet' has abundant clusters of double, deep pink flowers in late spring. Like C. monogyna, it is suitable for towns and coastal areas.

Fagus sylvatica 'Dawyck Good', Dawyck beech
Height 18 m/60 ft, spread 7 m/22 ft • Partial shade
• Almost any well-drained soil, including chalk

This column-shaped but compact beech has bright yellow young foliage, later turning green and finally orange-brown in autumn.

Malus 'Royalty', Crab apple
Height and spread 8 m/26 ft
• Full sun – partial shade
• Fertile, moist, well-drained soil

A small, spreading tree with richly coloured, dark red-purple leaves that mostly remain this colour to turn red in autumn. Almost matching, crimson-purple flowers appear in mid- to late spring, followed by small, brightly coloured dark red fruit in autumn.

Prunus padus, Bird cherry
Height 15 m/50 ft, spread 10 m/33 ft • Full sun •Moderately fertile, moist, well-drained soil

A spreading tree that is more conical in shape when young and produces fragrant white flowers in pendulous streamers in spring, followed by small, glossy black fruit.

Prunus serrula, Cherry
Height and spread 10 m/33 ft • Full sun • Moderately fertile, moist, well-drained soil

This is a rounded tree with richly coloured, peeling, glossy chestnut-brown bark. As the leaves emerge in spring, white, single flowers appear in small clusters, to be followed by edible, but unpalatable cherries.

Robinia pseudoacacia 'Frisia', Black locust / False acacia
Height 15 m/50 ft, spread 8 m/25 ft • Full sun; needs shelter from strong winds
• Tolerates poor, dry soil but prefers moderately fertile, moist, well-drained soil

A fast-growing tree that is roughly columnar and has golden yellow foliage, which turns a more yellow-green in summer and orange-yellow in autumn.

Satin matsudana 'Tortuosa', Twisted willow
Height 9–25 m/30–80 ft, spread 25 m/80 ft • Full sun • Deep, moist, well-drained soil; not suitable for shallow chalk

A fast-growing upright tree with twisted, contorted stems that are most obvious in winter.

Malus x soulardii ' Red Tip'

when the leaves are off the tree. Bright green leaves and spring catkins are a yellow-green.

Sorbus aria, Whitebeam
Height up to 15m/10ft, spread 7m/22ft • Full sun – partial shade • Moist, well-drained neutral to slightly alkaline soil

With young leaves of a silvery grey in a rounded, cloudy shape, this is a very pretty tree. Older leaves are a dark green with white hairy undersides that show up in a breeze. White flowers appear in late spring, followed by red berries.

Syringa, Lilac
Height and spread up to 4 m/12 ft • Full sun • Fertile, well-drained, neutral to alkaline soil

Lilac has spikes of fragrant white, pink, magenta-red or blue-grey flowers in spring. Syringa vulgaris 'Mme Florent Stepman' has white flowers, 'Paul Thirion' has magenta-red flowers, and 'Charles Joly' has deep purple-blue flowers.

Syringa palibiniana

(continued from opposite)

Tease out some of the thick roots that have run around inside the edge of the pot if planting a container-grown tree.

Place the tree in the hole and put a cane across the hole to check that the soil mark on the tree matches the soil height. Fill the hole with soil, water in, and tread in firmly to ensure that there are no air pockets around the roots.

Water thoroughly and apply a 5 cm/2 in depth of mulch to help conserve moisture. Water in dry weather for some months until the tree is well established.

EVERGREEN TREES

Planting a tree in a tub or container

Trees grown in tubs can be used to add interest to a patio and are much less trouble than annuals. This is the only method of successfully growing larger plants on a roof garden or balcony.

Choose a container larger than the pot the tree comes in and at least 30 cm/12 in in diameter. If using a ceramic pot check that it is frostproof. Insert a drainage layer at the bottom before adding a layer of compost. Where weight is not a priority use heavy, loam-based compost for stability.

Remove the tree from its pot and tease out some of the larger roots. Stand it on the new compost and trickle more compost around the sides and up to the original height of the soil on the trunk.

(continued opposite)

A round-the-year outline to the garden is provided by those trees and hedges that keep their leaves. They can provide a valuable screen as well as a constant form. Those that clip well for example box, holly and privet, make neat, sculptured hedges and can be shaped to form decorative and fun topiary shapes. Evergreens come in a wide range of shapes and colours with many different leaf forms, textures and colours.

Buxus sempervirens, Box
Height up to 5 m/15 ft spread 5–6 m/15–20 ft • Partial shade • Fertile, well-drained soil
This small, bushy tree has glossy, dark green leaves and is ideal for clipping to form a hedge or for topiary, particularly in the forms *Buxus semper-virens* 'Handsworthensis' or B. *sempervirens* 'Suffruticosa'. Variegated varieties are B. *sem-pervirens* 'Marginata', with a golden edge to the leaves, and B. *sempervirens* 'Elegantissima', which has white leaf margins. Select dwarf box for edging.

Cryptomeria japonica, Japanese cedar
Height up to 25 m/80 ft, spread 6 m/20 ft • Full sun – partial shade • Fertile, moist, well-drained soil but tolerates most well-drained soils, includ-ing chalk
A cedar that grows as a tall, cone-shaped column with glossy green leaves that take on a warm russet tint in autumn. The bright orange-brown bark shreds attractively and the female flowers produce small brown cones.

Eucalyptus gunnii, Cider gum
Height 9–25 m/30–80 ft, spread 6–15 m/20–50 ft • Full sun • Fertile, neutral to slightly acid soil
Rounded leaves are silvery grey-green when young, turning lance-shaped and blue-green later. They have an aromatic smell when crushed. *Eucalyptus gunnii* can grow large, so cut it back regularly to encourage

Box tree clipped to spiral shape.

young leaves and maintain a bushy, compact shape in a small garden. Cream flowers appear in summer. The grey bark peels away to reveal yellow-grey new bark below, sometimes flushed with pink.

Ilex aquifolium 'J.C. van Tol', Holly
Height up to 6 m/20 ft, spread 4 m/12 ft • Full sun – partial shade • Moderately fertile, moist, well-drained soil
Hollies are slow-growing, neat and compact. This columnar female holly with shiny, plain green, rounded leaves, is self-fertile, so if only one tree is grown it is still able to produce a mass of bright red berries. 'Golden van Tol' has golden edges to the spineless leaves.

Juniperus scopulorum 'Skyrocket', Rocky mountain juniper
Height up to 6 m/20 ft, spread 50–60 cm/20–24 in • Full sun – lightly dappled shade • Well-drained, sandy, chalky or dry soil
This juniper, as its name suggests, forms a tall, slender spire and provides a strong, sculptural shape that fits neatly into a small garden. It can be used to provide a good contrast with lower-growing plants. Its leaves are grey-green.

Laurus nobilis, Bay
Height up to 12 m/40 ft, spread 9 m/30 ft • Full sun – partial shade • Fertile, moist, well-drained soil
The aromatic, glossy, dark green leaves of bay are com-monly used in cooking. Bay can also be clipped into topiary shapes. In spring small balls of tiny creamy yellow flowers appear. Clip well. The plant is suitable for a container.

Cryptomeria japonica.

Laurus nobilis, Bay, in flower.

Ligustrum lucidum 'Excelsum Superbum', Chinese privet

Height and spread up to 9 m/30 ft • Full sun – partial shade • Any well-drained soil

A cone-shaped privet with yellow-edged, glossy green leaves, and white flowers in late summer and early autumn. It is suitable as a specimen tree or for hedging.

Ligustrum ovalifolium 'Aureum', Golden privet

Height and spread up to 2 m/6 ft • Full sun to partial shade • Any well-drained soil

This bushy privet is grown for its sunny, golden variegated foliage and is suitable as a specimen tree or to grow as hedging.

Magnolia grandiflora, Bull bay

Height up 6–18 m/20–60 ft, spread 15 m/50 ft • Full sun – partial shade; needs shelter from strong winds • Fertile, moist, well-drained, preferably acid to neutral soil

A dense, conical evergreen with decorative, dark glossy green leaves that have a paler green underside, usually with rusty hairs. Large, fragrant flowers appear in late summer.

Photinia x fraseri 'Red Robin'

Height and spread up to 5 m/15 ft • Full sun – partial shade;

needs winter shelter in frost-prone areas • Fertile, moist, well-drained soil

A compact, globe-shaped tree with bright red new leaves in spring. Grow it as a specimen tree or grouped with other trees or shrubs.

Prunus laurocerasus, Cherry laurel

Height and spread up to 5 m/15 ft • Full sun – partial shade • Moderately fertile, moist, well-drained soil but not shallow chalk

Dense and bushy, the cherry laurel has shiny green leaves and can be cut back to keep its shape. Fragrant white flowers appear in upright spires in mid- and late spring, followed by cherry-like red fruit. Use this shrub as a specimen or for a hedge.

Quercus ilex, Holm oak

Height up to 25 m/80 ft, spread up to 20 m/65 ft • Full sun – partial shade • Deep, fertile, well-drained soil

Slow-growing and rounded in shape, the evergreen holm oak has holly-like, glossy green leaves that are silvery-grey

Taxus baccata, Yew, with berries.

when young. It bears short, oblong acorns.

Taxus baccata, Yew

Height up to 10–20 m/33–65 ft, spread up to 9 m/30 ft • Sun – deep shade • Fertile, well-drained soil, including alkaline and acid soils

A slow-growing, long-lived tree with needle-like, dark green leaves and bright red autumn berries. Yew creates a fine hedge and wonderful topiary shapes but it is very toxic.

A colourful border based on carefully chosen mixed colours.

(continued from opposite)

Work the compost firmly down around the root ball to make sure that the tree will remain stable in wind. Water well, and make sure the plant has adequate moisture, even when it is well established.

ARCHITECTURAL PLANTS

Training a tree to the shape you want

For a multi-stemmed tree or one with branches close to the ground buy a plant with shoots along the length of the trunk. Prune out only those branches that are badly positioned or cross others. Shorten the remaining sideshoots to within 5–10 cm/2–4 in of the trunk. Do this only once.

For a tree with a clear trunk and a spreading top cut back all new shoots on the trunk and above the branching head to about 10–15 cm/4–6 in during the summer. When the tree is dormant, cut the shoots right back to the stem.

(continued opposite)

Where shape is all-important these plants are the stars. They stand out on their own to form a living sculpture and provide a strong focal point Alternatively, you can use the bold shape, texture or stunning colour of one of these plants as a contrasting feature to highlight softer, more muted effects created by other plants positioned around it.

Acer palmatum, Japanese maple
Height up to 8 m/25 ft, spread up to 10 m/33 ft • Sun – partial shade; needs shelter from cold winds and frost • Fertile, moist, well-drained soil

A deciduous tree with beautiful, fringed, fine-fingered green leaves that curl delicately earthwards and turn a wonderful rich red in autumn. Some are variegated, such as *Acer palmatum* 'Filigree', with pale green, cream-mottled leaves that turn golden; *A. palmatum* 'Garnet' has leaves that are very finely fingered and deep crimson in colour.

Cordyline australis 'Torbay Dazzler', New Zealand cabbage palm
Height 3–10 m/10–33 ft, spread 1–4 m/3–12 ft •Sun – partial shade; needs shelter from cold winds and frost • Fertile, well-drained soil

A palm with long, slim, sword-like leaves that arch to form a rosetted head. The green leaves are margined in cream and have cream stripes along their length. *Cordyline australis* 'Atropurpurea' has leaves flushed with purple.

Cornus controversa, 'Variegata'.

Acer palmatum, Japanese maple

Cornus alternifolia 'Argentea', Pagoda dogwood/Green osier
Height and spread up to 15 m/ 50 ft • Sun – partial shade • Fertile, well-drained, neutral to acid soil

This softly layered tree is often described as being shaped like a wedding cake, because of the way it displays its white-margined leaves in clearly defined tiers.

Cornus controversa 'Variegata'
Height and spread up to 15 m/ 50 ft • Sun – partial shade • Fertile, well-drained, neutral to acid soil

A shapely tree with branches that are arranged in tiers. The green leaves are strongly marked with creamy white margins.

Fatsia japonica, Japanese aralia/fatsia
Height and spread 1.5–4 m/ 5–12 ft • Sun – light, dappled shade • Well-drained soil

This is a very striking plant with its large, leathery, toothed,

hand-shaped, dark green leaves, which are up to 40 cm/16 in in size. Fist-like knobs of creamy white flowers appear in autumn, followed by small, round, black fruit. Suitable as a container plant.

Festuca glauca, Blue fescue grass
Height up to 30 cm/12 in, spread up to 25 cm/10 in • Full sun • Poor to moderately fertile, dry, well-drained soil

Grasses, with their tufty, long, slim, arching leaves, provide a stunning contrast to low-growing and earth-hugging plants. This blue-green evergreen perennial grows in cushion-like hummocks and produces violet-flushed, blue-green flowers in summer.

Liquidambar styraciflua, Sweet gum
Height up to 25 m/80 ft, spread up to 12 m/40 ft; 'Golden Treasure' grows to height of 10 m/33 ft, spread 6 m/20 ft • Full sun • Moderately fertile, moist, well-drained, acid to neutral soil

Festuca glauca.

Stipa gigantea, Giant feather grass.

Grow this sweet gum as a specimen where its vibrant autumn colour can be clearly admired. The glossy green, hand-shaped leaves turn a rich red and orange. *Liquidambar styraciflua* 'Golden Treasure' is a slow-growing alternative which has green leaves with yellow margins.

Phormium tenax, New Zealand flax
Height up to 4 m/12 ft, spread up to 2 m/6 ft • Full sun, with protection from frost • Fertile, moist, well-drained soil
The long, slim, sword-shaped leaves of New Zealand flax, folded into a V-shape at the base, grow to form striking, spiky, rosette-shaped plants. The more compact hybrid *P. tenax* 'Dazzler' has stunning red, orange and pink stripes.

Rhus typhina 'Dissecta', Stag's horn sumach
Height up to 2 m/6 ft, spread up to 3 m/10 ft • Full sun • Moderately fertile, moist, well-drained soil
The velvety textured, red shoots of this deciduous shrub look like stag's antlers, giving it its common name. Long, curving fronds of lance-shaped leaves turn a brilliant orange-red in autumn and the furry flower buds turn into red, nobbly flowerheads.

Stipa gigantea, Giant feather grass/golden oats
Height up to 2.5 m/8 ft, spread up to 1.2 m/4 ft • Full sun • Moderately fertile, medium to light, moist, well-drained soil

Dense tufts of tall, arching, blue-green leaves up to 30 cm/12 in long quiver in the breeze on long stems and are highlighted in summer by silver panicles of taller feathery flowers with a hint of purple that go golden as the seeds ripen.

Yucca filamentosa 'Bright Edge', Adam's needle
Height up to 75 cm/30 in, spread up to 1.5 m/5 ft • Sun • Any well-drained soil
Rigid, long, spiky leaves that are dark green with broad golden yellow margins form clump-like rosettes which appears to be bathed in constant sunlight.

Yucca filamentosa 'Variegata'.

BAMBOOS

The delicate, arching stems and curving, feathery leaves of bamboos make these plants a contrast to the bolder and firmer leaf shapes of other architectural plants.

Nandina domestica, Heavenly bamboo
Height up to 2 m/6 ft, spread up to 1.5 m/5 ft • Sun • Moist, well-drained soil
The mid-green leaves of heavenly bamboo curl downwards to show off their striking, serrated shape, which is highlighted by reddish-purple winter colour. Star-shaped white flowers appear in spring, followed by long-lasting clusters of red fruit.

Phyllostachys nigra, Black bamboo
Height 3–5 m/10–15 ft, spread 2–3 m/6–10 ft • Full sun – light, dappled shade; give shelter from frost and cold wind • Fertile, moist, well-drained soil
The arching, slender, green canes of black bamboo grow in clumps and in their second or third year turn an eye-catching shiny black shown off by the many lance-shaped green leaves.

Pleioblastus pygmaeus var. distichus, Pigmy bamboo
Height up to 1 m/3 ft, spread up to 1.5 m/5 ft • Full sun • Fertile, moist well-drained soil
This low-growing, upright, woody bamboo has mid-green, hollow canes and hairless, long, slim leaves.

Phyllostachys nigra, Black bamboo.

(continued from opposite)

For a tall and upright tree with a dominant central leading shoot, make sure that it has not developed two leaders. If so prune one of them back to its point of origin, leaving the more upright leading shoot to continue growing upward.

GREY AND SILVER FOLIAGE PLANTS

Pruning grey-leaved shrubs

To prevent them becoming unattractively straggly small plants like *Santolina pinnate* cotton lavender, and *Helichrysum italicum serotinum*, curry plant, need to be pruned every spring.

Cut back close to the base, to a point where new shoots can be seen. If plants are pruned regularly this may be only 10 cm/4 in from the ground. A neglected plant will shoot higher up.

The plant will look rather bare immediately after pruning but new shoots will soon begin to grow.

(continued opposite)

Beautiful effects can be created by mixing foliage shape, texture and colour so that a garden never looks dull at any time of the year. Grey-green foliage acts as a highlighter, showing up as a haze of silvery light against the dark-green leaves of its neighbours.

Armoracia rusticana 'Variegata', Variegated horseradish
Height up to 1.2 m/4 ft, spread up to 2 m/6 ft • Full sun • Fertile, well-drained soil
This is a perennial closely related to the horseradish with roots which are used for the hot and spicy sauce. It grows in clumps and has long stalks with green, serrated leaves which are splashed with decorative white markings. Clusters of white flowers appear on the plant from spring to late summer.

Astelia chathamica
Height up to 1.2 m/4 ft, spread up to 2 m/6 ft • Sun - partial shade • Moist, fertile, peaty soil
A clump-forming plant, this perennial produces arching leaves of an interesting silver-green which have a metallic and woolly texture on the upper-side. This plant is not frost-hardy: in frost-prone areas grow it in pots and take indoors during winter.

Ballota pseudodictamnus
Height up to 45 cm/18 in, spread up to 2 m/6 ft • Full sun • Well-drained soil
This low-growing, mound-shaped shrub has silvery, egg-shaped leaves that curl upwards on erect, white, woolly stems. In late spring to early summer it has unusual, pink-flushed, white flowers with funnel-shaped green calyces.

Brachyglottis Dunedin hybrids/ Senecio
Height up to 1.5 m/5 ft, spread up to 2 m/6 ft • Full sun • Fertile, well-drained soil
This bushy shrub has scal-loped green leaves with white hairs that create an overall

silvery effect. Loose clusters of yellow, daisy-like flowers appear from late summer.

Buddleja crispa, Buddleia
Height and spread up to 3 m/ 10 ft • Full sun • Fertile, well-drained soil
A deciduous shrub with arching stems and woolly white young shoots and leaves. Mauve, fragrant flowers appear in mid-and late summer. *Buddleia davidii* 'Harlequin' has mid-green leaves with creamy coloured margins.

Dianthus species, Pinks
Height 25–45 cm/10–18 in, spread 30–40 cm/12–16 in • Full sun • Fertile, well-drained alkaline soil
Pinks form a decorative edg-ing for the front of a border or alongside a path. They grow to form mounds of slim, silvery foliage topped by a huge range of fragrant flowers, mostly in shades of pink and white, some with petals edged in a second colour, and others with 'eyes' of a different shade.

Buddleia crispa

Elaeagnus angustifolia 'Quicksilver', Oleaster
Height and spread up to 4 m/ 12 ft • Full sun • Fertile, well-drained soil; tolerates dry soil and coastal winds
A very decorative deciduous shrub which shows off its silvery shoots and slim, silvery leaves to perfection in spring. Even the flower buds are silvery, opening into small, fragrant, creamy yellow flowers in early summer.

Grey and silver plants generally thrive in dry, sunny places.

Dianthus deltoides, Maiden pink.

Helichrysum italicum serotinum, Curry plant
Height up to 40 cm/16 in, spread up to 75 cm/30 in •Full sun • Moderately fertile, neutral to alkaline soil

An evergreen, low-growing shrub, the curry plant has narrow, silvery leaves and a strong aroma of the mixed spices it is named after. Yellow daisy-like flowers appear from summer through to autumn.

Ilex aquifolium 'Silver Milkmaid', Holly
Height and spread up to 4 m/ 12 ft • Full sun • Fertile, well-drained soil; tolerates dry soil and coastal winds

This holly forms a spreading, open shape, rather than the dense bush usually associated with hollies. It has sharply spined dark green leaves which are strongly marked, with an uneven silvery-white centre.

Lavandula species, Lavender
Height and spread up to 1 m/ 3 ft; Lavandula lanata has height 75 cm/30 in, spread 90 cm/36 in • Full sun • Moderately fertile, well drained soil

The silver-grey foliage of most lavenders forms a complementary background to the strongly aromatic blue-mauve, pink or white flowers, according to species. Flowers are dried to scent linen or pot-pourri and

the essential oils are used for both cosmetic and medicinal purposes. Lavandula lanata has the lightest coloured foliage. Some lavenders are only half-hardy and need to be grown in a protected spot.

Perovskia atriplicifolia, 'Blue Spire', Perovskia
Height up to 1.2 m/4 ft, spread up to 1 m/3 ft • Full sun • Poor to moderately fertile, well-drained soil; tolerates coastal conditions and dry, alkaline soils

This tall plant with its silvery, furry stems and deeply divided silver-grey leaves is topped by clusters of violet-blue flowers in late summer and early autumn.

Salix exigua, Coyote willow
Height up to 4 m/12 ft, spread up to 5 m/15 ft • Full sun • Deep, moist, well-drained sandy soil; does not tolerate shallow, chalky soil

This beautiful, upright, spherical shrub, with slender shoots bearing long, grey-blue leaves that are covered in silvery grey hairs when young, is ideal for use as a focal point in a small garden.

Lavandula 'Bowles' variety.

Santolina pinnata, Cotton lavender
Height up to 75 cm/30 in spread up to 1 m/3 ft • Full sun • Poor moderately fertile, well-drained soil

Keep this decorative, round to low bushy shrub in a neat shape by pruning hard in spring. It will then provide good ground cover or can be used to form a low hedge. It has deeply indented and slightly aromatic silvery leaves. In summer creamy white to lemon-yellow flowers rise above the leaves.

Border with mixed coloured and and silver foliage planting.

By summer a compact, well-clothed shrub will have been formed. Santolina pinnata, cotton lavender, is illustrated.

GOLD AND BRIGHT GREEN FOLIAGE

Taking heel cuttings

This method works well for *Elaeagnus* x *ebbingei* 'Gilt Edge' as well as elders (*Sambucus*), rhododendrons and azaleas.

Pull off the cutting to leave a sliver of bark at the end. Pull downwards so that the sliver of bark comes away at the base. This is the point where the hormones that stimulate rooting are most concentrated.

Using a sharp knife, trim off the long 'tail' close to the base of the cutting and at an angle, then insert the cutting in compost in a pot and cover with a polythene bag or use a cold frame or propagator.

In the colder wintertime, or when the weather is dull and uninviting, plants with golden coloured foliage create bright spots in the landscape and give a hint of sunnier days. They also look very effective in a special bed mixed with plants that have sunny flower colours of yellow, rust or orange. Alternatively, mix them with white for a fresh, clean look or blue for a striking contrast.

Carex hachijoensis 'Evergold', Sedge
Height up to 30 cm/12 in, spread up to 35 cm/14 in • Sun – partial shade • Fertile, moist, well-drained soil

The long, slim, grass-like leaves of this evergreen, clump-forming sedge are decoratively striped in green and yellow. In spring spikes of small brown flowers appear on 15 cm/6 in-long stems.

Catalpa bignonioides 'Aurea', Indian bean tree
Height and spread up to 10 m/ 33 ft • Full sun • Fertile, moist, well-drained soil

Giant, lime-yellow, pointed, heart-shaped leaves adorn this slow-growing deciduous tree, which appears as a haze of gold when the young leaves first unfold. Very decorative, white, foxglove-shaped flowers with throats of yellow and purple appear in summer, and these are followed by slim, trailing seed pods. Indian bean tree needs shelter from strong winds and young trees should be protected from frost.

Euonymus fortunei.

Choisya ternata 'Sundance', Mexican orange blossom
Height and spread up to 2.5 m/ 8 ft • Full sun • Fertile, well-drained soil

This dome-shaped evergreen shrub with its attractive divided and slightly aromatic golden yellow leaves provides a sunny feature, even in the gloomiest months of the year. The white orange blossom-scented flowers which appear in spring on other Mexican orange blossoms are rarer and less abundant on 'Sundance'. A sunny position gives the best colour. Provide shelter from frosts.

Elaeagnus x ebbingei 'Gilt Edge'
Height and spread up to 4 m/ 12 ft • Full sun – partial shade • Fertile, well-drained soil

This dense and slow-growing evergreen shrub provides round-the-year brightness with its colourful, pointed leaves, dark green in the centre and surrounded by a wide margin of bright creamy yellow. Slightly smaller, *E.* x *ebbingei* 'Limelight' provides more subtle colour with silvery young leaves that later become marked with yellow and pale green at the centre.

Euonymus fortunei 'Emerald 'n Gold'
Height and spread up to 90 cm/ 36 in • Full sun • Moist, well-drained soil

This low-growing, bushy ever-green shrub has leaves of bright green edged with a wide margin of sunny yellow that becomes tinged pink in winter.

Elaeagnus x *ebbingei* 'Gilt Edge'.

Hedera colchica 'Sulphur Heart', Persian ivy
Height and spread 5 m/15 ft; H. helix 'Buttercup' 2 m/6 ft • Full sun • Fertile, moist, well-drained, preferably alkaline soil

This is a vigorous climbing ivy with large, elongated, mid-green leaves splashed with yellow. Full sun produces the strongest coloration. An alternative choice is the small-leaved ivy *Hedera helix* 'Buttercup', which needs full sun to bring out its brilliant yellow colouring.

Hedera helix 'Buttercup'.

(continued opposite)

Hosta fortunei 'Aureo Marginata'.

Hosta 'Gold Standard' Plantain lily/hosta

Height 65 cm/26 in, spread 1 m/ 3ft; 'Sum and Substance' height 75 cm/30 in, spread 1.2 m/4 ft • Partial shade • Fertile, moist, well-drained soil

Clump-forming hostas are grown for their colourful and shapely leaves. 'Gold Standard' has golden, strongly veined leaves edged with bright green. Funnel-shaped, lavender-blue flowers appear on tall stems in mid-summer. An alternative is 'Sum and Substance', which has heart-shaped, glossy, yellow-green leaves and bell-shaped, pale lilac flowers. Prone to slug and snail damage hostas need good mulching as they will not tolerate drought.

Humulus lupulus 'Aureus', Golden hop

Height up to 6 m/20 ft, spread up to 2 m/6 ft • Bright sun – partial shade • Moderately fertile, moist, well-drained soil

Sambucus racemosa 'Plumosa Aurea'.

This fast-growing and vigorous climber is best trained over a fence, through a tree or up a tall frame, where its golden foliage can be seen to advantage. It dies down in winter, producing fresh growth in spring.

Ilex aquifolium 'Golden Milkboy', Holly

Height up to 6 m/20 ft, spread up to 4 m/12 ft • Sun • Moderately fertile, moist, well-drained soil

The spiny leaves of this holly are mainly a creamy gold, high-lighted by an outer dark green marking. The plant is dense and upright with purple-green stems. A position in full sun produces best colour.

Lonicera nitida 'Baggesen's Gold'

Height and spread up to 1.5 m/5 ft • Full sun – partial shade • Any well-drained soil

The long, arching shoots of this evergreen, bushy shrub produce small, bright yellow leaves and minute, creamy white flowers in spring. Grown in partial shade the plant is less prone to aphids but it needs sun for the best colouring.

Philadelphus coronarius 'Aureus', Mock orange

Height up to 2.5 m/8 ft, spread 1.5 m/5 ft • Partial shade • Moderately fertile, well-drained soil

This deciduous shrub is a shade-happy plant that displays leaves that are golden yellow at first, turning golden green later.

Sambucus nigra 'Aurea', Golden elder

Height and spread of up to 6 m/ 20 ft • Full sun – partial shade • Moderately fertile soil

This deciduous shrub is related to the common elder. *Sambucus nigra* 'Aurea' is a decorative form of the shrub, with yellow foliage developing from bronze new leaves on pink-flushed leafstalks.

Ilex aquifolium 'Argentea Pendula'.

Choisya ternata 'Sundance' (below, middle right), mixed with other foliage plants.

VIGOROUS BACKGROUND CLIMBERS

Pruning a rambler rose

After flowering and in late summer cut out very old, dead and diseased shoots right to the base. Leave all the young and healthy shoots.

On the remaining main shoots go along the length and prune all sideshoots, cutting them down to between two and four pairs of leaves from the main stem.

These vigorous climbers have a wide range of uses. They will quickly clothe a pergola or archway or cover an arbour. Alternatively use one to hide an unsightly building or train up trellis to screen a coal bunker, bin or garden shed. Grown up a wigwam or obelisk they can soon obscure an upright eyesore. Some of these climbers rely on leaf colour for decorative effect, others form a fine curtain of flowers for part of the year, and a number provide fragrance too. All spread generously.

Actinidia kolomikta
Height to around 5 m/15 ft
• Sun, with shelter from strong wind • Fertile, well-drained soil
The green leaves of this twining climber have tips strongly splashed in pink and white to give a colourful cover to walls, fences or the branches of a tree, until the leaves fall in autumn. Full sun gives the best colour variegation.

Ampelopsis brevipedunculata 'Elegans'
Height to around 5 m/15 ft
• Sun – partial shade, in a sheltered position • Fertile, moist, well-drained soil
Divided leaves of dark green mottled with pink and white decorate this deciduous climber. Small, inconspicuous green flowers appear in summer, and these are followed by decorative, marbled, pink and purple fruit that turns blue in late autumn. It makes an ideal plant for clothing a wall, fence, pergola or tree.

Hedera colchica 'Dentata', Persian ivy
Height to around 10 m/33 ft; Hedera helix 'Goldheart' grows to around 5 m/15 ft • Sun – full shade • Fertile, moist, well-drained soil
This ivy has dark green, elongated, heart-shaped leaves with stems and leafstalks flushed purple. Excellent for ground cover or can be used to conceal a wall or fence in the shade. Its blue-black winter berries are poisonous. Hedera helix 'Goldheart' is another ivy that also grows well up a shady wall.

▲ Actinidia kolomikta.

▼ Parthenocissus quinquefolia, Virginia creeper.

Hydrangea petiolaris, Climbing hydrangea
Height to around 15 m/50 ft
• Shade, in a sheltered position
• Moderately fertile, moist, well drained soil
This hydrangea is a vigorous climber, clinging to its support by aerial roots. It will grow over a shady wall or structure, and in summer it produces small, creamy white flowers with flower heads similar to those of a lace-cap type.

Jasminum humile 'Revolutum', Yellow jasmine
Height to 2.5 m/8 ft, spread to

Vitis coignetia.

3 m/10 ft • Sun – partial shade, in a sheltered position in cold areas • Fertile, well-drained soil
Grow this bushy shrub to hide an unattractive view. The delicate, pointed, slim, dark green leaves are semi-evergreen. Masses of fragrant, buttercup-yellow flowers add colour from late spring to early autumn.

Parthenoncissus quinquefolia, Virginia creeper
Height to 15 m/50 ft • Sun – partial shade as • Fertile, well-drained soil
To provide quick cover for a wall, fence, or even a large tree, use this creeper with its serrated green leaves that turn a glorious warm, golden russet in autumn.

Schizophragma integrifolium
Height to 12 m/40 ft • Sun – partial shade • Moderately fertile, well-drained soil
The large, dark green leaves of this plant, which climbs by aerial roots, are almost obscured in mid-summer by the unusual, creamy white, fragrant flowers which have long creamy bracts around the edges.

Vitis coignetiae, Crimson glory vine
Height to 15 m/50 ft • Sun – partial shade • Well-drained, neutral to alkaline soil
Climbing by tendrils, this hardy vine has large, heart-shaped green and strongly veined leaves that turn brilliant yellow, orange and scarlet red in autumn. The small, blue-black grapes are inedible.

Wisteria sinensis, Chinese wisteria
Height to around 8.5 m/28 ft • Sun – partial shade • Fertile, moist, well-drained soil
This twining climber needs a firm support for its vigorous growth. In late spring to early summer it is covered by trailing, pendent streamers of scented lilac or white flowers.

Wisteria sinensis is grown over a pergola showing its lilac flowers.

RAMBLER ROSES

These vigorous roses will soon clothe a sunny wall or fence, or clamber through a tree. They only flower once but the mass of clustered, sweetly scented flowers more than makes up for this.

Rosa 'Albertine'
Height – to 5 m/15 ft, spread up to 4 m/12 ft
An old and vigorous rambler with prickly red-green stems, mid-green leaves and rusty-orange buds that turn into very sweetly scented, light salmon pink, cup-shaped flowers in mid-summer.

Rosa filipes 'Kiftsgate'
Height up to 10 m/33 ft, spread up to 6 m/20 ft
Huge clusters of small, open, creamy white, fragrant flowers cover this exceptionally rampant rambler in summer.

Rosa 'Paul's Himalayan Musk'
Height and spread up to 10 m/33 ft
Large clusters of double, pale-pink, rosette-shaped, pleasantly fragrant flowers cover the trailing shoots of this climber in summer.

▲ *Rosa filipes* 'Kiftsgate'.   ▼ *Rosa* 'Albertine'.

PLANTS FOR PROBLEM AREAS

Almost every garden has problem areas where few plants thrive. These may consist of shaded patches where the soil never dries out, or, conversely, shady places where the soil is always much too dry, such as under a tree or large shrub, next to the house or close to a hedge, wall or fence. Equally, few plants can survive in sun-baked areas, which go with dry conditions, while in exposed areas harsh, cold winds can burn leaves, break stems and damage flowers.

Luckily there are plants which can survive each of these problems and some of the best are described in the following pages. Something can also be done to improve the situation. Soil can always be made more fertile (see pages 102–105), shade can be provided from strong sunlight, and shelter from wind.

PLANTS FOR SHADE

Most plants find it difficult to flourish in the extremes of very moist or very dry shade. You can offer some aid to plants in these inhospitable conditions if you dig in lots of bulky organic matter, which helps to improve the soil's structure, retaining water and nutrients within the soil while improving drainage. On dry soil, after watering well, add mulch, which will help to stop the soil drying out so quickly in the future. Choose plants which are most able to cope with the conditions.

Ferns

Many ferns are ideal for damp, shady conditions and their arching, verdant leaves create beautiful effects. Some suitable species are *Asplenium nidus*, Bird's nest fern and *A. scolopendrium*, Hart's tongue fern. Both are evergreen and very decorative with their long, lance-shaped leaves.

In a shady corner ferns can be grown by a pond, to be reflected in the water. Moss will gather and add more shades of green.

Plants for moist shade

Dicentra formosa, Bleeding heart
Height 45 cm/18 in, spread 60–90 cm/24–36 in • Partial shade • Moist, humus-rich, neutral to slightly alkaline soil

In late spring and early summer arching stems of beautifully spaced pendent flowers appear above the fern-like green leaves. The unusual, almost heart-shaped flowers are pink fading to white.

Epimedium pinnatum ssp. *colchicum* Barrenwort/ Bishop's mitre
Height 30–40 cm/12–16 in, spread 4 m/12 ft • Partial shade • Humus-rich, moist,well-drained-soil

With its evergreen, hairy leaves barrenwort makes an excellent ground-cover plant for

Epimedium pinnatum ssp. *colchicum,* Barrenwort.

Dicentra formosa, Bleeding heart.

areas of shade under trees and shrubs. In spring spikes of yellow, open, four-petalled flowers with pretty brown flecked spurs are produced.

Mimulus luteus, Yellow monkey flower/ Monkey musk
Height 30 cm/12 in, spread 60 cm/24 in • Sun – light, dappled shade • Fertile, humus-rich, very moist soil

The ornate trumpet-shaped flowers of this spreading perennial appear in late spring to summer and are yellow, spotted with purple-red on the petals and within the throat. Other species come in red, apricot, pale and deep pink.

Symphytum, Comfrey
Height up to 1.5 m/5 ft, spread up to 2 m/6 ft • Sun – partial shade • Moderately fertile, moist soil

Comfrey provides excellent ground cover in a shady area, with its large, coarse and hairy green leaves. In late spring to

summer small groups of drooping purple violet, pink or creamy yellow flowers add extra interest.

Tellima grandiflora, Fringe cups
Height up to 75 cm/30 in, spread 30 cm/12 in • Partial shade • Moist, humus-rich soil

On this shade-loving plant pretty serrated leaves are topped from late spring to early summer by tall stems of tiny, greenish white to white trumpet-shaped flowers.

Uvularia grandiflora, Merrybells
Height 75 cm/30 in, spread 30 cm/12 in • Partial – deep shade • Fertile, moist, well-drained-soil

Hanging, bell-shaped, yellow flowers appear in mid- to late spring amongst the drooping, green, sword-shaped leaves of this unusual shade-loving plant.

Symphytum grandiflorum, a small, neat, spreading comfrey.

Plants for dry shade

Alchemilla alpina, Alpine lady's mantle
Height 8–12 cm/3–5 in, spread 50 cm/20 in • Sun – partial shade • Humus-rich soil

This mat-forming ground-cover plant has very divided, finger-like leaves with silvery-haired undersides. Tiny yellow-green flowers appear in summer.

Bergenia cordifolia, Bergenia
Height up to 60 cm/24 in, spread 75 cm/30 in • Sun – partial shade • Humus-rich soil

The strongly veined, large, tough, rounded heart-shaped deep-green leaves of bergenia are tinted purple in winter. In late winter to early spring pale rose to deep pink flowers appear on long red stalks.

Digitalis purpurea, Foxglove
Height 1–2 m/3–6 ft, spread 60 cm/24 in • Partial shade • Humus-rich soil

The tall spikes of purple,

Digitalis purpurea, Foxglove.

Bergenia cordifolia.

pink or white foxglove flowers are produced in early summer. The flowers are hooded and trumpet-shaped, and beautifully maroon- or purple-spotted inside. Foxgloves often reseed themselves. You can grow them annually from seed.

Euphorbia amygdaloides var. robbiae, Mrs Robb's bonnet
Height 60 cm/24 in • Light, dappled shade • Moist, humus-rich soil

A spreading plant with dark green spoon-shaped leaves with red undersides. These are topped in late spring to early summer by large torches of small lime-yellow flowers.

Geranium phaeum, Mourning widow
Height 75 cm/30 in, spread 15 cm/6 in • Sun – partial shade • Well-drained, neutral to slightly acid soil

Unusual white-centred flowers in dark purple-black, deep maroon, violet-blue, light mauve or white appear in summer on this member of the cranesbill family.

Iris foetidissima, Stinking iris
Height 30–90 cm/12–36 in, spread 3 m/10 ft • Full sun –

partial shade • Well-drained soil

A beardless iris with tough, sword-shaped dark green leaves that have an unpleasant smell if crushed. Insignificant pale purple flowers, touched with yellow, appear in early summer, and these are followed in autumn by seed capsules that split open to reveal bright orange-red seeds.

Geranium phaeum

Vinca major ssp. hirsuta.

Vinca major, Periwinkle
Height 45 cm/18 in, spread indefinite • Sun – partial shade • Any but very dry soil

The open white, deep mauve or blue flowers of the evergreen periwinkle appear in spring and can continue right through until autumn. *Vinca major* 'Variegata' has white-edged green leaves that add light to a shady spot.

Iris foetidissima, Stinking iris.

PLANTS FOR FULL SUN

Planting a rock garden

Before you start, place the plants in their pots in position among the rocks and check you are happy with the effect. Move them around if you are not satisfied. Water plants well.

Knock each plant out of its pot as you plant it. Invert the pot, while holding your hand over the root ball. If necessary tap the edge of the pot on a rock to loosen it.

(continued opposite)

An exposed site in full sun often goes with light soil that drains quickly. Some plants can survive these conditions, but most wilt. To increase the choice of suitable plaints, improve the soil by regularly digging in lots of bulky organic matter such as well-rotted manure and compost. Mulch with a thick layer of ornamental bark or compost and grow ground cover plants to help to retain moisture within the soil. Never mulch soil that is already dry as this will make matters worse. Water well first.

Cistus hybrids, Rock rose

Height and spread 1.5 m/5 ft (C. x cyprius); C x purpureus and C. x skanbergii both have height 1 m/3 ft • Full sun • Poor to moderately fertile, well-drained soil

The open summer flowers of rock roses, with their paper-thin petals, come in a range of pinks or white with bright yellow centres and striking contrast markings. C. x cyprius has white flowers with deep purple marks, one on each petal, towards the centres, while C. x purpureus has dark pink flowers with maroon marks and C. x skanbergii has pale pink flowers.

Dianthus hybrids, Garden pinks

Height 25–45 cm/10–18 in, spread 30–40 cm/12–16 in • Full sun • Well-drained, neutral to alkaline soil

Pinks look decorative bordering a sunny bed or trailing over the edge of a container. They are renowned for their silver foliage and clove-scented, often bi-coloured flowers. 'Alice' is very striking with white, semi-double flowers and a large splash of dark crimson. 'Doris' is pale pink with a dark pink centre, and 'Musgrave's Pink' is an old-fashioned pink with single white flowers which have a green eye.

*Diascia species/*Diascia

Height 15–25 cm/6–10 in, spread 50 cm/20 in • Full sun • Fertile, moist, well-drained soil

Ideal for a sunny bank or a rock garden, diascias have a

long flowering season from summer to autumn and pretty trumpet-shaped flowers. *Diascia* 'Blackthorn Apricot' has clusters of apricot-coloured flowers, while *D. rigescens* has tall spikes of deep pink flowers.

Euphorbia polychroma, Euphorbia

Height 40 cm/16 in, spread 60 cm/24 in • Full sun • Light, well-drained soil

This clump-forming perennial

Cistus 'Sunset'.

is topped by a mass of short-stemmed and tight-headed lemon-yellow flower-like bracts from mid-spring to mid-summer.

Gaura lindheimeri 'The Bride'

Height up to 1.5 m/5 ft, spread 90 cm/36 in • Full sun • Fertile, moist well-drained soil

Pinks in a sunny border.

Diascia barberae.

From late spring to early autumn the butterfly-like white flowers of this pretty plant open at dawn from pale pink buds, changing later to pink again.

Inula helenium, Elecampane
Height 1–2 m/3–6 ft, spread 1 m/3 ft • Full sun • Deep, fertile, moist, well-drained soil
This tall perennial becomes a mass of striking bright yellow daisy-like flowers with very fine petals in mid- and late summer.

Iris sibirica
Height 50–120 cm/20–48 in • Full sun • Well-drained, moist, neutral to slightly acid soil
The deep purple-blue flowers of this iris, which appear in early summer, have white markings and darker veining. The foliage, which grows up in spring is an attractive mass of slim, grass-like leaves.

Knautia macedonica
Height 60–75 cm/24–30 in, spread 45 cm/18 in • Full sun • Moderately fertile, well-drained soil, preferably alkaline
In mid- to late summer the dark crimson-scarlet flowers of this vigorous perennial appear, to last over a long period. *Knautia arvensis* has lilac-blue flowers.

Lavandula species, Lavender
Height and spread 30–50 cm/

12–20 in (L. x intermedia); L. latifolia has height 1 m/3 ft, spread 1.2 m/4 ft • Full sun • Moderately fertile, well-drained soil
Lovers of sunshine, lavenders with their mauve, fragrant flowers and silver-grey foliage form an ornamental edge or low hedge for an open border. *L. x intermedia* has spikes of light blue to violet flowers, while the taller *L. latifolia* has mauve-blue flowers.

Leycesteria tormosa, Pheasant's eye
Height and spread 2 m/6 ft • Full sun – partial shade • Moderately fertile, well-drained soil
The deep wine-red bracts interspersed with tiny white bell-shaped flowers appear from summer to early autumn on this deciduous shrub. They trail decoratively amongst the pointed green leaves and the flowers are later followed by purple-red berries.

Sanguisorba minor, Salad burnet
Height and spread about 15–20 cm/ 6–8 in • Full sun – partial shade • Moderately fertile, moist, well-drained soil
A wild plant grown in gardens for its tiny deeply-toothed leaves with a hint of cucumber that provide a tasty addition to a salad. In summer it has pretty red bobble-like flowers.

Santolina chamaecy-parisus, Cotton lavender
Height 50 cm/20 in, spread

Santolina chamaecyparisus, Cotton lavender.

1 m/3 ft • Full sun • Poor to moderately fertile, well-drained soil
This attractive plant has fine-leaved silver foliage and pretty button-shaped bright yellow flowers. These appear in mid- and late summer, making this a delightful plant to grow in a rock garden, as ground cover or edging, and even as a low hedge.

Verbascum chaixii 'Album', Nettle-leafed mullein
Height 90 cm/36 in, spread 45 cm/18 in • Full sun • Poor, well-drained, alkaline soil
Tall spires of creamy white flowers with decorative deep mauve centres appear in mid- to late summer. A relation of the bright yellow wild mullein, this is a plant to show off in a herbaceous border or a wild or woodland garden.

Lavenders enjoy the baking conditions of a sunny patio.

(continued from opposite)

Use a narrow-bladed trowel to make a hole a little larger than the root ball. Trickle some gritty soil around the roots, making sure that the crown of the plant is not buried too deeply.

Firm well, then trickle coarse grit around the plant, keeping it off the leaves. Firm and level the grit with your hands to create a neat finish.

PLANTS FOR WIND AND POOR SOIL

Creating artificial windbreaks

When wind hits a solid object such as a wall or fence it goes over or around it, often causing severe turbulence a short distance from it on the leeward side. This can be very damaging to plants. Planting a hedge is the solution.

Hedges and screens of tall shrubs and trees make the most efficient windbreaks, because they reduce the velocity of the wind while causing less turbulence than a solid windbreak such as a wall or fence.

Moulded plastic windbreak nets give some protection to plants for up to ten years, or even longer. They are a very useful temporary addition to help while more natural windbreaks such as hedges and other living screens are becoming established.

Few plants can cope well with cold winds and poor soil. The plants listed here, some of them used in coastal conditions, will do better than most others in these situations, but they grow better in less exposed conditions and in more fertile, well-drained soil. By following the tips to cut clown wind turbulence, described on page 122 and in the left column, and by improving the soil condition, a wider range of plants can be grown.

Agapanthus, Agapanthus
Height 60 cm–1.2 m/2–4 ft, spread 60–45 cm/18 in • Full sun • Preferably fertile, moist but well-drained, soil
These eye-catching plants have huge globes of closely packed deep blue, bell-shaped flowers that top each tall stem in mid- to late summer. The long, dark green, strap-like leaves appear in early spring and arch decoratively outwards.

Allium, Allium species.

Allium, Allium species
Height up to 1.5–2 m/5–6 ft, spread 5 cm/6 in (A. giganteum); A. 'Globemaster' has height up to 75 cm/30 in, spread 20 cm/8 in; A. caeruleum has height up to 60 cm/24 in, spread 2.5 cm/1 in • Full sun • Preferably fertile, well-drained soil
Ping-pong balls of colourful, tiny flowers rise on tall stems on these decorative members of the onion family. *Allium giganteum* has strong pink-purple flowers in summer, *A. 'Globemaster'* has deep purple blue summer flowers and *A. caeruleum* has silvery blue

flowers which appear in early summer.

Alstroemeria, Alstroemeria
Height 50 cm–1 m/20 in–3 ft, spread up to 60 cm/24 in • Full sun – partial shade • Preferably fertile, moist but well-drained soil
In summer the trumpet-shaped flowers of alstroemerias appear in colours of pink, red, apricot and yellow, each with its own decorative tiger-like throat markings. *Alstroemeria hookeri* has soft creamy apricot flowers with yellow and brown markings and brown stamens, and *A. pelegrina* has magenta pink petals, white at the throat, also with the characteristic yellow and brown flecks. *A. aurantiaca* is bright orange or red, streaked in dark red.

Cortaderia sellowana 'Sunningdale Silver', Pampas grass
Height up to 3 m/10 ft, spread up to 2.5 m/8 ft • Full sun • Fertile, well-drained soil

Alstroemeria aurantiaca.

Agapanthus campanulatus.

This is a plant for a prominent position. With its tall silver-white plumes towering above the long, grass-like leaves it makes a striking display in late summer.

Crambe maritima, Sea kale
Height up to 75 cm/30 in, spread up to 60 cm/24 in • Full sun • Preferably fertile, well-drained soil
The thick and leafy stems, which are forced for use as a vegetable, bear fragrant flower heads in early summer. These are made up of masses of tiny white flowers.

Griselinia littoralis
Height up to 8 m/25 ft, spread up to 5 m/15 ft • Full sun • Light, fertile, dry, well-drained soil
A bold, evergreen shrub that is grown for its glossy, bright apple-green leaves. In 'Dixon's Cream' the leaves are strongly marked with creamy yellow centres.